THE MURDER CLUB

"Well, I do not like accidents," replied Mrs Mush, "there's no meaning in them: but," she added confidentially, "I dearly like a murder. Of course I do not wish for murders," she continued, in a tone of resigned virtue: "but when there is one, why, I like it. It is human nature."

(Julia Kavanagh, *Sybil's Second Love,* 1867)

THE MURDER CLUB

Guide to

THE MIDLANDS

Devised and Edited by Brian Lane

HARRAP
London

ACKNOWLEDGEMENTS

Sincere thanks go primarily to Derek Johns, Publishing Director of Harrap, whose imaginative response to the proposal for these *Guides* provided their initial impetus, and whose continued encouragement and practical support have ensured their realization. Thanks also to our editor, Roy Minton, whose knowledge and understanding has saved us from more than a few pitfalls; and to Tim Pearce, who helped turn our ideas into books.

On the Murder Club side there are people too numerous to mention whose contributions to our Archive of illustrations and texts have made the compilation of these books possible. In particular, credit must be given to Steve Wheatley, whose work on the overall concept of the *Murder Club Guides* was of immense value, as were his written contributions to Volume One. And to John Bevis whose creative application to the layout and overall appearance has helped make the concept a tangible reality.

For the kindness and generosity we have been shown in scores of libraries and museums, large and small, all over Britain, and for all those people who knew about things and were willing to share, we hope these books may represent our thanks.

First published in Great Britain 1988
by HARRAP Ltd
19-23 Ludgate Hill, London EC4M 7PD

ISBN 0-245-54681-2

Designed by Brian Lane and John Bevis

Typeset in Times by
Facet Film Composing Limited
Leigh-on-Sea, Essex

Printed by Biddles Limited,
Guildford and King's Lynn

THE MURDER CLUB GUIDE TO THE MIDLANDS

CONTENTS

GENERAL INTRODUCTION: On Apologias 7

KEY TO MAPS 10

THE MURDER CLUB 12

DERBYSHIRE
The Copy-Cat Murders
Michael Copeland (1960-2) 14
A Matter of Choice
Albert Edward Burrows (1920-23) 16
A Traveller's Tale
George Frederick Hayward (1927) 18
Murder in the Winnats
James Ashton, Nicholas Cook *et al* (1758) 19
The Madness of George Victor Townley
George Victor Townley (1863) 30

GLOUCESTERSHIRE
Arsenic in the Sheep Dip
Beatrice Annie Pace (1928) 38

HEREFORDSHIRE AND WORCESTERSHIRE
"I will never trust you more"
George Price (1738) 42
Here Comes the Murdering Major!
Herbert Rowse Armstrong (1921) 44
Skeleton in the Cupboard
Richard Hemming (1806) 52

LEICESTERSHIRE
Nearer my God...
James Cook (1832) 54
The Green Bicycle Mystery
Ronald Vivian Light (1919) 60
A Court of Peers
Earl Ferrers (1760) 66

LINCOLNSHIRE
The Dog it was that Died
Ethel Lillie Major (1934) 74
A Dead Post-Boy
Isaac and Thomas Hallam (1733) 75

NORTHAMPTONSHIRE
The Blazing Car Murder
Alfred Arthur Rouse (1930) 78
A Copy of Verses
Mary Clarke and Phillip Haynes (1821) 92
Honour thy Father and thy Mother
Thomas Gordon (1789) 93

NOTTINGHAMSHIRE

The Man Who Said Nothing
Frederick Nodder (1937) 96
"The Heathen in his Blindness"
James Brodie (1800) 99
"The Old Nurse, Death"
Dorothea Waddingham (1935) 99
"How I Met Murder"
Herbert Leonard Mills (1951) 103

SHROPSHIRE

Too Bad for his own Good
Jocelin Harwood (1692) 106

STAFFORDSHIRE

No Way Out
Leslie Green (1952) 110
Horrid Murder
George Caddell 112
The Black Panther
Donald Neilson (1975) 114
Better than the Workhouse
Joseph Jones (1906) 117
The Fatal Consequences of Gambling
Dr William Palmer (1855) 119
Victim of the Night-Mare
George Allen (1807) 123

WARWICKSHIRE

The Devil's Work
The Killing of Charles Walton (1945) 126
"Throw physic to the dogs"
John Donellan (1781) 129

WEST MIDLANDS

The Primrose and the Wretch
Abraham Thornton (1817) 134
Murder by Proxy
David Pagett (1980) 158
Money in the Bank
Frederick William Oakley (1936) 161
As Seen on the Radio
Stanley Eric Hobday (1933) 162

APPENDICES

One **Gaol Fever** 165
Two **The Coward's Weapon: 3** 167
Three **Some Notes on Street Literature** 170
Four **Epilepsy, Murder, and the Homicide Bill** 180
Five **Trial by Combat** 182

SELECT BIBLIOGRAPHY 183

INDEX 186

General Introduction

On Apologias

Madame Life's a piece in bloom
Death goes dogging everywhere;
She's the tenant of the room,
He's the ruffian on the stair.
(W.E. Henley, 1849-1903)

A disturbing by-product of the new fashionable 'humanism' and its inseparable partner 'attitude-baring' is that the individual is under constant pressure to apologize for his passions. And nothing needs an apologia quite as much as a fascination with the darker sides of humankind.

There can be few notions more difficult to promote than that an interest in, say, the ritual of Magic does not of itself lead to nocturnal harvesting of the parish graveyard; or that a diet of gangster movies results in St Valentine's Day madness. An interest in crime is viewed as decidedly sinister; but a fascination with the crime of Murder – be it as academic or aficionado – renders a person particularly vulnerable, particularly in need of an apologia.

And so, for all those members, and prospective members, and closet members of The Murder Club; for all those readers of these, its regional *Guides*, here are some excellent precedents for our common need to justify.

One of the earliest examples can be found in the first issue of what was to become a popular illustrated weekly paper for a number of years around the turn of the century. Though its name was *Famous Crimes Past and Present*, like so many similar magazines of the period "crime" meant "murder". Editor Harold Furniss wrote, "Down the vista of crime which stretches from the first transgression of our Father Adam to the last little boy punished for stealing a pennyworth of sweets, there stand at intervals landmarks – milestones, as it were – on the road of iniquity. These are the doings of great criminals, of men whose cunning, wickedness or brutality have thrown out their lives into relief against the sordid background of everyday transgressors. It is of these that we propose to write, and we do so with a two-fold purpose; firstly that those who are interested in criminology, and desirous of furthering the science by which the moral welfare of the country is preserved may have before them a reliable record of typical criminals; and secondly, that as the natural bent of man tends towards crime, we may provide him with reading matter, interesting and dramatic, which will afford him food for thought."[1]

That there was a lighter side to the "interest in criminology" even earlier is evidenced by David Jardine's *Criminal Trials* being published, in 1835, by The Society for the Diffusion of Useful Knowledge as part of its series 'The Library of Entertaining Knowledge'. Just why such material should be considered 'Entertaining' is spelt out by another chronicler of the Courts, Horace Wyndham: "Of course, the real truth is (as De Quincey, who was something of a connoisseur on such matters, has asserted) crime in itself is intrinsically interesting. We may protest to the contrary, but there is no getting over the fact that the traffic of the dock does make an appeal. An extended one, too. Still, there is abundant reason for this. After all, 'crime books' are concerned with human happenings, with real life, with the stir and fret and thrill of everyday occurrences. Again, crime is essentially dramatic, and touches the whole emotional gamut. Thus, there is tragedy; there is comedy; there is melodrama; and there is occasionally sheer farce. Even romance, too, at times. Anyway, plot and passion and swift moving incident from the rise to the fall of the curtain. Hence, not nearly so astonishing that such volumes are popular as that they are not still more popular."[2]

Other writers have sought to give equal stress to the 'Useful' and to the 'Entertaining' sides of the crime story. Few people have done more consistently to popularize the twilight world of the criminal than the much respected writer, broadcaster, and former barrister, Edgar Lustgarten: "The main aim of one approach is to probe psychology – and thereby to illuminate and instruct. The main aim of the other is to tell a story – and thereby to divert and entertain."[3] But whichever of these two caps Mr Lustgarten chooses to wear, he is clear on the moral foundation of his apologia, "Certainly the arrangement adopted in the construction of the book does not signify any departure by the author from the received opinion that murder is the wickedest and gravest of all crimes."[4]

A different approach is taken by Colin Wilson, whose prolific path has taken him through such dangerous territory as Black Magic, Extra-Terrestrialism, ESP, Assassination, and Murder. One of his contentions is that the study of murder is a necessity – indeed, an obligation – if one is to understand the counter-balance, which is man's great creative potential. We have to be very grateful to Wilson for much of our contemporary understanding of 'criminality', though it is an approach which has has led to accusations of pomposity – not much dispelled by his published feelings about some fellow-authors: "It will be observed that my references to certain other writers on murder – particularly Edmund Pearson, William Roughead and William Bolitho – are hardly complimentary. I dislike the 'murder for pleasure' approach. I consider this book, like the *Encyclopaedia of Murder*, as a tentative contribution to a subject that does not yet exist as a definite entity, a science that has not yet taken shape."[5] Wilson's co-author on the *Encyclopaedia of Murder* was Patricia Pitman, who took a rather less pedantic view of the task in hand, concluding that the fascination with murderers is that they are so utterly different from us, and that that fascination is perfectly natural. Further, she brings a refreshing down-to-earthness to it all by adding that, aside from psychological justifications, the *Encyclopaedia* can provide "...plots for novels, questions for quizes, and innocent entertainment for eerie winter evenings."[6]

But what of the "murder for pleasure" approach so despised by Wilson?

The late Edmund Pearson, tireless recorder of the classic American murders and controversial authority on the Lizzie Borden case does, it is true, seem to take a wholesome relish in the retelling of a great murder story; England's own 'Brides in the Bath' killer, George Joseph Smith, he laments as a man "who only went to ruin because, like so many great artists, he could not resist one more farewell performance" [see *Murder Club Guide No.2*].[7] In the essay 'What Makes a Good Murder?', Pearson treats 'collectors' of murders with the respect that he feels due to a discerning cognoscente, noting that "...failure to recognise the elementary principle of an attractive murder is characteristic of many who should be better informed".[8]

Back on this side of the Atlantic, Pearson would recognize a soul-mate in Nigel Morland, who steers a course happily between detective fiction and criminology; he too is adamant about quality in a murder – "the critical eyes of aficionados recognise two distinct divisions of murder in the United States. There are the common-or-garden majority, whose ultimate destiny is the pages of popular magazines with lurid covers. The second, numerically minute, division is concerned with murders acceptable to the discerning taste, and here time has made certain classics".[9]

Edward Spencer Shew was one of the pioneers, with Wilson and Pitman, of the encyclopaedic approach to the recording of murder, and in the frank introduction to his indispensible *Second Companion to Murder*, Shew comes dangerously close to appearing to enjoy his subject: "Here the emphasis falls upon naked violence, raw and uncompromising, like the mallet strokes which destroyed Francis Mawson Rattenbury [see *Murder Club Guide No.6*], or the blows of the iron-stone brick with which Irene Munro was battered to death upon the sands of the Crumbles [see *Murder Club Guide No.2*]. Here murder wears its most savage face;[10] a face that Ivan Butler recognises: "it is in the strange vagaries of human behaviour that the persisting interest lies...the bizarre, the mysterious, the tragic, the gruesome, the just plain vicious".[11]

Two novel and distinguished vindications are advanced by Gordon Honeycombe in his introductory pages to *The Murders of the Black Museum* – "But the Black Museum made me realise what a policemen must endure in the course of of his duty; what sights he sees, what dangers he faces, what depraved and evil people he has to deal with so that others may live secure".[12] And later, "Murder is a very rare event in England. Its exceptional nature is in fact part of its fascination."

A counterpoint to this approach is provided by journalistic investigators, such as Paul Foot and Ludovic Kennedy. Their immediate motivation is the righting of a particular injustice, but they also have a wider purpose. As Kennedy writes in his introduction to 'Wicked Beyond Belief': "...once we start selecting those whom we think worthy or unworthy of Justice, we shall all in the end be diminished; for even if Justice is sometimes rough in practice, it is not for Cooper and McMahon alone that this book has been assembled; but for all those who, if Justice is allowed to go by default, may come to suffer in their time."[13] Kennedy's intention is to expose those attitudes and processes of the police, the courts, lawyers and judges which create an institutional tendency towards injustice.

A more academic, but no less absorbing, motive for the study of Murder derives from the fact that murder cases have tended to be so much better documented than the less notorious fields of human endeavour. The wealth of detailed information which can be gleaned from Court testimony and newspaper reports provides an eloquent picture of the everyday behaviour, social conditions, and moral attitudes of times past. We would, undoubtedly, be far more ignorant of conditions in London's East End in the 1880s if it were not for Jack the Ripper; the description of repressive middle-class life presented by the cases of Dr Crippen and Major Armstrong [see *Murder Club Guide No.4*] is, surely, as vivid as any novelist could invent; an examination of the predicament of Florence Maybrick [see *Murder Club Guide No.3*] or Edith Thompson provides a telling case study of the moral taboos of their time.

To be generous to the field, an example should be given of the "There but for the Grace of God..." argument. Take Tony Wilmot's introduction to *Murder and Mayhem*, "Why do we like reading crime stories, especially murder? For murder, that most heinous of crimes, both horrifies and fascinates at one and the same time...Could it be that deep down, we suspect that we are capable of committing murder, or other serious crimes, if we knew we could get away with it? That, perhaps, the only thing that holds us back is the fear of being caught and paying the price?"[14]

Probably not. But the one certainty is that there are as many reasons for a fascination with the "ruffian on the stair" as there are people to be fascinated by him.

References

1 *Famous Crimes Past and Present*, Ed. Harold Furniss. Vol.1. No.1, 1903.
2 *Famous Trials Retold*, Horace Wyndham. Hutchinson, London, 1925.
3 *Illustrated Story of Crime*, Edgar Lustgarten. Weidenfeld and Nicolson, London, 1976.
4 *Ibid.*
5 *A Casebook of Murder*, Colin Wilson. Leslie Frewin, London, 1969.
6 *Encyclopaedia of Murder*, Colin Wilson and Patricia Pitman. Arthur Barker, London, 1961.
7 *Masterpieces of Murder*, Edmund Pearson. Hutchinson, London, 1969.
8 *Ibid.*
9 *Background to Murder*, Nigel Morland. Werner Laurie, London, 1955.
10 *Second Companion to Murder*, E. Spencer Shew. Cassell, London, 1961.
11 *Murderers' London*, Ivan Butler. Hale, London, 1973.
12 *Murders of the Black Museum 1870-1970*, Gordon Honeycmbe. Hutchinson, London, 1982.
13 *The Luton Murder Case*, Ed. Ludovic Kennedy. Granada Publishing, London, 1980.
14 *Murder and Mayhem*, Ed. Tony Wilmot. Harmsworth Publications, London, 1983.

Maps

The complexity of Britain's road system – particularly around the crowded inner-city areas – makes it impractical to provide a detailed road map to the regions covered in this series of *Guides*. Instead, individual cases are accompanied by a map of the immediate area, marked where possible with the nearest British Rail station as well as locational information relevant to the text.

To give an overview of the areas covered, each county is prefaced by a map on which the murder sites are numerically plotted and listed.

KEY TO MAPS

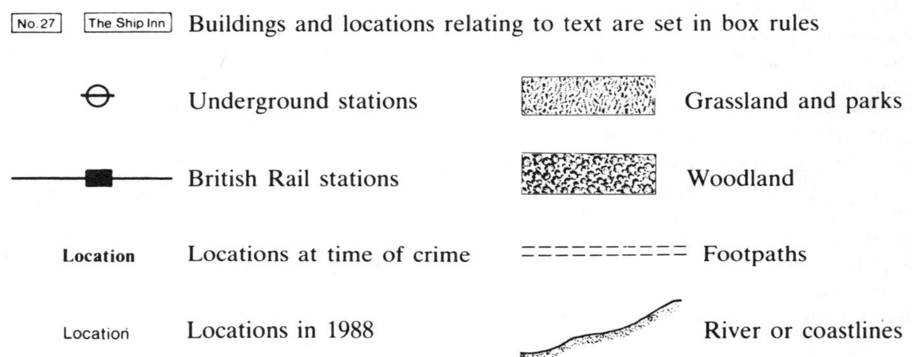

Location Photographs

In keeping with the status of this series of books as Guides, maps have been supplemented, where possible and appropriate, with photographs of buildings and locations relevant to the crime under discussion; in many cases, however, the precise spot on a landscape has been buried either by time or by the ubiquitous developer. Further research may unearth more precise information, and the compilers would be most grateful to receive it.

Public houses come quite naturally to the foreground in many of these cases, and provide a genuine excuse for refreshment in the amateur 'murder hunt'; but it should be remembered that those many private houses whose history has been blackened by dark deeds are not public monuments, and their present occupants' privacy should be respected.

Glossop
Hayfield
Castleton
Chesterfield
Wirksworth
DERBYS
Market Rasen
Kirkby-on-Bain
NOTTS
Newark-on-Trent
Nottingham
LINCOLNSHIRE
Kidsgrove
Barlaston
STAFFORDSHIRE
Stafford
Burton-on-Trent
Rugeley
Staunton Harold
LEICESTERSHIRE
Leicester
Little Stretton
Shrewsbury
SHROPSHIRE
Coseley
W. Bromwich
Birmingham
W. MIDLANDS
NORTHANTS
Warwick
Northampton
Hardingstone
Oddingley
WARWICKS
HEREFORD AND WORCESTER
Lower Quinton
Hay-on-Wye
Coleford
GLOUCESTERSHIRE

THE MURDER CLUB

Background

In the October of 1985, when Steve Wheatley and I first began to mould our mutual interest in Crime and Criminology into some more tangible form, it was as an occasional fireside activity. The first manifestation was the manuscript for a book of Execution Broadsheets. From there, as winter deepened, and the fireside became host to more frequent discussion, the ambitious concept for a new kind of periodical devoted to the Crime of Murder began to creep from our meditations. And the more of the blood-red wine that was sipped, and the more nimbly the shadows from the flickering flames darted about the room, the more of a good idea it seemed. It even stood up to the cold, thin reality of winter daylight.

It was, we decided, to be called *The Murder Club Bulletin* – though heaven knows why, the 'Club' wasn't due to emerge from the moving shadows until the next season's firelight. Indeed, at the time the first rough plans were put on to paper the 'Club' fitted round the editorial desk with more than enough room to spare.

It must have been around the mid-winter of 1986 that somebody said something like: "We've got the *Murder Bulletin,* what about the *Club*?"

I should say, though, that in the intervening months we had gradually begun to put together what will become a complete regional documentation of British Murders since the beginning of the seventeenth century; it's a big job. People in various parts of the country heard about it, and started to send us things – notes about famous local murders, regional press cuttings, pictures. We discovered people like Mr Mackintosh who had traced the last resting place of Bella Wright, the victim of the Green Bicycle Mystery in 1919, and had set up a fund to give Bella a modest memorial. We were becoming a Club!

Discussion began to revolve more and more around what we, as committed enthusiasts, would want out of a Murder Club if we were 'them'. The list on page 191 reveals some of those decisions which have already been adopted; other paths await discovery.

So, in the middle months of 1987 we had a prototype *Bulletin,* we had the partially clad skeleton of *The Murder Club,* and we had something else – we had a series of books demanding to be written; a series of Guides to the darker sides of Britain's landscape. Then came our first meeting with Harrap – long-established publishers of true-crime works – and their Publishing Director, Derek Johns. Derek it was who responded enthusiastically to the proposal for a series of eight *Murder Club Regional Guides;* Derek it was who enthusiastically adopted the suggestion to launch *The Murder Club* on the same date as the first four books – on the 30th of June, this year. And by the next season of flickering fires, Criminology will no longer be the exclusive preserve of the scientists, the lawyers, and the journalists. Our Members will already have become arm-chair detectives.

Brian Lane

London
April 1988

Derbyshire

1. Michael COPELAND 14
2. Albert Edward BURROWS 16
3. George Frederick HAYWARD 18
4. James ASHTON, Nicholas COOK, *et al* 19
5. George Victor TOWNLEY 30

The Copy-Cat Murders

The Murder of WILLIAM ARTHUR ELLIOTT and GEORGE GERALD STOBBS by MICHAEL COPELAND on Sunday June the 12th 1960, and Wednesday March the 29th 1961 respectively at Clod Hill Lane, Baslow, Chesterfield

MOOR BODY RIDDLE

Tuesday, 14 June 1960: On Sunday June 12th the shoeless body of 60-year-old William Arthur Elliott was found in isolated Clod Hill Lane which crosses the moor near Baslow. Mr Elliott was believed by the pathologist to have died of severe head injuries. The victim's 'bubble' car containing his shoes was subsequently found crashed in Park Road, Chesterfield. While police continue to search the desolate moorland for a possible weapon, detectives have been making inquiries around Mr Elliott's home at 9 Haddon Road, Bakewell, in an attempt to piece together his last hours alive; they are asking anybody who saw the ivory-coloured bubble car, registration number KLU 488, to contact them.

VICTIM'S DOUBLE TELLS OF ATTACK

Wednesday, 15 June 1960: Fifty-one-year-old bus cleaner William Atkinson, of Church Lane, North Wingfield, revealed today that he had been attacked about a week before the murder of Mr William Elliott in the same area where the bubble car had been found – Boythorpe Road, which runs close by Park Road. Mr Atkinson bears a remarkable physical likeness to the moors victim, and the police are working on the theory that he may have been assaulted in mistake for Mr Elliott. Furthermore, the two men were known to each other, being habitues of the *Spread Eagle* public house in Chesterfield. The inquiry is being headed by Detective Superintendent Leonard Stretton.

BUBBLE-CAR MURDER
Tip by Woman

Saturday, 18 June 1960: Mrs Gladys Vickers of Sutton Spring Wood, Chesterfield, told police last night that she may have seen Mr William Elliott attacked the night before his body was found. Mrs Vickers knew Mr Elliott and: "I saw him being chased along an alley outside the *Royal Oak* public house. The man chasing him was dark-haired, swarthy, and with thin features, and he caught up with him. Then I heard someone say 'Oh' and groan."

MAN DEAD IN BUBBLE-CAR MURDER LANE
'Carbon Copy Theory'

Wednesday, 29 March 1961: An unidentified man was found today dead from injuries in Clod Hill Lane, where 9 months ago William Elliott was found murdered. A police spokesman said that they were working on the assumption that it was a 'carbon copy' killing. The inquest on the late Mr Elliott returned a verdict of "murder by person or persons unknown"; he had been kicked to death. Although more than 100,000 people had been questioned, no arrest resulted. Detective Superintendent Stretton, who led the former inquiry, has taken over the present investigation; he revealed that an abandoned car had been found in exactly the same spot in Park Road that Mr Elliott's blood-stained bubble car had been left.

CARBON-COPY MURDER

Thursday, March 30 1961: Victim of what police have called the 'Carbon Copy Murder' has been named as 48-year-old Chesterfield chemist George Gerald Stobbs.

ANOTHER DRAMATIC SIMILARITY

Saturday, April 1 1961: Police issued a statement today which revealed another startling similarity to the 'bubble-car murder'. It would appear that a man named Gillespie, living near Stubbing Court, and who bears a great resemblance to victim Gerald Stobbs, was attacked shortly before the latest killing – police think that, as in the case of the assault on William Atkinson before the Elliott murder, Dr Gillespie was mistaken for the intended victim. The inquest called by Mr Frederick Nesbit, High Peak coroner, was adjourned to a date to be fixed.

PROBE INTO DOUBLE LIVES OF VICTIMS
Undercover Man in Hunt for Killer

Monday, April 3 1961: It was announced by officers investigating the 'Carbon Copy Murders' that they are to give an "undercover" man the task of infiltrating the circles in which both of the victims moved. Police now believe that both Mr Elliott and Mr Stobbs led double lives of which even their closest relatives were unaware. Both men had acquaintances in common and drank in the same public house – the *Three Horseshoes* at Chesterfield.

Despite continued investigations by the Derbyshire constabulary, the case remained unsolved over the succeeding months. The only further dramatic incident was the death of sixty-three-year-old Arthur Jenkinson shortly after he had been interviewed by the police. Although the coroner's jury returned a verdict of suicide, there was some persistent rumour that Mr Jenkinson had been murdered – had been overcome and had his head forced into the gas oven.

Month followed month and the likelihood of getting to the bottom of the Carbon Copy Mystery grew more remote. But three years later twenty-six-year-old Michael Copeland, a former regular soldier from St Augustine's Crescent, Chesterfield (near where the two cars had been abandoned) was arrested for the murder of William Elliott and George Stobbs. Furthermore, he was charged with the killing of Guenther Helmbrecht, a young German soldier, in Verden, in November 1960.

Copeland's confession (which he retracted before his trial) explained that "It was something I really hated" – a reference to the fact that both Stobbs and Elliott were homosexual.

Found Guilty of all three murders, Michael Copeland was reprieved and his sentence commuted to life imprisonment.

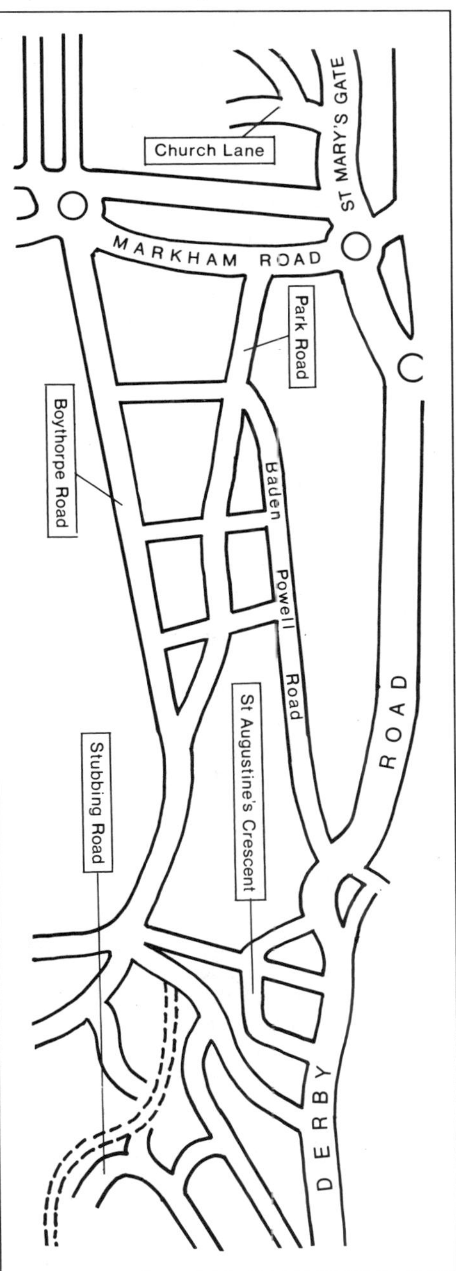

A Matter of Choice

The Murder of HANNAH CALLADINE and her two Children, ELSIE and ALBERT EDWARD by ALBERT EDWARD BURROWS on the 11th and 12th of January 1920 on Simmondley Moor, outside Glossop

There are singularly few notorious murderers about whom nothing good, however grudgingly, can be said. Some, like George Joseph Smith, had charm, a certain culture; Crippen, despite his single fall from grace, was a loyal and loving companion. Even Charlie Peace, when he was not robbing and killing, could hold an audience with a good fiddle tune!

Albert Burrows possessed none of these qualities, or any other of which a normal person would want to boast; in fact, like many of the dull-witted, brutish type to which he belonged, he was a sad and very incompetent gladiator in life's battle, and only his bluff, loutish approach ensured his survival – such as it was. Despite this, there were two women of whose eyes he seems to have been the apple.

We do not know when, or in what circumstances, he took Mrs Burrows as his wife; neither do we know much about her save that she was (perhaps necessarily) a hard and rather grasping woman, though clearly not astute enough to see through Albert.

Of his mistress we know a little more. She was christened Hannah Calladine, though Albert called her 'Nance'; she was nearly thirty years younger than Burrows, and in October 1918, when she was twenty-eight, Hannah did him the disservice of producing a son. Typically – though perhaps through pressure from Nance – Albert panicked, and 'married' the woman. This earned him six months in Derby Gaol for bigamy, and when he came out it was to be presented with a bastardy order requiring him to pay Miss Calladine seven shillings a week. Of course, he did not pay her a single farthing, and November 1919 found him once again a guest of His Majesty, convicted of default.

Hannah, though she did not record it for posterity, must have felt decidedly peeved over the shabby treatment that had been her lot, and maybe out of cussedness, or perhaps in a genuine attempt to drag reason from her reluctant lover, she departed from her home in Nantwich and pursued Burrows to his marital seat in Glossop. On December 17th, she was face to face with Mrs Burrows. Not unnaturally, Mrs Burrows felt very put out, and packed her bags; she remained in town just long enough to make a maintenance application against her husband. The case was ordered to be heard on January 12th, 1920.

Albert Burrows was at least bright enough to know that he had landed himself in a mess.

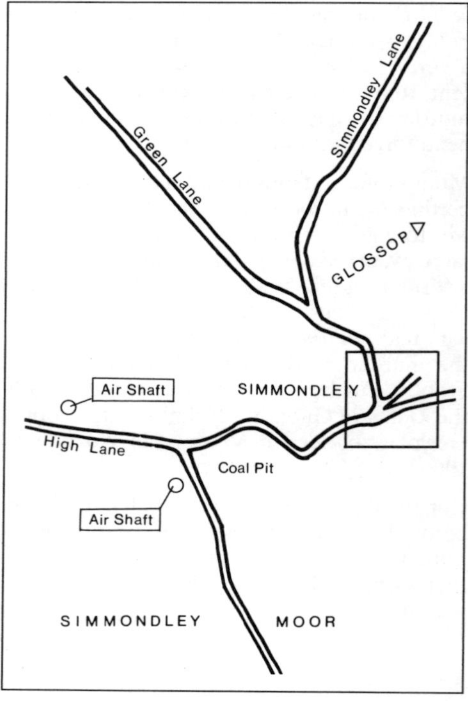

The options were straightforward enough; on the one hand, he could live with Nance and pay his wife maintenance; on the other, he could beg his wife's forgiveness and pay the bastardy order. Both of which solutions must have seemed academic anyway, because he didn't have any money.

Faced with this dilemma, most men would have weighed up the possibilities and tried to work out an acceptable compromise; some might simply have run away, started a new life with a new identity – an easy matter in the less bureaucratic climate of the 1920s.

That Albert Burrows chose a less articulate means for disposing of his problems should come as no surprise. Possibly on the basis of "the devil you know" principle, it was poor Hannah and her luckless children who became the objects of the disposal. On one pretext or another – it is hardly important in light of future events – Albert persuaded his 'second' family, young Nance and 14-month-old Albert Edward, out on to the lonely Simmondley Moor.

Beneath Simmondley Moor lies part of the Derbyshire coalfield; on the surface the visible traces of the once thriving industry that dug out the coal. It was at the bottom of the Dinting Airshaft which had ventilated one of these disused mines that Hannah Calladine and her son began their eternal rest.

On the following morning, the 12th of January – significantly, the day on which Mrs Burrows's maintenance claim was set to be heard – Albert was once again at the opening of an airshaft on Simmondley Moor. It was time for three-year-old Elsie Calladine to join her mother and stepbrother.

Speeding back to town, Albert was in time to catch his wife before she went into court; in time to try to persuade her to drop the maintenance application; to try to persuade her to return to the conjugal home: "Nance has gone!" he announced, with a macabre certainty. To her credit, Mrs Burrows stuck it out (at least as far as the court case was concerned), and the maintenance order was duly granted. In fact, the Burrowses were subsequently reunited, although with what success is best left unguessed.

We do know, though, that Albert was kept quite busy explaining away the sudden disappearance of Hannah Calladine and her two children. Hannah, he made it known, was living and thriving in Stretford, where she was employed selling bacon in the shop of a relative of his. Clearly, nobody was interested in making the thirty mile round trip to check on Albert's story, but still he continued to give out 'news' of Nance's well-being. Later, in a moment of gross arrogance, he went so far as to send a letter purporting to come from Hannah, signing off with the sentiment that Albert was "the best husband in the world", and that any who would say nay "are not fit to black his boots".

As for Hannah's children, Burrows, in his magnanimity, had "found them a good home". He didn't reveal where. Indeed, it is likely that Hannah and her babes would have remained 'lost' for a lot longer, their murderer have remained unvisited by Nemesis for many years; but Albert Burrows had a habit only slightly less repellent than killing children. He liked to rape little boys.

It was three years after the Calladines had disappeared, in March 1923, that four-year-old Thomas Wood went missing. Rescuers found the boy's abused and broken body three days later – at the bottom of an airshaft on Simmondley Moor. Burrows's luck had clearly been pressed too hard for too long, and in a short time the police had associated him with the latest vile crime, and had begun to check the whereabouts of Hannah, Elsie, and little Albert Edward. From beneath the years' accumulation of debris, their pathetic remains were taken out of the ventilating shaft.

At the Derby Assizes in July 1923, Burrows was tried only for the murder of Hannah Calladine and her children, but the thought of little Tommy Wood cannot have been far from the jury's thoughts. After an adjournment of only eleven minutes, they rejected the prisoner's defence that Hannah had committed suicide, and thus empowered Mr Justice Shearman to hand down the only sentence then possible for such a crime.

It is characteristic of this blustering bully that Albert Burrows's only reaction was: "I shan't be like Charlie Peace – I shan't tremble when I go to the scaffold."

He got his chance to prove it at Nottingham Gaol on the 8th of August 1923.

A Traveller's Tale

The Murder of Mrs AMY COLLINSON by GEORGE FREDERICK WALTER HAYWARD on Tuesday the 11th of October 1927 at the *New Inn* (now the *Lantern Pike)*, Hayfield

The *New Inn* at Little Hayfield is still standing, though it is called the *Lantern Pike* now, and Little Hayfield has been absorbed into Hayfield itself. But not a lot more has changed in the past sixty years there on the High Peak, an oasis between Sheffield and Greater Manchester.

In 1927 the licence of the pub was held by a man named Collinson, who with his wife Amy kept the business ticking over without too much strain. It was then, as now, a modest house – which is why, on the morning of the 11th of October, Mrs Collinson was alone in the pub. She was probably not much surprised by the visit of George Hayward; not, that is, until he began to bludgeon her with a piece of lead piping previously hacked from his own kitchen waste-pipe. Then, having dragged the poor woman across the parlour, he cut her throat with a carving knife.

George Hayward was a local, and his home, the White House, was near at hand. He had been a commercial traveller until very recently but was neither successful nor honest; which is why he was not only out of a job but being pressed by his former employers for money which he had collected from customers in the course of business and had failed to pay over. This debt amounted to some £70, but it was by no means the only debt clouding George Hayward's bleak financial horizon.

Murder, to be sure, is far less honest than embezzlement, but even George Hayward must have hoped that it would be more profitable. With the proceeds of ransacking the *New Inn,* Amy Collinson's murderer stood less than £40 better off. This is probably why he caught a bus to the neighbouring town of New Mills to draw his unemployment benefit from the Labour Exchange. From here he went on to Manchester where he bought a money order for £4 to prevent his hire-purchase furniture from being repossessed.

The continually luckless George Hayward remained a free man for half a day longer; time enough to hide the rest of the proceeds of his killing in the flue of his bedroom chimney. Where the police found it the next day when they arrested him.

In February 1928 the presiding judge at Hayward's trial at Derby Assizes was Mr Justice Hawke; the following month, the presiding hangman at his execution was Thomas Pierrepoint.

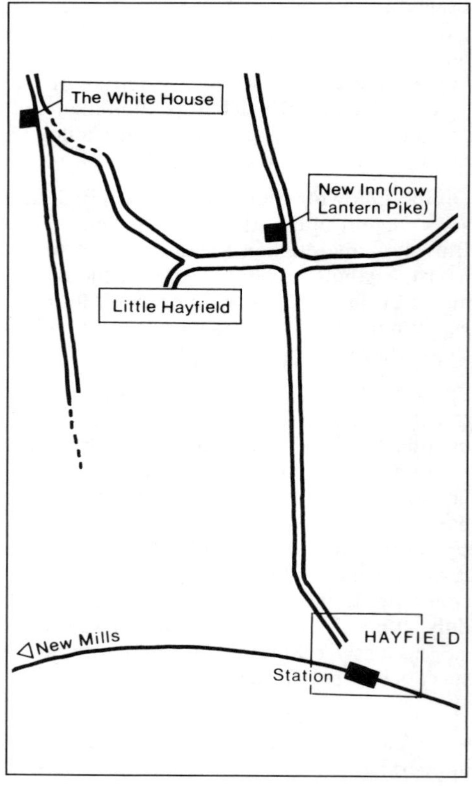

Murder in the Winnats*

The Brutal Murder of ALLAN and CLARA by JAMES ASHTON, NICHOLAS COOK, and Others around mid-April 1758 in the Winnats Pass, Peak District

The tasteful tourist will not, I opine, omit during his recreative visit to Castleton spending an hour in the very singular chasm or dell, happily designated the Winnats, more correctly Wingates – or more poetically rendered, "the portals of the wind." "Happy! happy! indeed," says some tourist, "was the imagination that first suggested its name – the gates or portals of the wind." This wild ravine is bounded on each side by perpendicular rocks of an amazing height; yet it is not wholly devoid of beauty: numbers of rare and elegant plants picturesquely adorn the steep sides of this, in other respects, deep, lone, and dreary pass. It is not a description of this long, winding, and deeply interesting defile which is here intended; no: it is to give a few hitherto unknown particulars concerning a tale of blood connected with the local history of this ghost-haunted dell – the Winnats. To detail the particulars of a brutal and horrible murder is not the most fascinating subject even for a juvenile writer; and, perhaps, far from being at all interesting to the general reader. But the story of the Winnats murder is full of circumstances of an extraordinary character; love on the part of the victims; awful ferocity on the part of the murderers; and the most striking instance on record of Divine judgement! These, with other minor attendant circumstances, must be the apology for giving notoriety to a deed which has no parallel (taking all the particulars into consideration) in the annals of crime. Let us, however, just observe that some diffidence exists in lifting or putting aside the veil which has to the present hid, in partial obscurity, the minute particulars of this fearful tragedy; the more so, as the perpetrators of the black deed may have descendants, or other kindred, who must necessarily wish all accounts of the dreadful action to be henceforth buried in oblivion. In consideration of this, the following details will not contain the names of the unfortunate actors in this deed of guilt – notwithstanding their being so well known throughout the Peak – but will distinguish them by the initials of their family names as follows: A—; B—; B—r; C—; H—**: they being five in number; and before commencing this story, let us fervently express our sincere hope that they have found that mercy in heaven, which they so barbarously refused to their trembling victims, after the most earnest and pathetic supplication that is possible to be expressed, by pitiful gestures and impassioned language.

About the middle of April, AD 1758, the then isolated inhabitants of Stoney Middleton, a small village near Eyam, and about twelve miles from Buxton, were more surprised than could scarcely be imagined now, at the arrival in the village, very early in the morning, in apparent great speed, of two very richly caparisoned beautiful steeds; mounted by a tall and sprightly-looking young gentleman, and a somewhat younger (and as the rustic villagers expressed themselves) 'angel-like' looking lady. Their astonishment was increased by the fair strangers galloping up to the *Royal Oak* inn; an inn, if so called, of very humble appearance. Arrived at the door they were soon dismounted, but not before they were encircled by a small concourse of the

---

* The title and text are taken from a Victorian travel guide.

** Perhaps time has given us the privilege of now revealing the villains' true names; they were, respectively, James Ashton, John Bradshaw, Francis Butler, Nicholas Cook, and Thomas Hall.

home-spun cloth clad village 'younkers', who gazed at the rich attire of the strangers, until their eyes bid fair for a trip from their sockets. The gentleman rapped first gently and then louder at the half-open inn door, asking frequently for the ostler; when after a lapse of six or eight minutes, a girl about thirteen appeared, bearing evident marks on her frontlet that she had been busily engaged in adjusting the pot-hooks in the chimney. "The ostler!" repeated the gentleman, "Mastur hasna nau oster," replied the 'browney', after having cleared her nasal pipes by taking three or four sniffs. The gentleman handed his fair companion into a room and immediately proceeded to assume the office of ostler himself. During his short absence how did the lady gaze around the place: chairs, tables, fire-irons, coal-ashes, and broken pots were promiscuously squandered on the floor: satisfactory evidence of the quality of the preceding night's company. Here lay a broken chair, there a legless table, and other numberless mutilated domestic articles, which had been the weapons and shields of the 'pot-valliants' of the late Bacchanalian orgies. The lady sat in mute astonishment, for never before that fatal journey had she seen such evidence of the great disparity in the manners and modes of life. By this time the host and hostess had descended from the realm of morpheus; they entered the lady's room, but almost involuntarily started back on beholding the costly garb and the entrancing beauty of their unexpected female guest. The gentleman now rejoined his fair one, and after having interrogated the hostess respecting her articles of provision in the house, he briefly and politely apologized by observing that he and his female companion would content themselves, as their stay was so very short, with the little provisional delicacies that they had brought along with them, and would pass along to the next place for breakfast. The two strangers are now alone in a room apart. The host was in the kitchen corner hemming and swelling with pride at the quality of the guests, fully persuaded that they had been recommended to his house for its reputed *respectability* and *accommodation*. The servant, before alluded to, was busy among the dishes, and frequently one cried "smash" on the floor, occasioned by her imagining she could feel in the palm of her hand the shilling she *should* receive from the illustrious guests. The wily hostess was listening to the conversation of the stranger, through a lattice, which adjoined the room where they were partaking of their repast. The prying dame had pinned up her mobbed cap from over one of her ears, which she kept as closely fixed, and equally steady to the lattice as was the head of Sisera to the ground when pierced by the nail of the heroic Jael. According to the hostess, the lady did not take of the repast; but, to the gentleman's solicitations for her to take some little refreshment, she only answered by deep heart-bursting sighs. The hostess also ascertained the gentleman's adopted name to be Allan; and the lady's Clara; furthermore, she heard the following dialogue, which, she averred, fixed her to the lattice in breathless fear; adding, that she could not understand all they said for "sha thute tha wur fariners, tha tak'd sa quarely."

Allan: Clara, my dear, pardon me for saying that I imagine I have perceived, during this morning's ride, a shade of despondency upon your angel brow; pray let me hear if aught – ah! if even a thought – disturbs your mind, that I may willingly bear the suffering it occasions.

Clara: Ah! my Allan, your anxious gaze has long bespoken some interrogation; but alas! what weighs so heavy at my heart cannot! cannot be alleviated by human sympathy!

Allan: Come, my adored, my ever dearest Clara, come tell me what it is that has produced this change in your still now soul-gladdening countenance? surely your love has not, during our journey, suffered the least diminution?

Clara: Allan, my faithful Allan, speak not of impossibilities. Do you forget the numberless expedients which have been used to estrange my affections from you: but in vain. Let me now tell you that, on the night I left my father's house to meet you to fly to Derbyshire, I more than fully proved the intensity of my love! Ah! that evening! that evening! I sat beside my father, whose eye, methought, almost discovered our secret in my face. Jocund were my dear brothers and sisters, while I, feigning illness, early retired to bed: but not to sleep. when midnight came, the appointed hour, I arose; my sisters, sleeping, I kissed again and again, leaving their cheeks suffused with tears. Softly I stole into my parents' room. I stood beside their bed, and sighed farewell, farewell! O! never can I forget the conflicting emotions that, during those few moments, rent my soul. I saw, in imagination, my aged parents aroused from their slumber in the morning by the wailings of my sisters, "O! father! mother! our Clara's gone! our Clara's fled!" The consequent distraction which I imagined had nigh compelled me to retract from my vow, when I heard your signal, and in a moment I was in your arms. Allan! my Allan! why doubt the unchangeability of my love?

Allan: Then why this change which I have so painfully noticed this morning?

Clara: Allan, I will tell you: 'tis a dream which I had last night: a dream so full of horror that, the chilliness of death creeps through my body at the thought of reciting it: yet I will essay. Methought that we alone were walking among some barren hills which, I imagined, as we rode along this morning, much resembled those which we beheld in the distance. There was a stillness and strangeness in the scene which affected me most peculiarly as we walked along. After a while we descended a hill into a valley, the most romantic and picturesque that imagination can conceive. A rivulet was winding through the vale, singing a song of peace, most enchantingly delightful. In the centre of the valley we sat down on a daisy-decked knoll, reciprocally vowing the fervency of our affection and love. It was at this moment that I felt a consciousness of someone being near, I turned my head to the right, when lo! I saw the shade, or image of, a little brother of mine, who had been dead twelve years. I started with the most intense surprise; his countenance was pale and ghastly as when I saw him in his last moments; his eyes were fixed on me, with some kind of meaning or expression, perfectly indiscribable. A tremor agitated my frame as I attempted to call him by his name; however, I repeated his name twice, and the last time, he lifted up his ashy hand, pointed to the top of the opposite hill, shook his head and vanished. I then, absorbed in thought, looked for a while towards the hill to which my brother had pointed; when I could perceive for or five distinct beings advancing towards us, yet I could scarce believe them to be human. Soon they reached us, and their terrific aspects made me tremble with horror; for although they were men, their garb, demeanour and brutal countenances induced me to imagine or think they were monsters unknown to mankind. Now, my dearest Allan, commenced the terrible scene which has left so deep and indelible an impression on my mind. Methought they seized us both, and hurried us away into a gloomy cavern, the interior of which filled me with the most painful horror imaginable. And what increased my agony to the uttermost was, I beheld them mangle your body in the most bloody and awful manner; then did they fix their deadly glance on me; and with a suffocating shriek I awoke, and for some moments, with open eyes, I struggled hard with the dread phantoms of my dream.

Allan: 'Twas horrid, surely; but calm your mind, my love; dreams are only freaks of fancy, which take their hue and character from circumstances, often, if not always, ideal and unsubstantial.

Clara: Allan! Allan! I think! I fear not! that which has received the concurrent and universal testimony of mankind in all the ages of the world, is entitled to some respect and credence. That some calamity awaits us, I have a most agonizing dread.

Allan: Be comforted, my fond Clara – banish from your bosom such doleful thoughts. I have a thousand times over dreamed of our happy union in the bonds of matrimony; dreamed of leading you to the altar, and felt, during these blissful moments, a happiness that I should in vain attempt to describe; but which I now hope, ere the sun sets behind the western hills, to enjoy in reality. Come, my Clara, take some little refreshment while I speak to the host and see our horses in readiness.

The host and Allan were now in the stable, and Allan took the opportunity of asking the following questions: "How far is it to a place named the Forest of Peak?" "Why about eight miles," replied the host. "What is the distance from there to Buxton?" said Allan. "Not a many miles," said the host. "We shall go through Castleton to the Peak Forest, I suppose?" said Allan; "Ah belike, and then through the Wunnats," replied Boniface. "Well, good host, you will bring the horses to the door in a few minutes, will you?" "Ah Sir, ah Sir, I wull," replied the *polite* and *gentlemanly* host. Allan again rejoined his loved one who sat absorbed in thought; "come, my dear," said he, "we must away, the horses are ready – they will now mount the hills, like Apollo's steeds, up heaven's steep." Clara rose from her seat and deeply sighed; a dark presentiment of evil entwined round her heart; and her agitation greatly affected Allan, although he endeavoured to conceal it from her notice. Soon they were mounted on their fleet-footed coursers, and very quickly out of sight. A few villagers had been conning the strangers anent the inn, to whom when the strangers had gone, the host approached, and thus immediately vociferated, "Na, I'st bet ony one on ya, my new drab cloth coat that yon two are for a Gretna Green job that are for th' Peak Forest, and yo know jobs a that sort is done thare welly same as Gretna Green."

The hapless pair are now wending their way to Castleton, where they intend stopping a short time. Allan looks with wonder on the langerous vales and the manifold mist-capped hills which bound their view on every side; Clara rides by his side, silent and thoughtful, her bosom heaves at intervals with bursting despair; unconsciously; with trembling hands she guides the rein; for ah! her thoughts are full of that dream:

And through her veins a chilling terror glides
(Tasso)

It is a merciful dispensation of Providence that a foresight or knowledge of the tragical end or termination of life, to which numbers are doomed in all countries, is impenetrably veiled from their mental vision until the almost actual transpiration. Indeed, were it otherwise, human existence would be unsupportable; a torrent of despair would overwhelm and utterly destroy those mental emanations which so unequivocally evince the glory and wisdom of the Great Author of our being. It is, however, difficult to account for the opinion which has been held with such tenacity by great numbers, that they have had prognostications of their fates; presages their or others tragical destinies; and in a manner convincingly impressive. By the especial interposition of Providence alone can this opinion be accounted tenable; and when Providence does interpose cannot be determined infallibly by the evidence of human testimony.

There was, however, something in the dream of Clara, as we shall see hereafter, strikingly coincident with the fate of herself and her unfortunate lover. Her despondency increased during their journey from Stoney Middleton to Castleton, which was about nine miles; a journey amid mountains which wore their unchanging garb of thousands of years; mountains mist-shrouded, when man may:

Look down
On towns that smoke below, and homes that creep
Into the silvery clouds, which far off keep
Their sultry state! and many a mountain stream,
And many a mountain vale, and ridgy steep;
The Peak, and all his mountains, where they gleam
Or frown, remote or near, more distant than they seem.
([Charlotte] Elliott)

It was near ten o'clock of the fatal day when the unfortunate pair reached the village of wonders – Castleton; they rode up at a brisk pace to one of the Inns, but not the principal; this plan they had, besides taking a circuitous route, invariably adopted during their journey: a necessary expedient to avoid being traced and overtaken by Clara's father and brothers, who had the most inveterate antipathy to Allan. They alighted from their smoking steeds at the Inn-door, and were shown into a room somewhat more respectable and comfortable than that at the *Royal Oak* Stoney Middleton. Allan, after having ordered the horses to be stabled and fed, called for breakfast to be served with greatest despatch. Clara took her seat in a corner of the room, leaned her head against the wall, and deeply sighed; Allan placed himself by her side, and in the most endearing, loving, and pathetic language he could command, conjured her to raise her dropping spirits; and then, in the glowing colours of heart-born affection, portrayed the years of unalloyed happiness with which they should be henceforth blessed. The earnest exhortations of Allan aroused Clara to some degree from her death-like stupor; she turned her head, gazed him steadfastly in the face, until the burning tears:

Rushed from her clouded brain,
Like mountain mists, at length dissolved to rain.
(Byron)

Breakfast was served, and Allan was in the act of endeavouring, in the most kind and persuasive language he could summon to his aid, to induce his Clara to partake, when an opposite room door was thrown open and he beheld, with some emotion, four uncouth, savage-looking men seated round a table, evidently in a state bordering on inebriation. While he looked on them with some surprise, one, seemingly by his glaring eyes the most intoxicated, broke out in a voice rough as his garb and nature, with an attempt to mouth or sing the following doggerel lines:

"Come fellows drink – drink your fill,
Full soon we must gang up the hill,
Where Odin rich in shining ore
Shall give us glasses – hundreds more;
Then luck to Odin – golden mine,
With metal bright, like th' sun doth shine."

The last couplet was a sort of chorus, in which they all joined with a bawl so loud that "roof and rafters a' did dirl". The worthy host now appeared among them, and thus politely voiciferated: "As you've been these five days and netes, fellows, and as you've now begun awanting to *chalk* I'd rather you'd mizzle – I've a gentleman and lady i th' parlour, so bounce!" On this they all arose; swung their groove-clothes on their backs – gave the landlord a hearty curse, and reeled out of the house. Staggering down the village they went; halting, however, at all the other inns; but at every one of which they met the door 'slap-bang' in their faces, accompanied by the significant exclamation: "Go where you've been, sots!"

These drunken Bacchanalians (the initials of four of whose names are mentioned in the commencement of this narrative, were A—; B—r; C—; H—;) now repaired towards Odin, where they were employed – a mine which was worked, as its name imports, in the time of the Danes: a thousand years ago. It is about a mile north-west of Castleton: and it was on the way thither that the following criminous conversation transpired among the miners alluded to – conversation darkly ominous: – "I say, chaps," said A—; "what dud ye think about th' old d—l of a landlord t'order us awey because we'd no money, and he'd better company i th' parlour?" "Why," replied B—, "I didna think sa mich about that as about summat else as crost my ene." "What's that, old buck?" asked C—; "Nay, nout very mich," replied B—r. "Na, I know, as sure as Mam Tor and that old Castle, what B—r means," H— immediately exclaimed. "Ah, out weet! out weet," said A—, "wear aw one, aint us?" "Belike, belike," rejoined C—; "well na, if B—r al not deny it, I'll guess and guess reet," H— said immediately. "Come then, at it," the other three replied. H— then commenced, and said, "na, B—r, didst na see the gentleman with the lady, tak saddle bags off his horse at th' Inn door, and dist na think they were full of money, they seemed sa heavy, and didst na think that shud like sum of it?" "Well, I did lad," replied B—r; "an I yoan amind, we'll go o'er th' hil here, an meet em i th' Winnats, and tak it on um – they'll go up there I'mh sure!" "By the d—l hee's B— leaving his work," said H—, "we must take him with us, we'll make him go, or crack a pick shaft on his skull: now be plucky, we'll have him with us." After a hot but short altercation with B—, they agreed to B—r's proposal, and they wended their way swiftly towards the Winnats.

The sun was near its meridian heights, when Allan and Clara left Castleton. Rapidly they rode along into the Winnats; but what pen can describe the agonizing fear of Clara, when, on entering the most secluded part of the defile, up sprang the five human savages, and seized the bridles of both horses, and with horrid imprecations bade the riders dismount, Allan with a countenance pale as death looked towards Clara, who with quivering lips faintly ejaculated: "Allan, my dream! my dream!"

H— and B—r had hold of the bridles, while the other three paced around the horses, and, with their pickaxes uplifted, swore that if they did not immediately alight they would bury the steel in the horses heads, and after that in theirs. Allan in the most beseeching manner, said: "I hope, my friends, you intend no injury to two strangers. See! see! the lady is falling from her horse with fear! Pray, have mercy on us! spare our lives, and you shall have everything we have; but in mercy injure us no further, for this dear lady's sake!" "No cavil," said A—, and springing up, he seized Allan's cloak and brought him to the ground. "Somebody'll be coming: let's haul 'em into the barn there," said H—, and they immediately hurried Allan away, piteously supplicating for mercy! This done, some of them returned for Clara, whom they:

"Dragged from among horses' feet"

and carried her away, in a state of insensibility, to the same fearful and fatal place.

The awful suspense – the indescribable agony experienced by Allan while these inhuman beings were gone for Clara, language cannot portray! H— had been left to prevent Allan from escaping, or giving any alarm during the others' absence; and Allan, in this bitter extremity, would fain have won him over by promises and tender supplications; but the callous-hearted villain, who stood in the doorway of the barn, swore vehemently that if Allan moved one limb or spoke one word more, he would bury his uplifted pickaxe in his body; on which Allan shuddered and said no more.

On the savages entering the barn with Clara, Allan received them on his knees, and, with his purse in his hand, said: "for Heaven's sake take this! take this; take our all, but O! in mercy spare our lives! do not, my dear friends, for that dear lady's sake, injure us any further." B— snatched the purse from Allan, while the others rifled his pockets. This done, they retired outside the building to consult on further proceedings.

"I wish," said A—, "we'd na com'n a'te a Castleton t'dey; we's be fun a'te shure enough, an be hanged." "Wa," replied B—r, "if we are fun a'te, we's know ar doom: but we mun stop that if we can." "Stop it!" exclaimed B—, "there's naught but one chance a that, na." "What's that?" asked C—; "Why," said H—, "he means t'kill 'em; an I'm it same mind." "I dunna like that," A— emphatically rejoined. "Well," H— swore, "if tha's qualms o' conscience, we's be obleeg'd to do it arsels; an if wer fun a'te after, tha mun swing wa us – not for murder – but for company; come, B—r, let's all into um, or shure we's be catched with horses standing yonder."

During this awful consultation, Allan had crept to Clara, whom he had by the most tender caresses brought back to sensibility. He endeavoured to persuade her that the worst was past; but, her wild gaze around the barn, and her faint ejaculations, "my dream, Allan! my dream! my dream!" filled his despairing soul with bitter agony. Returning footsteps now fell on their ears with all the terrors of immediate death. H— entered first; and Allan fell upon his knees again and said: "O, my friends! if you will but spare this lady's life, I will with my own hands take mine before your eyes! Do not, I implore you, injure her, do what you will with me!" This heart-rending appeal had little effect. The heartless monsters were busy about the door – making it fast inside – when Clara suddenly sprang up from the corner of the barn where she had laid, and in an attitude of humble prostration thus exclaimed: "If ever woman's tongue did raise a thought of pity – if ever signs and tears could move the heart of mortal man, let me now beseech you, in pity to spare the life of my companion, my love, my Allan! 'tis me! 'tis me! ah! 'tis through me alone that we are here. Come, in this my naked bosom plunge a weapon; but O! in mercy spare my loved, my dearest Allan!" Clara, as she finished this pathetic exclamation, closed her eyes, hung back her head, and presented her snow-white naked bosom to the savage monsters. Meanwhile Allan, roused by the moving appeal of Clara, sprang to his feet, and rushed between her and the heartless murderers; a moment elapsed, and he, in the agony of despair, leaped towards the savages, seized B—r by the throat and dashed him to the ground. Then, with the fury of a tiger, he sprang upon the others, who instantly surrounded him, and a struggle ensued which only the pencil of a Salvator Rosa could portray. In a few minutes Allan was overpowered and fell; yet, against their united strength he had almost gained his feet again, when H— or B—r struck Allan on the head with a pick, and he fell senseless, to rise no more. In what manner they took the life of Clara is not known; but it is said their blood comingled together on the floor of that fatal barn. Silent and horror-struck the murderers looked on their victims as they lay stiffening with death, wishing intensely, when also too late, they had spared their lives. Then it was that the enormity of their crime overwhelmed them with a life-lasting anguish; then it was that blood-bought guilt stamped their accusing minds with the deadly seal of horror implacable. They gazed on each other in speechless awe; the beautiful form and features of Clara aroused their attention, for oh!

A form of wax
Wrought to the very life was there;
So still she was, so pale, so fair.
([Shackerley] Marmion)

These miserable wretches who had dyed their hands with innocent blood, remained in the barn until the shades of evening chased the weary day from every mountain side. During their stay in the fatal place a violent thunder storm occurred, which added immeasurably to their perturbation of mind. The lightning flashed on the bloody faces of their fated victims; the thunder rebellowed in the horrible dell, and the guilty murderers trembled with excessive fear. Conscience-stricken, they heard in every crack the appalling voice of justice calling aloud for vengeance, and worlds they would have given to have undone their bloody deed.

Night had approached when they divided the booty, which was £200 in money and other valuables. They stripped Clara of her outer silken vestment, and placing her beside Allan, covered them with some unclean straw, and retired, having first agreed to return to the barn at midnight and inter the bodies. Midnight came and they repaired to the solitary place; but their 'blood-guiltiness' peopled the shades of night with horrid forms! They heard in imagination the shrieks of woe, and they retreated with precipitation from the dismal place. The following night they ventured again; but on their arrival at the scene of blood, two steeds, each mounted by a spectre, with hair

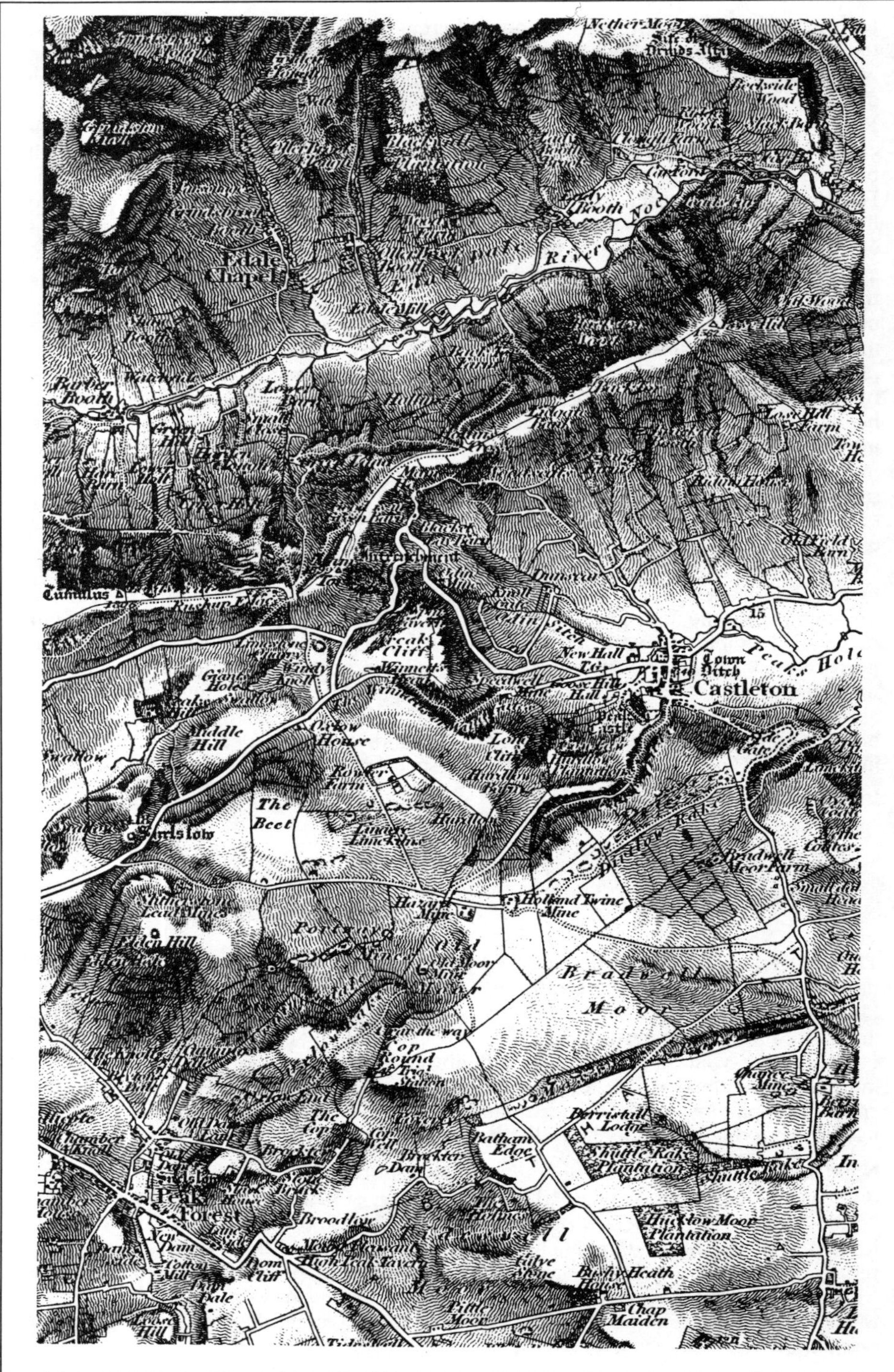
Edale Chapel
River
Castleton
New Hall
Town Ditch
Middle Hill
The Beet
Peak Cliff
Windy Knoll
Bradwell
Moor
Cop Round
Peak Forest
Batham Edge
Holland Twine Mine
Hucklow Moor Plantation
Bushy Heath
Chap Maiden
Eldon Hill
Shuttle Rake Plantation

dabbed with gore, rushed past them, and entered the barn; on which they retraced their steps more terrified than before. On the third night they again repaired to the place, determined of accomplishing their purpose; at the door they heard the same dismal wailings of distress, and were about to return, when B—r exclaimed: "it's only the d——l, he'll not hurt us," on which they entered: put the bodies in two sacks, and by the dim light of a solitary lantern, buried them at a little distance from the scene of their horrible death. This done they returned, but not alone; visibly they behold;

Two ghastly spectres,
For ever rising to their view
Eyes wide glaring – face distorted,
Quiv'ring lips of livid hue.

(Jewett)

The day following the interment of these hapless lovers their horses were found, saddled and bridled, in the forest adjoining the Winnats; and when brought into Castleton, great surprise was thereby excited. The probability of the riders having been murdered and thrown into Eldon Hole, was generally entertained; but a descent into that fearful chasm, and nothing found appertaining to them, proved the supposition erroneous. The horses were, in due time, removed from Castleton to Chatsworth, as waifs; the Duke of Devonshire being tenant to the Duchy of Lancaster, for the manorial rights of Castleton.

A many years after this circumstance, some miners in removing the earth to sink an engine shaft, discovered two skeletons, which were generally believed to be those of the gentleman and lady who belonged to the horses; this was further corroborated by one of the skulls having all its teeth perfect except one in the front, a deficiency that had been observed in Allan, both at Castleton and at Stoney Middleton. The skeletons were buried in the church-yard at Castleton, but no positive evidence of the murderers had been discovered. After the discovery of these human remains there were, now and then, a few dark hints dropped respecting the supposed guilty persons; originating chiefly, in the sudden change in circumstances of the suspected individuals, and in words spoken by them in unguarded moments. A— bought horses with his share of the booty, but they died in rapid succession; and when on his journeys, he frequently said: "I have always a beautiful lady with me – she rides on my horse." C—'s daughter went to the church not long after in a very rich silk dress, which excited the notice of the whole village. As no inquiry was made after the two unfortunate lovers, there was less possibility of ascertaining who the perpetrators of the murder were, except by the voluntary confession of one or all of the murderers; which, as the reader will see, was the case with A—.

Though the hand of human justice did not reach these guilty beings, yet the hand of God found them out, even on earth. C—, some years after the discovery of the bodies, fell from a precipice in the Winnats and was killed on the spot; a stone fell from a hill near the place of the murder and killed B—, and in a manner which astonished those who saw it B—r went mad and died in a most miserable state, after having attempted several times to commit suicide; H— hanged himself; and A—, after lying ten weeks on his death-bed, declared that he, C—, H—, B—, and B—r did rob, murder, and bury the gentleman and lady whom they met in the Winnats; adding that she was "the handsomest woman I ever saw," – he died the same day.

What can escape Thine eye, just God?
Ah! who can fly Thy vengeful rod?

Who these unfortunate victims were, and whence they came, is not satisfactorily known: Clara was supposed to be an English nobleman's daughter, and Allan a gentleman from the South of England. Some unusual opposition to their union by

Clara's haughty father, caused them to come to Derbyshire to be married at the Peak Forest, which was at that time extra-parochial, and where persons were united in matrimony without the slightest inquiry whence they came. – Jewitt, in the notes to his *Wanderings of Memory,* fixes the date of this direful tragedy in 1768; but the confession of A— (published in two popular periodical works) makes the date of the murder 1758. The same author represents them as having been married on the day of their murder. This, for reasons, I believe to be an error. The author of the *Peak Scenery* thinks the whole story is fabulous. Of the truth of this tale of blood, the following proofs may be instanced – A—'s confession, committed to paper at his death; the finding of the bodies; the horses without riders (one of the saddles is now in the Speedwell Cavern Museum, bought at a sale of articles from the museum of the late Thomas Bateman, Middleton, near Youlgreave. It was purchased off Mrs Willis, Grindleford Bridge, one of whose ancestors obtained it at Chatsworth, where he was a groom at the time of the tragedy. This saddle belonged to the horse rode by Clara; it is made of, or covered partly with, red morocco leather, and has a stirrup-shod, or shoe); the recognition of the horses on their way through Stoney Middleton to Chatsworth, by the host of the *Royal Oak* inn; the testimony of the landlord's servant who was married to Mr John Andrew, Eyam, and who died after having a thousand times repeated the circumstances of the gentleman and lady calling at the *Royal Oak* inn, always adding *a la* A—: "O! she was a pretty woman!"; the remains of the barn is still pointed out close by the shop at the entrance to the Speedwell Cavern; and the unexceptionable, concurrent impression of the truth of the melancholy story among the inhabitants of the Peak. Many more corroborative proofs might be brought foreward; among the rest, a Mrs Simpson, of Oakard, near Hope, remembered seeing a pair of stays and a chemise when she first went to Oakard, after becoming the second wife of Mr Simpson. On observing these articles in the house, she asked her husband who could have worn such things at Oakard, to which he replied, that they came with his first wife from Castleton, and belonged, he believed, to the lady of the Winnats. A Mr Hallam of Stoney Middleton answered them some question on their leaving Stoney Middleton, and saw the horses on their way back to Chatsworth.

Readers, do not imagine that the barbarity of the perpetrators of the foul deed in the Winnats is still the prevailing characteristic of the inhabitants of the Peak. Thanks to the humanizing effects of mechanical genius – the mountain-barriers of this wild district are now penetrated, and these wonder-working excavations operate as channels of civilization! It may be added, that the inhabitants of Castleton, and the Peak in general, are now distinguished by many excellent traits of humanity, kindness, and social importance. That the inhabitants of this mountainous locality a generation back should have been rough and uncouth, yea, even savage and ferocious, may be accounted if not apologized for by the generally stated fact that the North of Derbyshire was, during and after the Septarchal ages, a penal settlement; that criminals were sent here to work in mines (under captains) as a fit punishment for certain crimes. I was surprised that my good neighbours of Castleton should have been a little chagrined on the first appearance of this tale in print: I am certain it cannot affect their material interests; and their being otherwise sensitive would be exhibiting finer or more touchy feelings than even a very many of the most eminent of mankind: Dr Johnson, for instance, told his wife, while he was paying his addresses to her before marriage, that his grandfather was hanged. And as to places where crimes have been committed, it may be said of them as the poet sings of cities:

Thou canst not find a spot whereon no city stood.

THE END

The Madness of George Victor Townley*

The Murder of BESSIE CAROLINE GOODWIN by GEORGE VICTOR TOWNLEY on Friday the 21st of August 1863 in Wigwell Lane, Whatstandwell, Nr. Wirksworth

The winter of 1855 will long be remembered as one of the severest ever known in England. As week after week went by with no sign of the cruel black frost breaking, even men at home were able to realize from their own experiences something of the awful sufferings and hardships which our gallant soldiers were enduring in the trenches before Sebastopol.

Among the incidents of that remarkable winter, one lingers with special vividness in my recollection. It was a Twelfth Night children's party, and the life and soul of the party was a handsome girl of fifteen, one of the jolliest, merriest lasses I have ever met. She seemed born for a happy life; and who would have dreamed that a terrible and tragic end was in store for that bright young creature before she was eight years older.

For that handsome, high-spirited girl was Bessie Goodwin, whose murder by her lover thrilled all England with horror and created a sensation which I have hardly known paralleled in my time.

At the time I knew them, Miss Goodwin and her parents resided in Chester. Her father, Mr Henry Goodwin, had been an officer in the Austrian cavalry, and was one of the finest amateur flautists in England. Mrs Goodwin, I think, kept a ladies' school in which she was assisted by her daughter Bessie. But when she was about twenty, the latter left home to keep house for her grandfather, Captain Goodwin, of Wigwell Grange. Captain Goodwin's eldest son was a doctor in Manchester, and in the year 1859, just before she went to live with her grandfather, Bessie met at this uncle's house a young man named George Victor Townley, between whom and herself there quickly sprang up a strong attachment.

Townley was the eldest son of a well-known commission agent in Manchester, who resided with his family at Hendham Vale, about a couple of miles from the city. George Victor, in addition to well-developed musical gifts, had refined literary tastes, considerable acquirements as a linguist, and fascinating manners. He was, in short, a cultured and intellectual gentleman. In Bessie Goodwin, he found a congenial and sympathetic companion; he fell in love with her, and she with him, and they became engaged.

But as George Victor's position and prospects offered no immediate hope of his being able to marry, the engagement was not recognized by either family; so strong, indeed, was the disapprobation of Miss Goodwin's relations, that the engagement was broken off. But the young people were sincerely attached to one another, and after an interval of a few months, during which, I believe, they kept up a clandestine correspondence, they met again, and the engagement was renewed. At this time I think there can be no doubt that Bessie really was in love with George Victor, though her passion was never so deep and strong as his.

So matters went on till the summer of the year 1863, when an incident occurred which quite changed the spirit of Bessie's dream. There came to Wigwell Grange on a visit a young clergyman of good family and excellent prospects – an attractive, agreeable man – in every respect a most eligible suitor. He was fascinated by Miss Goodwin the moment he saw her. His attentions soon became pronounced, and Bessie did not resent them. On the contrary, she found herself more and more drawn to this new lover, who had already become a great favourite with her grandfather.

---

*Adapted from *Famous Crimes Past and Present,* 1903.

The absent are always in the wrong, says the French proverb, and the more Bessie Goodwin reflected on her absent lover, George Townley, the less she liked him. Here she had the prospect of an early marriage with a man who could give her the comforts and even the luxuries of life...and when the young clergyman proposed, she accepted him.

So the deed was done, and on the 14th of August, 1863, Bessie Goodwin wrote to George Victor Townley asking him to release her from their engagement; a letter which was destined to be her death-warrant. Unfortunately that letter was destroyed, and there was nothing but the imperfect recollection of Townley's mother, to whom he had read the letter, to prove how it was worded.

We can gather, however, from Townley's reply to the effect which the letter produced upon him. He took a whole day to consider his answer, and on the 16th of August, he wrote as follows to Miss Goodwin:

> Hendham Vale, Sunday
>
> My Dearest Bessie, – Dearest you will always be to me; to say that I am not terribly cut up would be a lie, but, at any rate, you know I am not the man to stand in your way...Before I go I wish to see you once again, and for the last time...Say in your next where you will meet me. I will come by the first or second train from Derby on Tuesday or Wednesday morning, whichever suits you; of course, without anyone knowing. – Ever, dearest Bessie, your affectionate
>
> George.
>
> p.s. Will you write by return?

On the Monday, he wrote again:

> Dearest Bessie, – It is doubtful whether you will get the letter I wrote you yesterday till tomorrow...this is simply to say that in my haste I mentioned Tuesday or Wednesday forgetting that I should have to leave here today in order to see you tomorrow...I think if we say Thursday evening or Friday morning it would be best...I suppose anywhere between your house and Whatstandwell would do. Address care of W. Arrowsmith, Gilnow Mills, Bolton, where I am going tomorrow.
>
> G.V.T.
>
> p.s. Trains – I can arrive at Whatstandwell Bridge at 4.02 afternoon, or at 9.34 or 11.37 in the morning, whichever you like.

On Wednesday, the 19th, he wrote as follows:

> Gilnow Mills, Bolton
>
> My dear Bessie, – I will only say here that I arrive by the 11.37am Friday morning, and that I hope, dear Bessie, you will not bother yourself about this as far as I am concerned...You can still write to the Midland Hotel, Derby, where I shall stay tomorrow night...if you like to call at the inn I will not stir out till you come; but I leave this to your judgement. – Ever yours affectionately,
>
> G.V.T.

On the same day, Miss Goodwin wrote a letter to Townley:

> My dear George, – I write this in the greatest haste to tell you not to come on any account. I leave here today, and can't tell when I shall or can be back again. I do not wish to see you if it can possibly be avoided, and, indeed, there will be no chance now, so we had better end this state of suspense at once, and say 'Good-bye' without seeing each other. I feel sure I could not stand the meeting...Yours truly,
>
> Bessie

This letter reached Hendham Vale on the Thursday morning, and Townley's mother, perceiving from whom it came, opened it, and immediately telegraphed to her son who was then staying at Mr Arrowsmith's:

> Letter from B[essie]. Come at once. Will meet you at the station. Will wait. Immediate.

Immediately on receipt of the telegram, Townley left Bolton and returned to Hendham Vale. From there he went on the same day to the Midland Hotel, at Derby, where he slept. On the following morning, Friday the 21st of August, he left Derby, and went to Whatstandwell, the nearest station to Wigwell Grange, which is about a mile and a half distant. At twenty minutes to six he arrived at Wigwell Grange and asked for Miss Goodwin. Bessie escorted him into the garden to avoid her grandfather's knowing, and they remained there in earnest conversation for half an hour. Then Townley left, but evidently on the understanding that they were to meet again, for at a quarter to seven Miss Goodwin set out from the Grange in her walking dress to keep an assignation.

She met her former lover in Wigwell Lane, and they were seen walking together there between eight and nine o'clock. Reuben Conway, a labourer in the employ of a Mr Bowmer described what followed:

> As I was going along the turnpike road towards Wigwell Lane end, I heard a moaning noise which appeared to come from the direction of the Mill Lane end. I ran forward, and found Miss Goodwin guiding herself by the wall, and coming towards the house. Her face and the front of her dress were covered with blood. She asked me to take her home, and said there was a gentleman down there had been murdering her. I put my arm round her and carried her about twenty yards. She asked me whether I could see anyone, and on looking down the road I saw Mr Townley sixty or eighty yards below the lane end, and nearer the lane end than the place where the blood was afterwards found. He was crossing the road, and then came towards me. When I first saw him he was about forty yards away from the hunting gate. As he came up I went towards him and asked who had been murdering Miss Goodwin. He said he had stabbed her. I asked him to go and help me, and he took hold of her head and I of her body, and we carried her towards Wigwell. He called her "Poor Bessie" several times, and said "You should not have proved false to me." She said nothing. We laid her down near a gate, and he asked me for something to put round her neck to stop the bleeding. I said I had nothing, and he asked me to go for help. I asked him if he would stop with her, and he said he would. I went to Mr Bowmer's yard for help, leaving Mr Townley with Miss Goodwin.

Conway returned to find Townley holding a shawl tightly round Miss Goodwin's throat to staunch the flow of blood. They were joined by a Mr Seeds and his brother, and between them the four men raised the now unconscious lady and bore her homewards. For an instant the pathetic girl regained her senses, and a sigh was followed by a groan, and then the whispered words "I am dying! I am dying!"

That was her last utterance on earth. The rest was silence. When they carried her a little farther, Townley suddenly said: "Stop! She is dead!" They laid her down. George Victor bent over and kissed her tenderly; then, lifting her head, said sadly: "Yes, she is dead! I have killed her!"

It was true. Bessie Goodwin had breathed her last.

As the four bearers carried their lifeless burden within the gates of the Grange they were met by Captain Goodwin and his housekeeper, Ann Poynter: "What's amiss? What have you there?"

"It is your granddaughter, Bessie, murdered", blurted out Seeds.

"What nonsense are you talking? Who would murder my granddaughter?"

Townley stepped forward and said quietly: "I have done it."

"You, who are you, Sir?"

"My name is George Victor Townley."

"My God! my God! – You – you murder my poor Bessie! You villain! What made you do it?"

Coldly and calmly George Victor made reply: "She has deceived me, and the woman who deceives me must die. I told her I should kill her. She knows my temper."

In the meanwhile a police constable had been sent for. On the officer's arrival at Wigwell Grange, Townley walked up to him and said: "I wish to give myself up for murdering the young lady." He handed over to the policeman a bloody knife, and added: "I am far happier now that I have done it than I was before, and I trust she is." He expressed no repentance for the cold-blooded murder, but rather regarded it as a duty imposed upon him – an act of stern justice which the circumstances of the case compelled him to execute.

The trial commenced at the Derby Winter Assizes on the 12th December 1864 before Mr Baron Martin.

The case for the Crown was as I have already

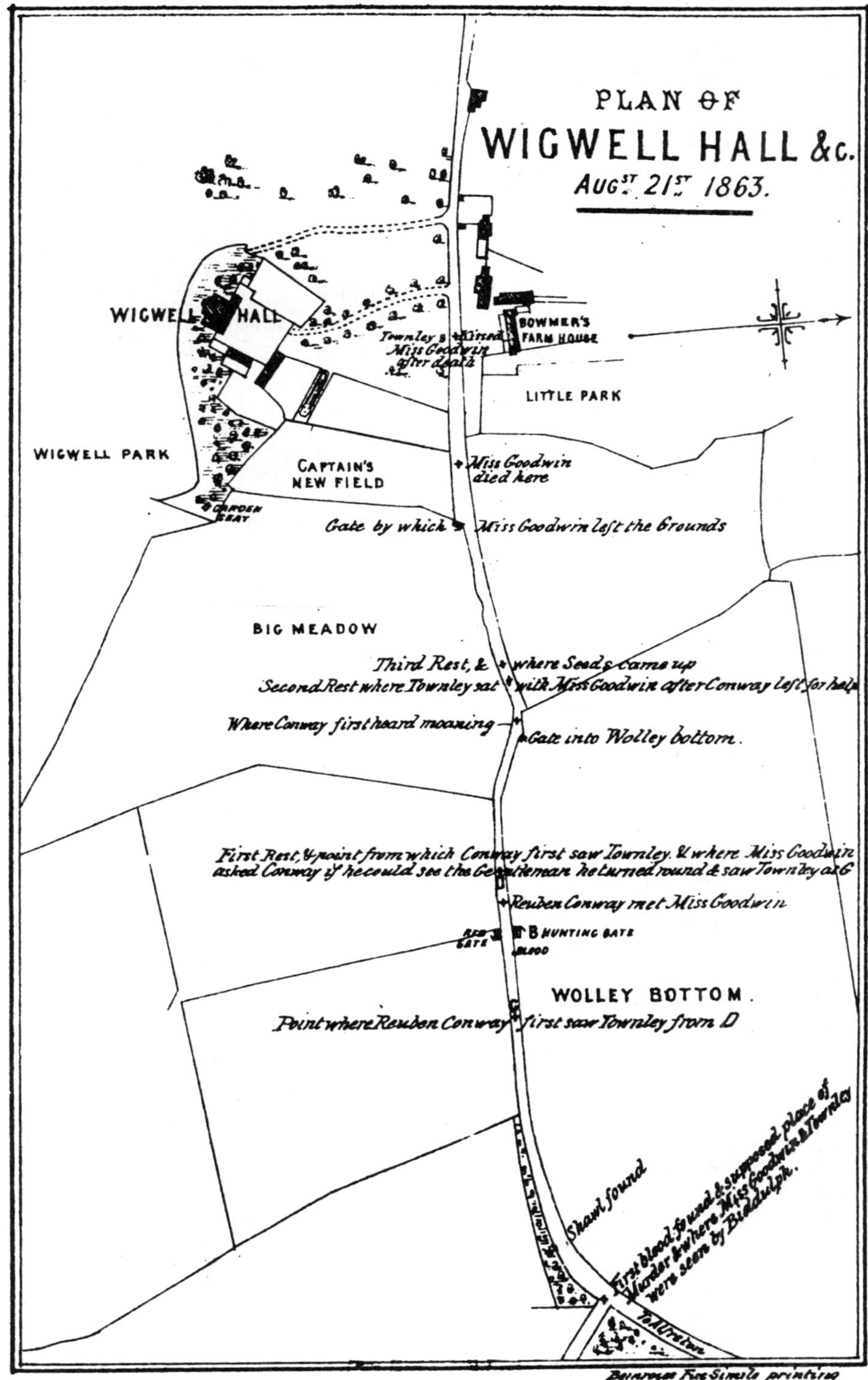
PLAN OF
WIGWELL HALL &c.
AUG.ST 21ST 1863.
WIGWELL HALL
BOWMER'S FARM HOUSE
Townley kissed Miss Goodwin after death
LITTLE PARK
WIGWELL PARK
CAPTAIN'S NEW FIELD
Miss Goodwin died here
GARDEN SEAT
Gate by which Miss Goodwin left the Grounds
BIG MEADOW
Third Rest, & where Seads came up
Second Rest where Townley sat with Miss Goodwin after Conway left for help
Where Conway first heard moaning
Gate into Wolley bottom.
First Rest, & point from which Conway first saw Townley. & where Miss Goodwin asked Conway if he could see the Gentleman he turned round & saw Townley at G
Reuben Conway met Miss Goodwin
RED GATE
B HUNTING GATE
BLOOD
WOLLEY BOTTOM.
Point where Reuben Conway first saw Townley from D
Shawl found
First blood found & supposed place of Murder & where Miss Goodwin & Townley were seen by Biddulph.
To Alfreton
Bemrose Fac-Simile printing

unfolded it to the reader. The only evidence I need quote in addition is that of Dr Newton Mant, who thus described the nature of the wounds inflicted:

"... there were three wounds on the right side of the neck, one a stab behind and below the right ear; the second a stab in front of this, superficial; the third wound, still farther in front, three inches long, and extending nearly to the chin. The back part of the wound appeared to have been produced by a stab directed downwards and backwards. The external carotid artery and the internal jugular vein were severed. These were severed by the third wound. The first wound was probably given from behind, and was not mortal. I should have thought that a person could not have walked after receiving the third wound. The knife produced here would have caused the wounds. I saw the prisoner that night ... there was much blood upon him."

There was a hush of breathless excitement in court when Dr Forbes Winslow, the celebrated expert in mental cases, stepped into the witness box. In reply to questions of the prisoner's counsel, Dr Forbes Winslow said:

"I have seen the prisoner twice in the presence of Mr Sims, the Governor of the jail... I talked to him largely on the subject of this crime, and I think at this present moment he is a man of deranged intellect. He was deranged on the 18th of November, and I thought still more so last night when I saw him for the second time. He repeated to me that he did not recognize he had committed any crime at all, neither did he feel any degree of pain, regret, contrition, or remorse for what he had done; he repudiated the idea of its being a crime either against God or man, alleging that he considered Miss Goodwin as his own property; that she had been illegally wrested from him by an act of violence; that he viewed her in the light of his wife, who had committed an act of adultery, and that he had a perfect right to deal with her life as he had with any other description of property, as the money in his pockets, etc.... He said he recognized the right of no man to sit in judgement upon him. He was a free agent, and, as he did not bring himself into the world by any action of his own, he had a perfect liberty to think and act as he pleased, irrespective of anyone else. I regard these expressions as the evidence of a diseased intellect."

The prisoner's mother then took the witness stand and deposed how badly her son, the prisoner, had taken the news of Miss Goodwin's breaking off their engagement. That he appeared excitable, his hands and feet twitching nervously, so that she felt constrained to give hime some morphia. There was, she confessed, hereditary insanity on her side of the family.

At the end of the prisoner's case, as presented by Messrs. MaCaulay QC, and Sergeant O'Brien, his lordship summed up the case to the jury. He concluded by telling them that the question they must address was: "Was the prisoner insane? and did he act under a delusion, believing it to be other than it was?" If he knew what he was doing, and that it was likely to cause death, and was contrary to the law of God and man, and that the law directed that persons who did such acts should be punished, then he was guilty of murder.

The jury retired, and after an absence of five minutes returned to court with a verdict of "Guilty" of wilful murder.

Mr Baron Martin put on his black cap...

On the day after the trial his lordship addressed the following letter to Sir George Grey, Secretary of State for the Home Department:

> Nottingham, December 13, 1863
>
> Sir – George Victor Townley was convicted yesterday before me at Derby of murder, and sentenced to be executed. I have directed a copy of my notes to be made for you should you desire to have it; but there is a full report of the trial in the newspapers. The conviction was, in my opinion, right; but Dr Forbes Winslow and Dr Gisborne were examined at the trial, and both deposed in the strongest manner that the prisoner is now of diseased mind and absolutely insane. I think it right to call your attention at once to the subject, with a view to a correct opinion being formed as to the propriety of execution.
>
> Yrs. etc.
> Samuel Martin

In fact the Home Secretary concurred with his lordship's opinion as to the rightness of the conviction and went so far as to declare himself unimpressed with the medical evidence submitted to him. In consequence the matter was passed on to the Commissioners in Lunacy for their opinion as to the condemned's state of mental health. The Commissioners' letter of reply arrived a mere two days before the execution was due to take place and, in rather indistinct terms, stated that the prisoner could not be considered to be of sound mind but was, according to the law laid down in court, responsible for his actions. In the meantime a letter had been received at the Home Office from three Derby Justices of the Peace who, having been instructed to report upon Townley's sanity from Derby Jail found it necessary to "certify that the said George Victor Townley is insane."

Sir George then, with the concurrence of the Lord Chancellor sent yet another quartet of "medical gentlemen of much experience in cases of lunacy" to visit and report on Townley. Meanwhile Townley had been removed to the Bethlehem Hospital. Messrs. Hood, Bucknill, Meyer, and Helps duly reported their unanimous conclusion that "George Victor Townley is of sound mind."

The Home Secretary, upon receiving the report of these four Commissioners, perversely announced that the capital sentence on Townley would be commuted to one of penal servitude for life. Understandably, this provoked an extraordinary outburst of public and newspaper outrage; and the controversy raged many weeks among the learned and the lay.

Gradually the excitement over the case died out and the memory of it faded from the minds of most people, when a twelvemonth later it was recalled to them by the startling announcement in the newspapers dated Monday, February 13th, 1865, that George Victor Townley had committed suicide in Pentonville Prison on the previous evening.

At the close of the sermon in the prison chapel on the afternoon of Sunday, February 12th, the convict who always sat next to Townley in chapel noticed to his surprise that his neighbour, whom he had never known to open his lips in chapel before, sang the last two verses of the concluding hymn – *Abide with me* – in a particularly loud voice. He closed his book sharply and, clasping it tightly in his hand, filed with the rest out of the chapel.

Suddenly there was a shout of alarm, followed by a dull, sickening thud. Townley had thrown himself, as bathers dive, clean over the railings of the circular gallery, and plunged head foremost on to the stone floor three-and-twenty feet below.

So by his own act, George Victor Townley was held to have solved the problem of his sanity or insanity.

George Victor Townley's Statement to the Commissioners in Lunacy

"What have I been guilty of? I am guilty of nothing. I don't admit I am guilty of anything. I don't believe that I have done any harm. Bessie Goodwin was my property, and I had a right to do what I did because she was false to me. I was not myself when I did it. I might have been mad at the moment. I am quite sane now.

I have done her no harm. She is better where she is than if she had lived. I believe there is a future state. I am waiting to go to her. I shall be too happy to join her. They set her against me. She was my property. I saw her, and took away what belonged to me; what else could I do? I think she in the same circumstances would have had an equal right to do the same.

I consider that a man has the right to kill his wife if she is an adultress. I think Bessie Goodwin was guilty of adultery in engaging herself to another. She was as much my property as if we had been married. I look upon marriage as a mere ceremony.

I never thought deeply about religion. I did not give religion any thought. I am not troubled by the thought of being punished. Why should I be punished? There is no reason for it.

The results of the trial are nothing to me. I know what was pleaded for me. I could not have pleaded guilty, because I was not guilty of anything.

If they take my life it is because they have the power to do it. I took hers because it belonged to me. Their right is that of might. Mine is the right of possession to recover possession of my property.

Other men think and act differently, because their temperament and circumstances are different. A man who has a particular temper, and finds himself in circumstances that compel him to act as I did, is not accountable. Other people might not act as I did. The fact that I have acted as I have done is proof that a man is not accountable in those circumstances.

I am not sorry for the parents of Bessie Goodwin, or for any of those that brought me to this. I only prevented them taking away what was mine; I only took what belonged to me. She is now waiting for me. I shall join her in a short time.

The persons who combined to take her from me were no friends of mine; they were always my enemies. They had a personal enmity to me. I do not think they would combine to take my life. But they did combine to injure me in the most tender part by taking her away.

I have done nothing but what is right and proper. I cannot alter these opinions. You will see that I will die with them. I have no positive hope that my life will be spared. I have always looked on the worst side. I only pray God that I might die at this minute, as I sit here, and then it would all be finished.

Before I committed murder I tried to get her to say the name of the man who had replaced me, but she would not. I never mentioned B. to her then, because I did not, from what she had written to me, once think of him. I certainly used no threats before I stabbed her. But I don't remember anything at the very last."

Gloucestershire

Beatrice Annie PACE 38

Arsenic in the Sheep Dip

The Death of HARRY PACE from Arsenic Poisoning on Wednesday the 18th January 1928 at Fetterhill Farm, Coleford

and the Trial and Acquittal of his Wife BEATRICE ANNIE for his Murder

It must have seemed like adding insult to injury to Mrs Pace when she was accused of murdering her bully of a husband. Harry Pace had never been easy to live with, and the long-suffering Beatrice would not have been normal if it had never crossed her mind how pleasant life would be without him; especially after one of those periodic outbursts of sadistic rage which always left her scarred and bruised, inside and out, for months afterwards: "We have been in our present house nearly four years, and on two occasions my husband thrashed me severely, once about two years ago and again in March before I was having my baby. The first time was with a strap and the second time with a stick. In the early part of last year he threatened to shoot me and I called the police."

But now Harry *was* dead.

The facts of the matter were these. Harry Pace, quarry-man and part-time sheep rearer, living at Fetterhill Farm, in Coleford on the edge of the Forest of Dean, had been taken ill while dipping sheep in the early summer of 1927. Pace was clearly suffering so acutely from stomach pains and a burning sensation in his throat that it was thought prudent to confine him to the Gloucester Royal Infirmary for observation. Pace was discharged in October, but in December was stricken with a similar attack. On January the 10th 1928 he died.

The funeral was arranged for January 15th, and would have proceeded without interruption had it not been for the suspicions of Harry's brother Elton who obtained an order from the coroner, Mr Maurice Carter, to stop the funeral and conduct a post-mortem examination. In many respects it is comforting to know that the degree of power still rests in the hands of the ordinary citizen to effect this kind of dramatic action. In the case of Harry Pace it would probably have been best left alone.

Nevertheless, Harry's mortal remains were subjected to close medical scrutiny, and in his evidence to the inquest Professor Walker Hall testified that he could discover no signs of natural disease in the body's organs, but that the appearance of the stomach lining suggested the presence of a strongly irritant poison; furthermore, changes in the liver, heart and kidneys pointed to arsenic, the last dose of which must have been taken between six and forty-eight hours before death, but that the poison must have been present in the body at least three weeks before death; the total amount of arsenic found was 9·42 grains. Asked if it would have been possible for Pace to have absorbed the arsenic – which was a major active constituent of sheep-dip – through the skin, Professor Hall excluded the possibility of infiltration to the extent found.

During the inquest which was to span an incredible twenty-two hearings between January 16th and the end of May, Sir William Willcox, a senior medical adviser to the Home Office, was summoned to comment on the post-mortem findings, and submitted his report on March 23rd. The symptoms, he confirmed, were indicative and typical of arsenical poisoning, the analyses showing the substance to be present far in excess of a fatal dose. In addition, Willcox felt that the previous illness – in July 1927 – also suggested arsenical poisoning. Other symptoms exhibited by the late Mr Pace – pigmentation of the skin, slight jaundice, inflamed throat, and the retardation of putrefaction in a sample of blood were all suggestive of the same conclusion.

Dr Ellis gave evidence on the analysis of various preparations of sheep-dip found about the farm, and advanced several theories to the coroner's jury as to how the potentially lethal substance could have been secretly administered.

After the briefest of summations, the coroner emphasized that in his opinion there was no evidence to support the suggestion that Harry Pace had been accidentally poisoned. After an hour's retirement the jury's foreman was able to state that in the opinion of his colleagues and himself: "Harry Pace met his death by arsenical poisoning administered by some person or persons other than himself, and in our view the case calls for further investigation."

In a move that was subsequently to be heavily criticized (and quite rightly so), the coroner declined to accept this verdict: "Only the committal of a person after a coroner's inquiry can bring about an investigation, which cannot take place unless there is some person named. It is necessary for you to name a person if a person is to be charged." The jury retired for a further twenty-five minutes before returning with the amended verdict "that Harry Pace met his death by arsenical poisoning administered by Beatrice Pace."

Within moments Mrs Pace, sitting distraught in the body of the court, was arrested on the coroner's warrant. With cries of "I didn't do it! I didn't do it!" her pathetic figure was helped to the cells.

Beatrice Pace was committed for trial at the Gloucester Assizes on July 2nd 1928. Mr Justice Horridge presided, and the evidence for the prosecution, as is traditional in poisoning cases, was led by one of the Law Officers of the Crown – in this instance the Solictor-General Sir Frank Boyd Merriman KC. Such was the strength of sympathy for the plight of Mrs Pace that a public subscription was sufficient to enable her solicitors, Wellington and Matthews, to remain the services of no less an advocate than Mr Norman (later Lord) Birkett KC.

In his opening address, the Solicitor-General observed that there was no dispute whatever as to the cause of Harry Pace's untimely decease – he had died from a massive nine and a half grains of arsenic – more than four times a lethal dose. And that the sheep-dip – purchased, he emphasized, by Mrs Pace – contained at least 2,800 grains in a single packet! Mrs Pace, he reminded the court, had made two significant statements to the police: "I don't think it possible for any person who had visited him to have given him any poison to take"; and "It is my view, and I am convinced, that my husband poisoned himself and I don't think anyone else would have done it. If they had, I should have known."

In all, Sir Frank Merriman called seventeen witnesses fairly equally divided between medical experts and relatives of the deceased. Of the latter, Leslie, the eleven-year-old son of the Paces, had some of the most damaging evidence to relate. He described the day on which his father, lying on his sick-bed, had asked for a box in which he kept his sheep-dipping materials to be brought to him. After checking the contents he instructed the boy to lock the box away in a chest of drawers in the room. The implication was clear: Harry Pace already suspected that he was being slowly poisoned and was keeping the source under lock and key.

Pace's mother recalled how, two days before his death, her son had complained of the bitterness of the water that was given to him to drink, and asked her to bring a fresh glass from the tap. And then came Elton, whose suspicions had initiated this elaborate legal ritual. He claimed that he had heard – "with his own ears" – Mrs Pace wishing "the old bastard" was dead; wishing she could poison him. On one of his visits, Elton maintained, he found Beatrice Pace leaning across his brother murmuring "Harry, you're dying – we shan't see you much longer".

The medical witnesses in the main reiterated what they had presented to the coroner's court. It was Sir William Willcox that Norman Birkett met in cross-examination:

Birkett: Arsenic may find its way into the body through the mouth? – *Willcox:* Yes.
Sometimes through the skin? – If the skin is broken.
You have from time to time referred to cases of accidental poisoning from certain preparations such as sheep-deep, which contain arsenic? – Yes.
Also, that there is a danger of suicidal death from this preparation? – Yes, there is, of course, a risk.

There is a risk of chronic arsenical poisoning to those who carry out sheep dipping? – Yes. If the most perfect methods of cleanliness were not followed during the process, some of the arsenic might be absorbed when taking food? – Yes, if the person did not wash his hands, or if there were rashes on the hands.

As the case for the prosecution closed, Norman Birkett rose to take one of the biggest and most successful gambles in the whole of his long career at the bar. He submitted to Mr Justice Horridge, in advance of any evidence being presented on behalf of the defence, that there was insufficient evidence for the trial to continue further; the scientific evidence was, he suggested, as consistent with self-administration as with any other possibility.

Amid general surprise, the judge responded: "My opinion is that it would not be safe to ask the jury to proceed further with it". He instructed them to return a formal verdict of "Not Guilty", and to evident public approbation Mrs Pace was acquitted.

The question remained – the question *remains* – who killed Harry Pace?

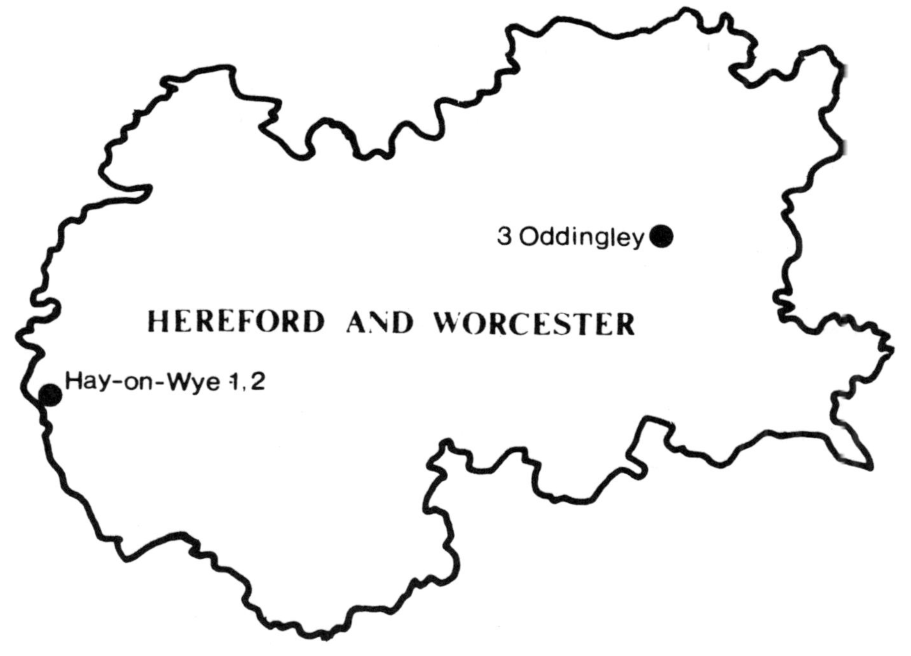

Herefordshire and Worcestershire

1. George PRICE 42
2. Major Herbert Rowse ARMSTRONG 44
3. Richard HEMMING 52

"I will never trust you more"

The Murder of MARY PRICE by her Husband GEORGE in the year 1738 on Hounslow Heath

GEORGE PRICE

Sentenced to Death for Murdering his Wife but Died of Gaol Fever on 22nd October, 1738

This malefactor was a native of Hay, in Brecknockshire, where he lived as a servant to a widow lady. Having lived in this station seven years, he repaired to London, and became acquainted with Mary Chambers, servant at a public house at Hampstead, whom he married at the expiration of a fortnight from his first paying his addresses to her; but Mr Brown, his master, disapproving of the match, dismissed Price from his service.

Soon after this he took his wife to Brecknockshire, and imposed her on his relations as the daughter of a military officer, who would become entitled to a large fortune. He was treated in the most friendly manner by his relations; and the young couple returning to London, the wife went to lodge at Hampstead, while Price engaged in the service of a gentleman in New Broad Street.

Mrs Price, being delivered of twins, desired her husband to buy some medicine to make the children sleep, which he procured; and on the children dying soon afterwards a report was circulated that he had poisoned them; but this circumstance he denied to the last moment of his life.

Price now paid his addresses to other women, and conceiving his wife as an obstacle between him and his wishes he formed the infernal resolution of murdering her. He told her that he had procured the place of a nursery-maid for her in the neighbourhood of Putney, and that he would attend her thither that very day. He then directed her to meet him at the *Woolpack,* in Monkwell Street. Accordingly she went home and dressed herself (having borrowed some clothes of her landlady) and met her husband, who put her in a chaise, and drove her out of town, towards Hounslow. When he came on Hounslow Heath it was nearly ten o'clock at night; when he suddenly stopped the chaise and threw the lash of the whip round his wife's neck; but drawing it too hastily he made a violent mark on her chin; immediately finding his mistake, he placed it lower, on which she exclaimed: "My dear! my dear! For God's sake – if this is your love, I will never trust you more."

Immediately on her pronouncing these words, which were her last, he pulled the ends of the whip with great force; but, the violence of his passion abating, he let go before she was quite dead; yet, resolving to accomplish the horrid deed, he once more put the thong of the whip about her neck, and pulled it with such violence that it broke; but not till the poor woman was dead.

Having stripped the body, he left it almost under a gibbet where some malefactors hung in chains [see *Murder Club Guide No. 2*], having first disfigured it to such a degree that he presumed it could not be known. He brought the clothes to London, some of which he cut in pieces, and dropped in different streets; but knowing that the others were borrowed of the landlady he sent them to her, a circumstance that materially conduced to his conviction.

He reached London about one o'clock in the morning, and being interrogated why he came at such an unseasonable hour, he said that the Margate hoy had been detained in the river by contrary winds.

On the following day the servants and other people made so many inquiries respecting his wife that, terrified at the idea of being taken into custody, he immediately fled to Portsmouth, with a view to entering on board a ship; but no vessel was then ready to sail.

He was drinking at an ale-house in Portsmouth when he heard the bellman crying him as a murderer, with such an exact description of him that he was apprehensive of being seized, and observing a window which opened to the water he jumped out, and swam for his life.

Having gained the shore, he travelled all night, till he reached a farmhouse, where he slept on some straw in the barn. On the following day he crossed the country towards Oxford, where he endeavoured to get into service, and would have been engaged by a physician, but happening to read a newspaper in which he was advertised, Price immediately decamped from Oxford, and travelled to Wales.

Having stopped at a village a few miles from Hay, at the house of a shoemaker to whom his brother was apprenticed, the latter obtained his master's permission to accompany his brother home; and while they were on their walk the malefactor recounted the particulars of the murder which had obliged him to seek his safety in flight. The brother commiserated his condition and, leaving him at a small distance from their father's house, went in and found the old gentleman reading an advertisement describing the murderer. The younger son bursting into tears, the father said he hoped his brother was not come; to which the youth replied: "Yes, he is at the door; but being afraid that some of the neighbours were in the house he would not come in till he had your permission." The offender on being introduced fell on his knees, and earnestly besought his father's blessing; to which the aged parent said: "Ah! George, I wish God may bless you, and what I have heard concerning you may be false." The son said: "It is false; but let me have a private room; make no words; I have done no harm; let me have a room to myself."

Being accommodated agreeable to his request, he produced half-a-crown, begging that his brother would buy a lancet, as he was resolved to put a period to his miserable existence; but the brother declined to in any way aid in the commission of the crime of suicide*; and the father, after exerting every argument to prevent his son thinking of such a violation of the laws of God, concealed him for two days.

It happened that some neighbours observed a fire in a room where none had been for a considerable time before, and a report was propagated that Price was secreted in the house of his father; whereupon he thought it prudent to abscond in the night; and having reached Gloucester he went to an inn and procured the place of an ostler.

During his residence at Gloucester two of the sons of the lady with whom he had first lived as a servant happened to be at school in that city, and Price behaved to them with

---

* The superstitious horror of suicide in European culture has partly pagan origins. The notion of suicide as a sin is not Biblical; it was invented by St Augustine of Hippo, and he intimates pretty clearly what his reason was. Some Christians were choosing to end their lives immediately after baptism, in the belief that this was the only way of avoiding sin and proceeding to heaven. To prevent this decimation of believers, Augustine taught that suicide was itself a greater sin than any that was likely to be committed by remaining alive. So English law stigmatized suicide as a felony; the *felo de se*'s property was forfeited, leaving his family impoverished; and his body was denied a Christian burial. Even when these unfeeling practices were given up, suicide remained legally equivalent to self-murder. The law was changed by the Suicide Act 1961, which enacts that "The rule of law whereby it is a crime for a person to commit suicide is hereby abrogated."

(*Textbook of Criminal Law,* Glanville Williams. Stevens, 1978).

so much civility that they wrote to their mother describing his conduct; in reply to which she informed them that he had killed his wife, and desired them not to hold any correspondence with him.

The young gentlemen mentioning this circumstance, one of Price's fellow-servants said to him: "You are the man that murdered your wife on Hounslow Heath. I will not betray you but if you stay any longer you will certainly be taken into custody."

Stung by the reflections of his own conscience, and agitated by the fear of momentary detection, Price knew not how to act; but at length he resolved to come to London and surrender to justice; and calling on his former master, and being apprehended, he was committed to Newgate.

At the following sessions at the Old Bailey he was brought to his trial, and convicted. He was sentenced to death, but died of the gaol fever [see Appendix One] in Newgate, before the law could be executed on him, on the 22nd of October, 1738.

Here Comes the Murdering Major!

The Death of Mrs KATHARINE ARMSTRONG on the 22nd of February 1921 at her home 'Mayfield', Hay-on-Wye and the Trial and Conviction of her Husband HERBERT ROWSE ARMSTRONG for her Murder

"'Scuse fingers," mumbled the Major, placing a fresh buttered scone on his guest's tea-plate. Oswald Martin smiled – he was enjoying his visit to Major Armstrong's house; he had almost forgotten what good company the old boy could be when he chose.

Both men shared the profession of solicitor, with offices at either end of the high street in the small town of Hay-on-Wye; but over the past year the relationship had been more than a little strained. In fact they were locked in a legal wrangle which had become so acrimonious that they could scarcely bear to acknowledge each other in the street, and Martin had felt constrained to threaten the Major with legal action for the recovery of a £500 deposit from a client which Armstrong had no right to retain, but which he was nevertheless stubbornly withholding.

'Mayfield'

Oswald Martin's office

The battle was still raging, but the two men had called a brief armistice on this agreeable afternoon in late October, and were reliving a happier acquaintance over currant-bread,

Armstrong's study at 'Mayfield'

tea, and scones. They chatted idly about this and that, and Armstrong was soon firmly entrenched in his favourite subject of gardening, and the ceaseless temerity of the dandelions in infesting his rambling lawns. The afternoon was fast fading when Oswald Martin thanked the Major for his hospitality and departed homeward.

As soon as his guest had left, the small, dapper figure of the Major could be seen carefully clearing away the tea things. Then he crossed to his desk and with deep concentration counted a number of little white-paper packages that he had taken from a drawer. Rubbing his hands with satisfaction, he replaced the packets and drifted into a deep reverie.

Not long after Oswald Martin reached home he began to feel distinctly uncomfortable. Soon the unfortunate man was engulfed by a terrible wave of nausea, vomiting and diarrhoea, which continued to plague him throughout a sleepless night. On the following morning, Mrs Martin called in Dr Thomas Hincks, who diagnosed a bilious attack and confined his patient to bed. It was in no time at all that the village grape-vine carried news of Oswald's illness to his father-in-law, Mr John Davies, local chemist, and a fussy old fellow, who soon materialized at the sick-bed's side with questions on recent diet. No sooner had he heard of the tea-party with Armstrong than an unmistakable cloud seemed to settle over the chemist. John Davies scratched his nose reflectively; "Oswald," he said, "I don't want to alarm you, but I very much fear that there's more to this bilious attack of yours than meets the eye. In fact, I'd almost stake my reputation on it being no less than a case of arsenical poisoning!" "Really, father," Martin expostulated, "Armstrong may be a bit of a shark legally, but dash it all, you can't go around saying the chap's a poisoner. There's such a thing as slander, you know..."

"Just a minute," Davies interrupted him. "You wouldn't know anything about this, Oswald; in fact nobody does, because I've kept it to myself for quite a while now. I've had my suspicions all along – ever since the death of poor Mrs Armstrong. Even before that. If I showed you my ledger... that man has bought enough pure arsenic to kill an army... always coming in for it he is; says it's for the dandelions. By God, Oswald, the most voracious weeds in all Christendom couldn't get through that lot. What's more, he's still buying the stuff when no self-respecting dandelion's shown its head above ground for weeks. You take care, boy, or you could end up like the Major's lady. Have nothing to do with that man, that's the best advice I can give you!" and John Davies

John Davies's chemist shop

strode purposefully out of the sick room. He took with him a determination to action; he was on his way to Dr Hincks's surgery.

Hincks listened carefully to all that the grim-faced Davies had to say – including a snippet of information about a certain box of Fuller's chocolates that had been sent anonymously to his son-in-law's house by post in September. The box had shown signs of having been tampered with, and Oswald's sister-in-law had been taken quite ill after eating a chocolate at a dinner party in early October. The postmark on the package had been unreadable, but Davies was prepared to hint at who *he* thought was the sender! Hincks was understandably alarmed by the accusation of poison; he paid a return visit to his patient and collected a sample of Oswald Martin's urine and (as they were still in the house) the box of suspect chocolates. Both specimens he sent to the Home Office for analysis – the regular procedure where there was a suspicion of poison being present. When the results came back the combined fears of Hincks and Davies were more than justified – the urine did indeed contain traces of arsenic, and on the top layer of the chocolates there were two into which had been injected a substantial amount of that same fatal substance.

Dr Hincks was a worried man, and in an attempt to divert his attention for a while from the awful implications of the analyst's report he saddled a horse and set out for an hour's vigorous riding...

...Suddenly he reigned in his horse and sat stationary in the saddle; an awful thought had grown in his mind. "What about Mrs Armstrong?" He had signed the certificate himself: death from natural causes. But now, going through each symptom and circumstance of her illness, it was impossible for him to overlook the fact that those causes could have been something very far from natural.

Mrs Armstrong had been a strong-willed and domineering woman; some six inches taller than her husband, she had ruled him with a firm hand that brooked no smoking, no drinking, and no answering back. She was also a neurotic and a hypochondriac, dosing herself with prodigious quantities of the most fashionable patent medicines. Hincks had treated her for rheumatism between

The Armstrongs on their wedding day

May and August 1919, and later for bilious attacks, insomnia, and delusions of guilt and inferiority that became so marked that in August 1920 she was admitted to a mental hospital. By December of the same year, however, both her physical and mental condition had improved dramatically, and the Major had insisted that she return home immediately, quite against medical advice. Armstrong obtained her discharge on January 22nd 1921, but no sooner had she returned home than she relapsed into another bout of serious illness; within a month she was dead. Thinking over the final path of her illness, Dr Hincks became more and more convinced that the certificate should have read "cause of death – arsenical poisoning".

The doctor had practised in the same locality for upward of twenty-three years; he was deeply respected – even loved – by his patients, many of whom invested him with an almost saintly infallibility. It thus took more than a little courage now for him to write to the Home Office confiding that he could possibly have been wrong in his diagnosis. But a good doctor will never shirk his responsibility, and Hincks at least aspired to competence in his professional duties; as a result he found himself a few days later on the way to an interview with Hereford's Chief Constable and the Director of Public Prosecutions. On his way to the meeting Dr Hincks's thoughts were completely centred around Major Armstrong. What sort of a man was he? He wore a mask of deep respectability, and yet he was currently undergoing treatment for venereal disease contracted during the period his wife was in hospital. Despite this illness, just three days after Mrs Armstrong's death, the Major had been seen in London in the company of an old flame from his army days; and three months later he had unsuccessfully proposed marriage to a local lady.

With vision clarified by hindsight, Hincks saw a new image of his patient with the anomalies of behaviour that caused the doctor to caution the Chief Constable to conduct his enquiries in the strictest secrecy: "If he gets to know about it, he might murder himself, his children, and me!" Hincks had by now convinced himself that Armstrong was a homicidal maniac, and he recollected with concern that the Major always kept a loaded revolver by his bed. He also remembered vividly the day that Armstrong had casually asked him, "By the way, doctor, what is a fatal dose of arsenic?"

But there was another reason for the police to tread warily in investigating the case; Major Herbert Rowse Armstrong, TD, MA (Cantab), solicitor, clerk to the local magistrates, and churchwarden, was a clever and educated man, and a highly respected pillar of the community.

During the time that the police were cautiously building their case, the unsuspecting Armstrong was positively bombarding Oswald Martin – now recovered and back at work – with further invitations to tea and dinner. Martin, not surprisingly, found one excuse or another to refuse the Major's 'hospitality'.

The evidence was building up against Armstrong. The police carefully noted the dates and amounts of arsenic that the Major had purchased and the fact that he owned a tiny spray-gun with which he individually eradicated the hateful dandelions – the nozzle of a similar gun exactly fitted the puncture marks discovered in the contaminated chocolates. It was also known that about six months before Mrs Armstrong's death her husband had drawn up a new will for her, leaving the £2278 estate and all her personal assets to him, and excluding their three children who would have been joint beneficiaries with their father under the terms of the previous will. The new document had been witnessed by the maid but not, as is legally required, in the presence of Mrs Armstrong herself.

At last the police were confident enough of their case to move in, and on New Year's Eve Major Herbert Rowse Armstrong was arrested in his office at Hay for the attempted murder of Oswald Martin. Armstrong appeared completely composed, and blustered: "This is not a very serious matter and I will help you all I can." But the statement that he made later was guarded, and when he was searched two tiny packets were found in his waistcoat pocket – one containing

The military and civilian aspects of Herbert Armstrong's life

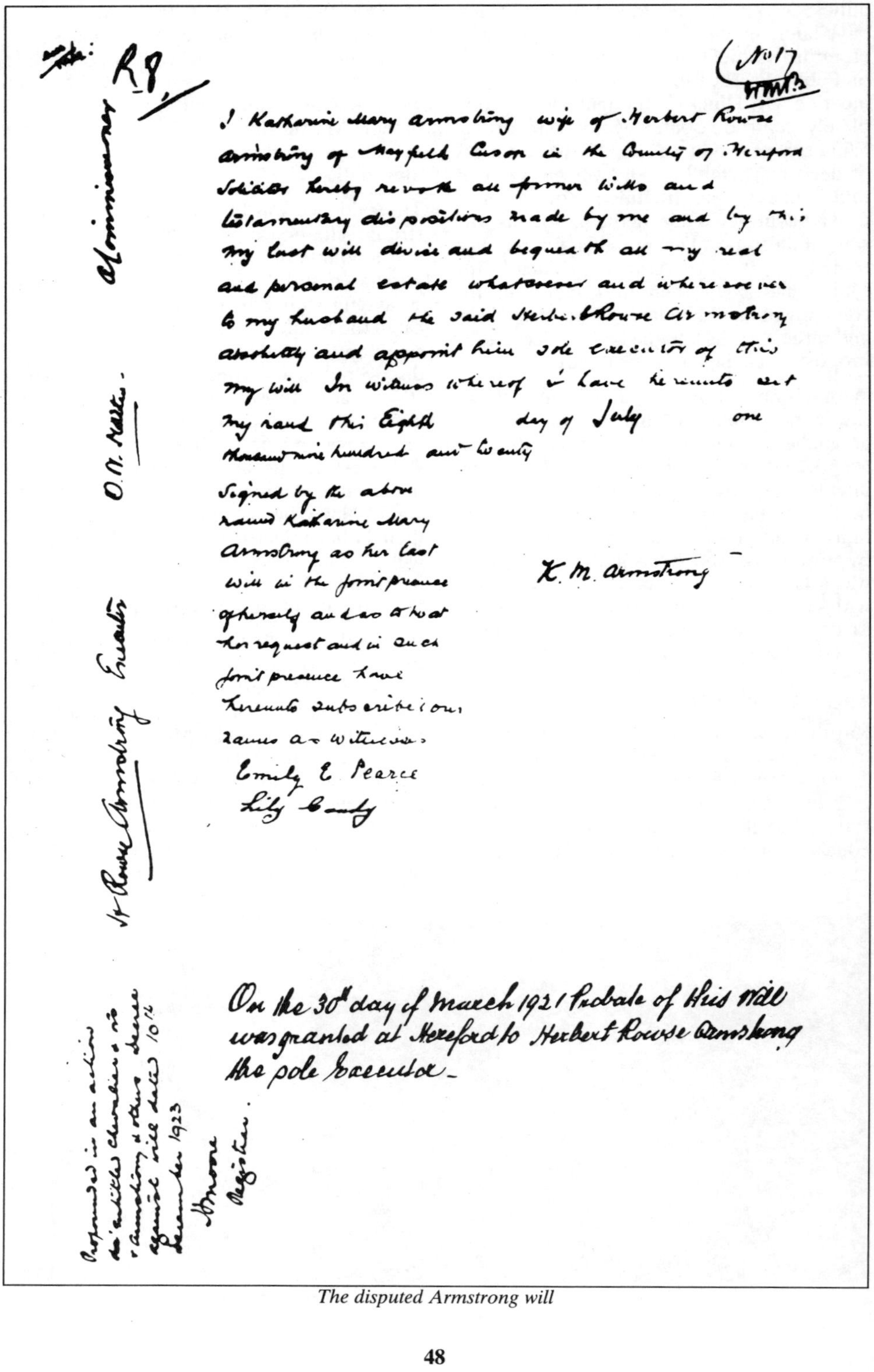

No 17

I Katharine Mary Armstrong wife of Herbert Rowse Armstrong of Mayfield Cusop in the County of Hereford Solicitor hereby revoke all former Wills and testamentary dispositions made by me and by this my last will devise and bequeath all my real and personal estate whatsoever and wheresoever to my husband the said Herbert Rowse Armstrong absolutely and appoint him sole executor of this my will In witness whereof I have hereunto set my hand this Eighth day of July one thousand nine hundred and twenty

Signed by the above named Katharine Mary Armstrong as her last will in the joint presence of herself and us who at her request and in such joint presence have hereunto subscribed our names as witnesses

Emily E. Pearce

Lily Candy

K. M. Armstrong

Herbert Rowse Armstrong Executor

On the 30th day of March 1921 Probate of this Will was granted at Hereford to Herbert Rowse Armstrong the sole Executor.

Propounded in an action Chevalier & others v Armstrong & others decree against will dated 10th December 1923 H. Moore Registrar.

The disputed Armstrong will

several grams of white arsenic*, and the other an arsenic and charcoal mixture. In the Major's desk at home more of the poisonous packets were found. Armstrong's explanation that he had divided the arsenic up into 20 equal-sized packets "for convenience in killing the weeds" fell very flat indeed. When he was asked why this method was more convenient than just pushing the stuff straight into the ground he maintained a dignified silence.

At 6.45pm on January the 2nd, 1922, the icy ground of the local churchyard at Cusop yielded up the exhumed body of Mrs Armstrong, and her organs were removed in a chilly cottage nearby to be sent for analysis. The analyst later reported: "It is the largest amount of arsenic I have found in any case of arsenical poisoning." Mrs Armstrong's suffering had been prolonged by constant and systematic dosing over a long period of time, resulting in the terrible mental and physical torment of her last unhappy years.

* For a note on Arsenic as a poison see *Murder Club Guide No.1.*

Armstrong now faced the dual charges of the murder of his wife and the attempted murder of Oswald Martin; it was ironic that he should appear in the very court – the Hereford Assizes – where he himself had acted so many times as Clerk to the Court. On this occasion his place had been taken by an 80-year-old stand-in, to whom Armstrong constantly offered advice.

When the case came to trial – which lasted for ten full days – Armstrong proved to be a stalwart witness, remaining for over five hours in the box; finally, after a deliberation of forty-eight minutes, the jury found him guilty and sentence of death was passed upon the murdering Major.

He was hanged at Gloucester on Wednesday the 31st May, 1922. Perhaps to this day his body lies beneath the triumphant heads of a host of golden dandelions!

[*Adapted from 'Here Comes the Murdering Major' by Susan Dunkley.*]

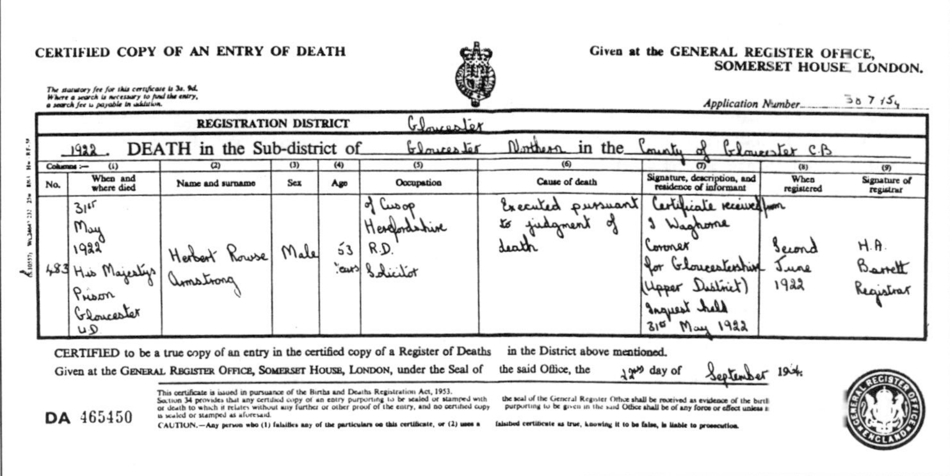

CERTIFIED COPY OF AN ENTRY OF DEATH

Given at the GENERAL REGISTER OFFICE, SOMERSET HOUSE, LONDON.

The statutory fee for this certificate is 3s. 9d. Where a search is necessary to find the entry, a search fee is payable in addition.

Application Number 307154

REGISTRATION DISTRICT Gloucester

1922. DEATH in the Sub-district of Gloucester Northern in the County of Gloucester C.B

No.	(1) When and where died	(2) Name and surname	(3) Sex	(4) Age	(5) Occupation	(6) Cause of death	(7) Signature, description, and residence of informant	(8) When registered	(9) Signature of registrar
483	31st May 1922 His Majesty's Prison Gloucester U.D.	Herbert Rowse Armstrong	Male	53 years	of Cusop Herefordshire R.D. Solicitor	Executed pursuant to judgment of death	Certificate received from J Waghorne Coroner for Gloucestershire (Upper District) Inquest held 31st May 1922	Second June 1922	H.A. Barrett Registrar

CERTIFIED to be a true copy of an entry in the certified copy of a Register of Deaths in the District above mentioned.

Given at the GENERAL REGISTER OFFICE, SOMERSET HOUSE, LONDON, under the Seal of the said Office, the 12th day of September 1984.

This certificate is issued in pursuance of the Births and Deaths Registration Act, 1953. Section 34 provides that any certified copy of an entry purporting to be sealed or stamped with the seal of the General Register Office shall be received as evidence of the birth or death to which it relates without any further or other proof of the entry, and no certified copy purporting to be given in the said Office shall be of any force or effect unless it is sealed or stamped as aforesaid.

CAUTION.—Any person who (1) falsifies any of the particulars on this certificate, or (2) uses a falsified certificate as true, knowing it to be false, is liable to prosecution.

DA 465450

Statement made by Herbert Rowse Armstrong to the Police

Broad Street, Hay

I, Herbert Rowse Armstrong, having been cautioned by Chief Inspector Crutchett that anything I may say may be used in evidence hereafter, wish to make the following statement:

Mr Martin is a brother solicitor in Hay. He had been married in June last but owing to ~~a personal bereavement~~* my wife's death in February last I had been unable to do any

* These alterations appear on the original document.

entertaining. I asked Mr Martin to have a cup of tea on Wednesday the 26th of October 1921. At that time I had two men working in my garden, which had been allowed to get in a very bad state: their names are McGeorge, who was working in the garden, and Stokes who was erecting a fowl-house. They both live in Bear Street, Hay.

I had no special reason for inviting Mr Martin to tea other than that I had not entertained him since his marriage, and at that time I was not entertaining on a very large scale.

On the day in question Mr Martin arrived at my house about 5pm. I had previously gone home to see that everything was in order. I took him round the garden and showed him the various improvements that I proposed to make. We then entered the drawing room where tea had been laid out by my housekeeper Miss Pearce. As far as I remember the food was placed in three plates on a wicker stand. ~~I can trace~~ remember that wicker stand as I have a more ornate one in brass, and my housekeeper had asked which I preferred. The food consisted of buttered scone, buttered currant loaf in slices, and bread and butter. I handed Mr Martin some scone on a plate. He took some, and I also took some which I ate and I afterwards placed the dish of currant bread and butter by his side on the table and asked him to help himself. I shall be able to ascertain by going to my house where the scone and ~~buttered bread~~ currant loaf were bought. I remember Mr Martin saying that buttered loaf was a favourite dish of his, and I know that he ate heartily and cleared the dish. Afterwards I asked him to smoke, and remember that he was off colour and instead of having a pipe said that he would smoke a cigarette. At the time both Mr Martin and I were working at high pressure on some sales of a Capt. Hope, and probably this was the reason for his being below par. Mr Martin and I discussed general office organization, and I remember telling him that I was under-staffed. I also was feeling the effects of hard work. It was light when we began tea, but it soon became necessary for me to light the gas, and as I did so the globe came off and fell which caused it to break. Mr Martin left about 6pm and drove home in his own car. All the food which Martin consumed was prepared by Miss Pearce and was waiting for us when we entered the drawing room; and either she or the maid brought the tea and hot water in when we had taken our seats. Miss Pearce had previously asked if the food (which was subsequently placed on the table) would be satisfactory, and I had said "Yes".

The following morning I went to Mr Martin's office to get various documents relating to Capt. Hope's sale which was to be completed on the 2nd November. It was a big property sale in which he was acting for several purchasers. I was told ~~that Mr~~ by one of his clerks (I cannot remember which) that he had been taken ill. I think now that it was Preen as I have a recollection of him saying that Dr Hincks had been called and had said that he thought Mr Martin was suffering from jaundice.

Mr Martin's illness was causing a great inconvenience as the completions were fixed for the following Wednesday, and there was a great deal to be done. I sent a message to Mr Martin by one of his clerks (I do not remember which), and said that if I could assist in any possible way, and he would authorize his clerks, that I would carry the matter through if he were not well enough. The next thing that I remember was that he was not down at his office on Saturday. I called at his house on the Sunday morning after church. I saw Mrs Martin, and she told me that he had been very sick but was better, and would be down at his office on Monday. It was not necessary for Mr Martin to accept my offer of assistance as he was able to attend his office and carry through the completions by the stated date. After Mr Martin's illness he told me that he had been very sick and that he had had a thorough clean out. Prior to his illness I had chaffed him about his practice of motoring to and from his office saying that if he did not take walking exercise he would be ill. I always walk to my office, not possessing a car.

I am continually meeting with Mr Martin professionally and he and his wife have a standing dinner invitation to my house when a date can be fixed.

The first time I purchased arsenic was in 1914. I think ~~I have got the receipt in my gardening book.~~ At this time I came across a recipe for weed killer consisting of caustic soda and arsenic which was very much cheaper than the liquid weed killer, which I and my gardener had previously been in the habit of purchasing. I therefore purchased caustic soda and arsenic from Mr Davies, chemist of Hay, and signed the book. I remember him telling me that the arsenic had to be mixed with charcoal and he mixed it accordingly. I made the weed killer at my house by boiling the caustic soda and arsenic in an old petrol tin. I think I put in all I purchased. It might have been in the proportion of equal parts of each but I don't remember. I think Miss Pearce will remember the preparation. It was all used in the garden as weed killer. I have always had considerable trouble with weeds on the path of my vegetable garden.

The purchase of half-a-pound of arsenic in June, 1919, was for the same purpose and was used in exactly the same way.

The liquid and powder weed killer were purchased to my order by Jay of Castle Gardens, Hay ~~(my gardener)~~ who attended to my garden at that time ~~to my order~~. I don't even know how much was purchased and I never saw it. I believe it was kept in the stable.

In January 1921 I made a further purchase of a quarter of a pound of arsenic at Mr Davies's shop. A small amount of this was used as a weed killer after being boiled with caustic soda by myself. It was not a success which explains why I have some left at my house. When I purchased this arsenic it was mixed with charcoal. I am keeping this to make a further trial later on. I remember talking to Mr Taylor, the Bank Manager of Hay, respecting my recipe for weed killer. I remember being pleased at being able to make my own weed killer at a much cheaper rate than the prepared article, which after the war was very dear and I could not afford it. This last preparation I carried out myself as before by boiling the arsenic with caustic soda in a petrol can. Although I have no motor car I use petrol for a petrol gas installation.

From the 2nd September to the 20th September 1921, as far as I can trace, I did not leave Hay, but on the 21st September 1921, I went motoring with Mr Lee, Surveyor of Taxes, of Derby, who took myself and my son to Bath where my son was returning to school. We returned on the Sunday following.

I don't take chocolates myself and have not purchased any of them since I bought a small box for my late wife in August 1920. These I bought in Hay but I can't remember the shop – they were certainly not Fuller's, which I was of the impression were not procurable in Hay.

During the period between the 2nd and 20th September 1921, ~~while~~ I was in Hay transacting business at my office and residing at my house. I did not leave the town. I may have called on friends socially but I do not remember.

I am unable to throw any light upon the finding of arsenic in Mr Martin's urine or as to the cause of his illness after having tea with me on 26th October 1921. I did not touch the food he ate in any way and partook of what was on the same dish. If arsenic got into the food, I cannot account for it being there.

The cupboard where I keep the arsenic at my house contains boot cleaning materials and is unlocked. Nobody in the house as far as I know is aware of the presence of arsenic in the house. This arsenic I speak of is the only poison in my possession anywhere, excepting of course any contained in medicine. I have a medicine chest in ~~my~~ a bedroom.

I make this statement quite voluntarily, and without being questioned.

H Rowse Armstrong

31 December 1921
Alfred Crutchett (Chief Inspector)
Walter Sharp (Sergeant)

Skeleton in the Cupboard

The Murder of the Reverend Mr PARKER by RICHARD HEMMING on Tuesday June the 24th 1806 in the Garden of Oddingley Rectory and the Murder of RICHARD HEMMING by THOMAS CLEWES and Others at about the same time

An extraordinary tale of village intrigue came to light during a murder investigation that took place almost twenty-five years after the crime at Oddingley, just south of Droitwich.

The story begins in 1806, a time when much of the Church's revenue came from tithes; this was a levy exacted at 10 per cent of the annual produce of land or labour, and was clearly not designed to be popular with the small farmer. It was particularly unwelcome when pursued with the aggressive disregard for circumstances that characterized the collecting technique of the Reverend Mr Parker, rector of Oddingley. He was, in short, a very unpopular man.

On the 24th of June, Midsummer's Day, in 1806, a shot was heard to come from the rectory garden, followed by the cry "Murder!" When villagers reached him the Reverend Parker lay dead, his clothes still smouldering from the gun wadding. As one of the villagers gave chase the assassin turned and levelled a gun at him; having scared his pursuer into flight the gunman threw his weapon over a hedge and made good his escape. But not before he had been identified as Richard Hemming, a carpenter and wheelwright of Droitwich. It is no doubt indicative of Parker's unpopularity that the fifty guineas "for information" remained unclaimed; and the mystery of why a comparative stranger with no connection with the rector should want to murder him remained unsolved.

It was in the year 1830 that the answers were uncovered to this puzzle. Since the relaxation of Parker's strangling grip on the collective agricultural purse, local farmers had been enjoying a modest prosperity. Thomas Clewes, though, seems to have been happy to exchange one master for another, and now gave the greater part of his profits to the brewer and the innkeeper. When through drink he became incapable of following the plough his Netherwood Farm was sold; it was the new owner who found the skeleton under the barn floor. And it was Mrs Hemming from Droitwich who identified the teeth – heaven knows how – as those of her missing husband Richard.

It was far too late, and now unnecessary, to punish Hemming for the Reverend Parker's death; but it was in time to arrest Clewes for the murder of Richard Hemming. The terrified farmer was quick, however, to give credit where it was due, for it was not his hand alone that cut off Richard Hemming in his prime. It transpired that a consortium of six local farmers had hired Hemming to dispose of the hated rector, and had then – whether as a precaution against exposure or because Hemming was trying a little blackmail on his own account – disposed of him in his turn. Of the guilty six, only Clewes and two others were still alive, and as the two others were by now prosperous and influential members of village society, it was thought best to put the skeletons back into the cupboard, so to speak, and withdraw any allegations and charges that had been made. Which seems to be a curiously satisfying conclusion.

Leicestershire

1. James COOK 54
2. Ronald Vivian LIGHT 60
3. Earl FERRERS 66

Nearer my God . . .

The Murder of Mr PAAS by JAMES COOK on Wednesday the 30th of May 1832 in his Workshop by Wellington Street, Leicester

Mr Paas was a respectable tradesman, and carried on business at No. 44 High Holborn, London, as a manufacturer of brass instruments used by bookbinders. James Cook, his murderer, was a bookbinder at Leicester. Mr Paas was in the habit of taking occasional journeys in the way of business, and in the course of his travels Cook became his customer, and ordered goods from him to the extent of about £25. Cook at this time was twenty-one years of age, and he had only recently entered upon the business of his deceased master in a small yard leading out of Wellington Street, Leicester, upon his own account. In the month of May, 1832, the usual period of credit had expired, and Mr Paas wrote to Cook, saying that he should visit Leicester in a few days, when he hoped to receive the amount of his bill. On Wednesday, the 30th of May, Mr Paas accordingly arrived in Leicester, and put up at the *Stag and Pheasant Inn.* In the afternoon he quitted that house and proceeded upon his rounds, for the purpose of collecting the accounts due to him in the town. He called at several places, and among others at the house of Cook. After he had left there he was seen by one of his old customers, of whom he made inquiries as to Cook's solvency. He told this man that he had already called upon Cook to pay an account, and that he had been requested to call again in the evening. Mr Paas was not seen alive again after this; and the result showed that he had been wilfully and most diabolically murdered by his customer and debtor.

The circumstances which attended the discovery of the murder were of an extraordinary and interesting nature. The workshop which Cook occupied was situated over a cow-house, in the occupation of a Mr Sawbridge, a milkman. In the early evening of Wednesday, the 30th of May, a very large fire was observed to be blazing in his workshop; but as considerable heat was known to be occasionally necessary for purposes of trade, no notice was taken of the occurrence. About eight o'clock Cook visited the *Flying Horse,* a beer-shop in the immediate neighbourhood of his workroom. He called for some drink, and played a game of skittles with an undisturbed aspect, and then requested the change of a sovereign. The landlord, Mr Nokes, produced the coin necessary, and Cook, on giving him the sovereign, took from his pocket a silk purse containing money to a very considerable amount in gold, silver, and notes. This excited some surprise, but no remark was made, and Cook went away, returning apparently to his workshop. After a short time, however, he went to Mrs Sawbridge, and told her that he was going to work during the night in order to finish some

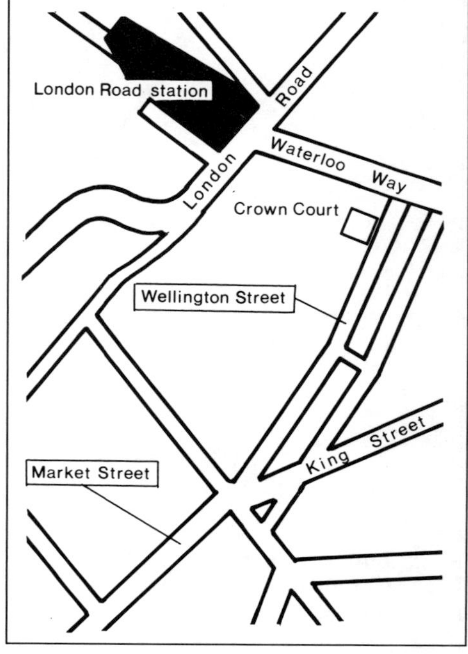

articles which he had in hand, and desired her therefore not to be frightened if she should see that he had a fire. At half-past ten o'clock he returned to his workshop, and was let in by Sawbridge. From that hour until half-past four o'clock the next morning nothing was seen of him, although it was evident that he had remained in his room, as he was unable to quit the premises without the knowledge of his landlord. A strong light was observed in his workshop, and he was heard occasionally to move about, both in the house and in the yard; but although his father went to look for him, and to inquire into the cause of his unexpected absence from home during the night, he made no answer.

On Thursday evening the murder was discovered. At about ten o'clock the appearance of an unusual degree of light in the workshop of Cook attracted observation, and the neighbours had assembled, as fears were expressed that the premises had caught fire. The window-blinds were down, and from without no distinct information could be obtained as regards the existence or non-existence of any conflagration, so an entrance to the building was in consequence determined on. Mr Timson, a broker who resided within two doors went to the top of the stairs leading to Cook's workshop, burst open the door, and immediately entered that apartment. He found that the fire which had been kindled in the grate was extended far beyond its usual bounds, and a large piece of flesh was burning on the top of it. The flesh was taken off and put upon the floor, and the fire was raked out and extinguished.

Cook was sent for, and he declared that the flesh was horseflesh, and that he had bought it with the purpose of feeding a dog; but a surgical examination showed that it was part of a human body.

The non-return of Mr Paas to his inn at once led to the belief that he had fallen victim to the barbarous machinations of Cook, that he had been murdered, and his remains thus mutilated and consumed. A sensation of horror was created as this idea gained ground, and the evidence which confirmed the general impression was soon obtained upon an examination of the premises of the supposed murderer. In the chimney of his workshop was found all that remained unburned or unscorched of the body of the unfortunate Mr Paas. Two thighs and a leg, separated from each other and from the main trunk of the body apparently with great determination with a knife and saw, were found suspended from a nail by a cord in the chimney, about a yard and a half above the fireplace, evidently only awaiting a favourable opportunity when they too might be consumed, and then all trace of the murder would be destroyed. In the room were also discovered the leg of a pair of black trousers covered with blood, together with a snuff-box, an eyeglass, a pencil-case with the letter 'P' engraved on it, and some fragments of cloth much stained with blood. Among the ashes were found the horrible remains of the deceased, in the shape of calcined bones; and there was also discovered a gaiter of the description known to have been worn by Mr Paas.

On Sunday, the 3rd of June, an inquest was held upon the remains of the deceased, at the *Dog and Gun*, in Market Street, and the jury returned a verdict that Mr Paas had been wilfully murdered by James Cook.

A few days sufficed to bring this atrocious malefactor to justice. Cummins, an officer of Leicester, started in pursuit of him, and he succeeded in apprehending him on Tuesday, on the point of joining a vessel just sailing from Liverpool to America.

On Wednesday the 8th of August, the prisoner was put upon his trial at the Leicester Assizes, charged with wilful murder. The indictment alleged the murder to have been committed in various ways, in order to meet all the circumstances of the case.

The prisoner, when called upon to plead, confessed himself guilty of the offence imputed to him. He declared that he was fully acquainted with the effect of his plea, and declined to withdraw it.

Sentence of death was then immediately pronounced by the presiding judge; and, in order that the heinous nature of the crime of the prisoner should be more especially marked, he ordered that his body be gibbeted in chains after his execution [see *Murder Club Guide No.2* for a note on Hanging in Chains]. On the following Friday, the 10th of August, the sentence was carried into effect, the convict being hanged in front of the gaol at Leicester.

NEARER, MY GOD . . .

The following extraordinary story of Christian persistence derives from a little-known volume published in 1832 by Messrs. Simpkin and Marshall. Entitled *Narrative of the Conversion (by the instrumentality of two ladies) of James Cook, the Murderer of Mr Paas,* the two ladies – one of whom is possibly the book's 'author', Mrs Lachlan, the other a young woman identified as Miss Payne of Sulby Abbey, Northamptonshire – by a formidable assault on the sensibility of James Cook, then captive in Leicester Gaol awaiting trial for his life, managed to convert his formerly brutal, ungodly attitude to one of pious submission. The documents in the case are terrifying in their sheer dogmatic determination to "win a soul for Jesus".

The story opens with the ladies discussing the case and, out of Christian charity, deciding to send a salutary letter to Cook, liberally spiced with Biblical sentiment and accompanied by a parcel of printed tracts, hand-bills, and books of verses – one ironically titled *Sunbeams for Dark Hours.* The following is extracted from that first letter:

July 13th

As being like yourself, born in sin, depending *wholly* on a Saviour's blood for *Salvation,* and without which I must be eternally condemned, I am bound to follow His Holy example, by proving myself the *Friend of Sinners* in *Their Time of Need.* Consequently, I take up my pen with the deepest feelings of my own unworthiness and his *Manifold* and *Great Mercies to point out to you a way by which even now your never-dying soul may yet be saved from Eternal Fire.* Yes, I repeat, *even now,* it is possible, notwithstanding all your sins, *That your precious soul may not perish, but have everlasting life.* Are you ready to hear of such a means of salvation? Oh! do not turn away and let that *Evil Spirit* which tempted you to the first most dreadful act, influence you to one *still* more awful, namely, *Despair of God's Mercy, but seize the present moment, ere it flies, to escape from his snares,* by seeking refuge in that *Redeeming* God *Who is able to save the uttermost of all* who call upon him in faithfulness for *"The*

Blood of Jesus Christ cleanseth from all sins"; and if you can only *Believe* this, you may *yet be saved,* since *"All things are possible to him that Believeth".* You may, perhaps, be inclined to say here, "No murderer can inherit the Kingdom of God", and *which the devil will endeavour to persuade you is the case to the very last, in order that you may not use those means* which he *knows* would, in all probability, *secure you to that Eternal Peace he is so unwilling you should ever enjoy.* That there is such a scripture as that respecting murderers, I grant, but Satan takes up the word of God itself frequently *to drive Sinners to Despair;* therefore it is my duty to inform you that *such* a threat is not *confined* to *Murder* only, but every other sin is as likely to keep men out of heaven...

...And since God is not a man that he should lie, or the Son of Man that he should repent, can you not *Depend* upon *His Most Holy Word,* and come unto him just as you are, exclaiming *"God be Merciful to me a Sinner! Gracious Saviour, wash me in thy Cleansing Blood,* and I shall be whiter than snow!"...

...Do you believe that the word of God is true? If you do, you must *also* believe that the *Greatest Sinner may entertain hopes of Pardon, through the blood of Christ.* Yes, if you had murdered *thousands,* that Precious Blood is all sufficient to wash away your stains; therefore repent and be converted, that your *Sins may be blotted out,* and since God is more willing to *Hear* than we to pray, *Draw near unto Him with a true Penitent Heart and lively Faith,* saying, *God be merciful to me a sinner.* Again I beseech you not to despair of His Mercy. Recollect the thief on the cross, *even at the very last minute,* was pardoned; therefore why not you likewise....

[This seemingly endless tirade continues for a further five pages in identical vein, with much exhortation to repentance and prayer, concluding on a cautionary note:]

...But if you will not be influenced by my advice, how *deep* will be your remorse to all eternity, and how awfully you will lament having neglected the *Present Opportunity Afforded You,* and in the midst of all your torments, exclaim: "I might even to the very last have been saved, if I had attended to the writer of that letter; yes, if I had only come to Christ, and cast myself on His Mercy, depending on His Blood, I might have escaped this place of torment; but, alas, *Now* it is too late, and I am for ever lost".

May the Lord give you grace to make a *Full Confession* of *All* the circumstances relating to this awful affair, as far as *you yourself* are concerned, for His Dear Son's sake, Jesus Christ our Lord and *Saviour. Amen.*

Should the Lord graciously permit this letter to be instrumental in promoting that repentence unto *Salvation,* which is not to be repented of "and without which no man can see the Lord" I should *much* like to hear *of* or *from* you; in which case you may direct to me thus:

[there follows an address, etc.]

Cook, so it is claimed, penned – or had penned – the following uncharacteristically modest and self-effacing reply:

Most Respectful Madam,
I scarcely know how sufficiently to express my gratitude for the very great kindness you have evinced towards me, who could not expect anything of the kind, considering my situation, and likewise being an entire stranger. I have attentively perused the papers which you wrote, and have derived great consolation from so doing, as they are so plainly expressed, and hold out hopes, even to the worst of sinners; which is certainly most comfortable to me, as I must class myself amongst those of that denomination. I may with truth add that they have offered me more room for pardon from our blessed Saviour than anything yet given me. This I hope will in some measure reward you for the very great pains you must have taken towards making me a good Christian. If

I am not asking too much, I should feel happy in either seeing you, or hearing from you again; if it is possible for you to come I shall be more pleased, as from what I have experienced from your pen, it makes me anxious to hold some conversation with the writer. If I have expressed myself in any way too freely in asking you to come, I most sincerely ask your forgiveness.

With every respect
Believe me, Madam,
Yours most thankfully,
JAMES COOK

True to their promise, the ladies turned up at the prison armed with "a new, large Bible, having marked some hundreds of verses, peculiarly suited to such a wretched criminal's case. . ."

"In a few minutes [they] were able to proceed to the prisoner's cell, and with indescribable emotion they rose, inwardly imploring the assistance of that Power, without which all human effort is in vain . . . they reached a small apartment, in which there was scarcely room for three iron bedsteads, a table, and several chairs; and there, behind the door, sat a youth of a most interesting, handsome countenance, heavily ironed, leaning over a table, on which was placed a writing-desk, and on this lay the little book called *Sunbeams*. . .

Presently the ladies took a seat opposite the criminal, and the gentleman accompanying them required whether [Cook] had read the contents of the parcel first delivered. Cook replied, "I have read the little book [*Sunbeams*] through two or three times." The ladies then took up the conversation:

"Do you think you have any feelings since you received that letter, which you had not before?"

"Yes, Ma'm."

"What are they?"

"They give me larger hopes of pardon."

"Hopes of pardon! Why, the hopes you may entertain through the Blood of Jesus Christ are as boundless as eternity itself. Had you committed a thousand murders, one drop of the Blood of the Son of God could wash them all away; but it must be applied to your soul through *Repentence;* the first proof of which is your open and full confession of your crime. This what I am most anxious to procure, for it is the first step towards repentence and amendment."

Hereupon Cook, hanging down his head, said: "I did confess when I was examined before the Magistrates; I dare say you saw that."

"Yes, I did see it; but that confession was false! You know it was."

He remained silent.

She then said with solemn earnestness, "Are you not wretched?"

"Well, I don't enjoy myself as much as if I had nothing on my conscience, certainly."

"Enjoy yourself! You know there does not breathe in existence a more miserable creature than you are at this moment. It is utterly impossible you should be otherwise, since God has declared there is no peace for the wicked; therefore you are assuming an indifference which you know you do not feel!"

He was again silent, which gave the ladies some hope that he was influenced by a power which prevented him from adding sin to sin by uttering additional falsehoods . . .

On Saturday, July 28th, the same two ladies revisited a much "improved" James Cook; it had been seen in the meanwhile "that for the first time he knelt on two knees, and put up both hands, and cast his eyes to heaven in fervent prayer".

Saturday, July 28. – Cook held out his hand to us, and looked quite altered, and so much happier. The following dialogue then took place:

Lady: Well, Cook, you know the last time we saw you, we endeavoured to convince you of the necessity of confessing your sins. Are you inclined to do so?

Prisoner: I have confessed.

Lady: We are rejoiced to hear it; and now how do you feel?

Prisoner (slowly, emphatically, and interrupted by many, many tears and sobs): I feel that I deserve to die fifty times; but I hope and trust I shall be forgiven, through the atonement and intercession of Jesus Christ. (Here he wept so much that he seemed exhausted, and leaned his head on the Bible before him; and then burying his face in his handkerchief. He still, though shedding floods of tears, repeatedly exclaimed: O, I am so happy! Oh dear, I never could have believed I should have felt as I do now.)

Lady: Why did you not confess to us when we were before with you?

Prisoner: To tell you the truth, I had it at the end of my tongue to confess to you the first day you came, but if any one had come and offered me my liberty, I could not have uttered a word.

Lady: How happened that?

Prisoner: I don't know how it was; I'm sure it must have been the devil.

Lady: We understand your brother has been with you this morning, and has endeavoured to persuade you to plead Not Guilty at your trial, and that your family will engage counsel for you and spare no expense on your account. What did you say in reply?

Prisoner: I decidedly refused; for I am resolved never to conceal from man what I must acknowledge before God; therefore I shall plead Guilty.

Lady: You have resolved well. How could you ever hope for pardon from God if you, on so solemn occasion as this, in his presence, and before an earthly tribunal and judge, were to utter a direct falsehood?

Prisoner: It is my full determination to plead Guilty. I deserve to die a hundred deaths.

Lady: What sort of life do you think you would now lead, if that were to be spared?

Prisoner: A life of holiness. Yes, it would be a useful life. I should be an ornament to society.

Lady: We have brought you some texts of Scripture pasted on boards, to hang up in your cell; these are the verses: 'Repent and Believe the Gospel', 'The Wages of Sin is Death, but the Gift of God is Eternal Life, through Jesus Christ Our Lord', 'Behold the Lamb of God, which taketh away the Sins of the World', and 'The Son of Man is come to Seek and Save that which was Lost'.

He appeared exceedingly pleased with these texts, and afterwards requested they might be allowed to remain in his cell, after his death...

Lady: We have brought you Fletcher's address upon "What must I do to be saved?"

Prisoner: O Fletcher, he is a nice man. But O, I now love every body! I feel that I should like to do good to all men.

Lady: Should you like us to receive the sacrament with you?

Prisoner: O I should love to receive it with you!

Striking while the iron was hot, the ladies visited Cook again on Monday, July 30th, when they found him wearing "an almost angelic expression, and beaming with joy upon seeing us". They popped in on Tuesday the 31st: "We found him seated at a table reading his Bible. Upon being asked whether it (the Bible) did not become more precious to him every day, he said: 'Yes, I love to read my Bible'". On August 1st, the diary notes, after a further visit to the Prisoner: "Oh what a beautiful work of Grace is there! Great God, thy power is indeed infinite, and thy mercy in Christ Jesus is as boundless as eternity itself". Saturday 4th of August, and Cook had received the Sacrament for the first time. The ladies' visits are interrupted by other of God's pressing work, though they do get an invitation to hear Cook sing, on Monday the 6th, at a private 'concert' for the benefit of his keeper, where he sang four hymns (one of which was the *Funeral Hymn*).

On Wednesday the 8th, Cook appeared on his Trial at the Leicester Assizes, and the ladies record "This day I beheld poor Cook before his earthly judge. May the Lord prepare him to stand before his Heavenly one, whose mercy endureth for ever!"

On the 10th August, Cook was executed (after receiving the Sacrament), and on the following day gibbeted in Saffron-lane, Leicester, not far from the Aylestone toll-gate: "The body was dressed in the same clothes that he was hung in – black coat, black waistcoat, white duck trousers, and a pair of Berlin gloves. His face was covered with a pitch plaster, and over it placed the cap he suffered in."

The Green Bicycle Mystery*

The Death of ANNIE BELLA WRIGHT on Saturday July the 5th 1919 on the Gartree Road, Nr. Little Stretton and the Trial and Acquittal of RONALD VIVIAN LIGHT for her Murder

WHAT HAPPENED?

On the evening of Saturday the 5th of July 1919, a twenty-one-year-old girl left her home at Stoughton (where her father was a farm worker), and cycled to Evington to get a stamp at the post office and to post a letter. She then returned, and proceeded on the road to Gaulby to visit her uncle, a Mr Measures.

*This text has been based on the researches of Mr A. W. R. Mackintosh into the murder of Bella Wright. With colleague Mr W. Richardson, Mackintosh has for many years pursued the minutiae of the Green Bicycle Mystery, and has opened many new avenues for investigation. By no means the least of their achievements has been to identify the spot where Bella was buried.

At about the same time a man of thirty-four, who lived in Highfield Street, Leicester, went out for a cycle ride and arranged to be back for supper at around 8pm. He turned left into the London Road and proceeded through Stoneygate and Oadby to Great Glen. He then turned left and proceeded to the left turn into Gartree Road. This would have taken him back to Leicester, but he looked at his watch just before he reached Great Stretton and realized that he would be home too soon; so he decided to return through Houghton-on-the-Hill. He therefore turned right, and when he came to the cross-roads where the Gaulby Lane crossed the Houghton Lane (see map [1]) he saw a girl bending over a bicycle. She raised her

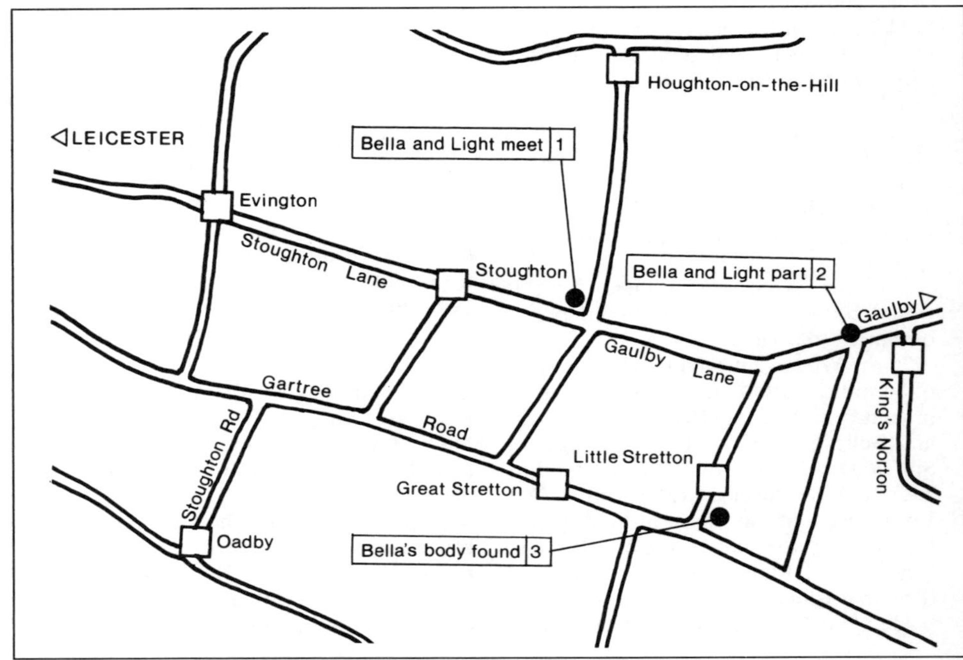

head as he approached and asked him if he had a spanner. He replied that he hadn't, but asked what the trouble was. She said that her back wheel was loose and while he did what he could to put it right he asked where she was going. When she said "Gaulby", he thought he might as well go with her as he could easily get to Houghton from there. When the couple arrived at Gaulby she said that she would only be about ten minutes and as that appeared an invitation to wait, he went with her to her uncle's house and waited outside. Mr Measures's daughter and her husband, a Mr Evans, happened also to be on a visit, and they asked about the man outside. When she told them of the circumstances they advised her not to go back with him as he looked "too old" for her. So she prolonged her visit until the man eventually tired of waiting and set off for home. His route took him uphill to Gaulby church, and when he arrived there he found he had a puncture. It took nearly an hour to mend it, and as the girl hadn't passed him during that time he went back to the house and got there just as she was coming out. They then cycled back together

Bella's uncle Mr Measures

Annie Bella Wright

the way they had come. When they got to the road junction beyond King's Norton (see map [2]) the girl said she would have to bid goodbye to her companion as her route was to the left. He, according to his subsequent evidence, proceeded directly back to Leicester via Stoughton and Evington.

At about 9.20pm Mr Cowell, a farmer, was going along the Gartree Road when he found a girl lying on the road alongside a bicycle (see map [3]); when he examined her he found she was dead. Returning to his farm at near-by Little Stretton, Cowell harnessed his pony and trap, and after arranging for someone to guard the body, proceeded to Great Glen to report the matter to Constable Hall, the local policeman. From there he phoned Dr Williams at Billesdon, and then returned to Little Stretton. It was dark by the time Dr Williams arrived so he gave instructions that the girl's body be removed to an unoccupied house at Little Stretton. At this point it was assumed that she had died in a cycling accident.

The next day, Sunday the 6th PC Hall returned to the scene and after a careful search found a bullet on the road. He then went to the house where the body had been deposited, and after washing the congealed blood from the face discovered a bullet wound. Dr Williams was immediately informed and he and another doctor carried out a full post-mortem.

It was subsequently established that the girl's name was Bella Wright and that she lived in Stoughton. When her relatives at Gaulby got to hear of her death the hue and cry went out for the 'Man on the Green Bicycle' as everyone jumped to the conclusion that he must have been the killer.

WHAT HAPPENED TO BELLA WRIGHT?

Until recently there was a doubt as to where Bella Wright had been buried, as there was nothing in the Stoughton Church records to indicate that she had been buried there. A contemporary report of the funeral was subsequently discovered in the *Leicester Daily Post* of 12th July, 1919:–

LEICESTERSHIRE MYSTERY
Burial of Murdered Girl:
Impressive Scenes at Stoughton

Simply and impressively the funeral took place in the pretty little churchyard of Stoughton Parish Church yesterday (Friday) afternoon of Miss Annie Bella Wright, the 21-year-old (she would have been 22 on the 14th July) victim of the brutal crime perpetrated on Saturday night at Little Stretton. The church was filled with people who knew the dead girl – representatives of her workpeople at Bates Rubber Mills, friends at Leicester and the villagers at Stoughton where her father and mother live, all of whom knew her well. The funeral bell tolled as the cortège was starting from an old world cottage at the other end of the village. People lined the route along which the cortège passed, rustic roads lined with grassy banks and over which the foliage of lines of trees hung impressively.

The principal mourners were Mr and Mrs Wright (father and mother), Archie Ward, HMS *Diadem* (the victim's young man), Philip, Tom, and Leonard (brothers), Mr and Miss Beaver (uncle and cousin), Mrs Harrison and Mrs Lambert (aunts), Mr and Mrs Measures (aunt and uncle), Messrs. T. Wright and Len Wright (uncles), Miss Ward, and Mr and Mrs Langley.

The hymn *Peace, Perfect Peace* was sung as the flower-laden coffin was borne up the aisle and many of the women wept silently.

The Vicar of Stoughton, the Rev. W. N. Westmore BA said he wanted to ask each one there why they had come to see the burial. He hoped it was to show sympathy to the relatives of the girl who had been so foully murdered. He trusted it was not a sense of curiosity that brought them to the church that afternoon. Curiosity would not lead forward on the path of righteousness, but they did want to show their sympathy at this poor girl being taken away from them. He wanted to say to those who thought that religion was at a discount, and Christianity had had its day, and that a man need not attend any longer to those things that the church persists in teaching, and that he was taught in childhood – he wanted them to think that in a question of this sort when a girl was suddenly and foully murdered on a country road, that in the midst of civilisation there was a heart of barbarism. Why were murders of this sort not

Located by Messrs Mackintosh and Richardson, the last resting place of Bella Wright has been marked and the grave lovingly tended by Mr Richardson

more common? It was because Society in the main was impregated with the spirit of Christianity. Men may not go to Church, but still the spirit of Christianity enters into their lives and they live with moral courage.

The hymn *Brief Life is Here our Portion* was sung, and to the recessional *Rest in The Lord* the murdered girl was borne to her last resting place. Hundreds filed by to take a last look at the coffin and numerous floral tributes, among which was a heart-shaped wreath from the dead girl's fellow-workers. The mother and father broke down at the graveside.

WHAT HAPPENED TO RONALD LIGHT?

Although the identity of the 'man on the green bicycle' was not to be known for many months, his name was Ronald Light, and at the time of Bella Wright's death he was living in Highfield Street, Leicester. Light was born in October 1885 and the first family home had been in Granville Road, Leicester. It is understood that his father had been the manager of Ellistown Colliery, near Coalville. After graduating as a civil engineer at Birmingham University, Ronald Light was employed as an engineer and draughtsman at the Midland Railway Works at Derby, but he usually returned to Leicester at weekends.

In May 1910 he purchased a green BSA bicycle from a firm named Orton & Co. of Derby. At about that time he also became a member of the Fortress Company, Royal Engineers, whose headquarters were at Buxton. From time to time, Light used to hire a motor cycle from Orton's to enable him to get into Buxton.

The Great War broke out in August 1914 and in February 1915, after undergoing training at Chatham, Newarke and Ripon, Ronald Light was granted a commission as a Second Lieutenant in the Royal Engineers. He was later posted abroad on active service, though for some reason he left the Royal Engineers in August 1916, and in the September he rejoined in the Honourable Artillery Company as a private. After undergoing further training Light was sent overseas again. He eventually suffered badly from shell-shock, and was invalided to a number of hospitals in England before his demobilisation in January 1919.

Ronald Vivian Light

Sometime in 1916 or 1917 Ronald's father died accidentally at Granville Road, and in May 1917 the home was moved to Highfield Street where Ronald lived with his mother and a maid-servant.

It was not until the Tuesday evening following his encounter with the girl cycling to Gaulby that Light read of the tragedy in the *Leicester Mercury,* and learned that the dead girl's name was Bella Wright. By this time the public and the press had decided that it was the man on the green bicycle who had been responsible for her death. According to his later evidence, Light was now in a serious dilemma. He worried over the matter for some time before eventually deciding to do nothing except remove the bike from where he usually kept it to the attic.

In October 1919, Ronald Light decided to get rid of his bicycle. He filed off the number at the top of the saddle column and took it down to the canal to a point near the Gas

The Green Bicycle as it was recovered from the canal

Works, and after detaching the back wheel (because it had a distinctive back-pedalling brake) he threw the parts separately into the canal.

When he was an officer in the Army Light had had a .45 revolver, but when he reverted to being a private and was posted overseas, he took the revolver with him but not the holster. According to his evidence, when he became a casualty, all his belongings, including the revolver, were left behind in France. But he still had the holster and some rounds of ammunition at home which he also threw into the canal.

In January 1920 Ronald Light took up an appointment as a mathematics master at a school in Cheltenham. On the 23rd of February in the same year a horse-drawn barge was going along the canal when suddenly its tow-rope tightened and up came a green bicycle. The manager of a cycle shop in Leicester, who examined the bicycle, found a number on the inside front fork, the duplicate of one usually stamped at the top of the saddle column. In no time ownership of the bike was traced to Ronald Light.

After the preliminary police-court proceedings, Light's trial was fixed for June 20th 1920, at Leicester Castle. He was defended by the celebrated advocate Sir Edward Marshall Hall, and to everyone's surprise, he was found Not Guilty.

If you ask any of the older generation today, you will almost invariably be told that "he done it", and it was only through the brilliance of Marshall Hall that he got off. What they don't tell you is that at the inquest proceedings Mr Robert Churchill, the ballistics expert, revealed that a carrion crow which was found dead nearby had also been shot. So it is almost certain that whoever shot the crow also shot Bella Wright. As this evidence was not given at the trial, it would appear that the police were very remiss in not properly following through with this line of investigation.

I, the writer, happen to be seventy-seven years of age; and in that very summer of 1919 I was staying at a farm belonging to a relative of my father in Strathglass in Inverness-shire. I was fourteen-and-a-half years of age at the time and there was a boy, Billy, at the farm who was about my own age. There was also an older member of the family who had been an officer in the army during the Great War and had later been in the Black and Tans. He had got quite an armoury of weapons in the house so Billy got hold of a couple of .45 revolvers with a supply of ammunition and we went about

Telephone 357 and 862.

LEICESTERSHIRE CONSTABULARY.

£5 REWARD.

At 9-20 p.m., 5th instant, the body of a woman, since identified as that of ANNIE BELLA WRIGHT, was found lying on the Burton Overy Road, Stretton Parva, with a bullet wound through the head, and her bicycle lying close by.

Shortly before the finding of the body the deceased left an adjacent village in company of a man of the following description :—

Age 35 to 40 years, height 5 ft. 7 in. to 5 ft. 9 in.; apparently usually clean shaven, but had not shaved for a few days, hair turning grey, broad full face, broad build, said to have squeaking voice and to speak in a low tone.

Dressed in light Rainproof Coat with green plaid lining, grey mixture jacket suit, grey cap, collar and tie, black boots, and wearing cycle clips.

Had bicycle of following description, *viz.*:—Gent's B.S.A., green enamelled frame, black mudguards, usual plated parts, up-turned handle bar, 3-speed gear, control lever on right of handle bar, lever front brake, back-pedalling brake worked from crank and of unusual pattern, open centre gear case, *Brooke's* saddle with spiral springs of wire cable. The 3-speed control had recently been repaired with length of new cable.

Thorough enquiries are earnestly requested at all places where bicycles are repaired.

If met with the man should be detained, and any information either of the man or the bicycle wired or telephoned to E. HOLMES, ESQ., CHIEF CONSTABLE OF COUNTY, LEICESTER, or to SUPT L BOWLEY, COUNTY POLICE STATION, LEICESTER.

County Constabulary Office,
Leicester, 7th July, 1919.

T H JEAYS & SONS, PRINTERS 7 ST. MARTINS, LEICESTER.

the place firing indiscriminately. At one stage we were going along a road on which you would not be likely to see more than about one person a week. Suddenly we saw someone coming towards us, so we hid our revolvers. I then said to Billy, "I know who that is." He said, "You can't possibly know." I said, "It's my uncle Charlie." The reason I knew him was that he was the only person I had ever seen with a Louis Napoleon beard. He was a civil engineer in London and I lived in Glasgow, so he was as surprised to see me as I was to see him. He said it was the first time he had been to the farm in thirty years. The point is that I could easily have accidentally shot my uncle. There were thousands of service revolvers about after the Great War, and it would have been well within the bounds of possibility for someone like myself to be shooting indiscriminately, and for poor Bella to unwittingly come within the line of fire.

The matter has never been satisfactorily resolved. In the meantime Ronald Light went to stay at the Isle of Sheppey, in Kent, where he lived unobtrusively until his death in May 1975 at almost ninety years of age. His funeral was at Charing Crematorium, near Ashford, and his ashes were scattered in the Garden of Remembrance there.

WHAT HAPPENED TO THE BICYCLE?

The Green Bicycle as it was retrieved from the canal – minus the back wheel – was the principal exhibit at the trial. When I discussed the matter with other people, I was often asked "What happened to the Green Bicycle?" So I determined to find out. I contacted the police but they didn't know anything about it; I contacted the Museum, and likewise they didn't know, but said that if I located it they would very much like to have it. It looked rather hopeless until one day I was talking to a lady in Evington and she told me that when she was a schoolgirl, in about 1930, she used to go to a shop where there was a green bicycle hanging on the wall. I checked up and sure enough it was still there, but the third generation proprietor, John Franckes, didn't want to let it go. We are still trying, and I have no doubt that it will eventually arrive at the Museum.

A Court of Peers

The Murder of Mr JOHN JOHNSON by LAURENCE SHIRLEY, EARL FERRERS on Friday the 18th of January 1760 at Staunton Harold, near Ashby-de-la-Zouch

An Unfortunate Appointment

Laurence, Earl Ferrers, was descended of an ancient and noble family, and the royal blood of the Plantagenets flowed in his veins.

This nobleman was married in the year 1752 to the youngest daughter of Sir William Meredith; but although his general conduct, when sober, was not such as to be remarkable, yet his faculties were so much impaired by drink that, when under the influence of intoxication, he acted with all the wildness and brutality of a madman. For a time his wife noticed nothing to cause her to repent her marriage, but he subsequently behaved to her with such unwarrantable cruelty that she was forced to flee his house, and, rejoining her father's family, to apply to Parliament for redress. And so an Act was passed granting her a separate maintenance to be raised out of her husand's estate; trustees being appointed, it fell the lot of the unfortunate Mr Johnson – remarkable only for the regularity of his manner, the accuracy of his accounts, and his fidelity as a steward – that he should act as receiver of rents to be paid over for her use. At first he was uneasy, and declined the office, but at the insistence of his master the Earl, consented to act.

His Lordship at this time lived at Stanton [Staunton Harold], a seat about two miles from Ashby-de-la-Zouch, in Leicestershire; and his household consisted of Mrs Clifford, a lady who lived with him, and her four natural daughters, besides five menservants, exclusive of an old man and a boy, and three maids.

Mr Johnson lived at the house belonging to the farm, which was held under the Ferrers lordship, called the Lount, about half-a-mile from Stanton. It seems that he was accustomed to visit his master with some regularity to settle the accounts which had been placed under his care as land steward; but by dint of Johnson's unenviable position as receiver of the Countess's maintenance, the Earl, his master, gradually conceived an irrational dislike for him, and charged him with having plotted with his wife's trustees to lose him a coal contract. Before long, the unfortunate Johnson was the brunt of many wild and extravagant accusations of conspiracy and treachery, resulting in the steward's dismissal from his farm. The trustees, however, as part of the Act of separation, had already granted him a lease of it, it having previously been promised to him by the Earl. It was probably this that decided Ferrers on his course of wicked revenge.

A Shot Fired in Anger

On Sunday, the 13th of January 1760, Earl Ferrers went to the Lount, and, after some discourse with Mr Johnson, ordered him to come to him at Stanton on the Friday following, the 18th, at three o'clock in the afternoon. His lordship's usual dinner-hour was two o'clock; and soon after that meal was disposed of on the Friday he went to Mrs Clifford, who was in the still-house, and desired her to take the children for a walk. She accordingly prepared herself and her daughters, and, with the permission of the Earl, went to her father's, at a short distance, being directed to return at half-past five. The men-servants were next dispatched on errands by their master, who was thus left in the house with three females only. In a short time afterwards Mr Johnson came, according to his appointment, and was admitted by one of the maid-servants, named Elizabeth Burgeland. He proceeded at once to his lordship's apartment, but was desired to wait in the still-house; and then, after the expiration of about ten minutes, the Earl, calling him into his own room, went in with him and locked the door. Being thus together, the Earl required him first to settle an account, and then, charging him with the villainy which he attributed to him, ordered him to kneel down. The unfortunate man went down on one knee; upon which the Earl, in a tone of voice loud enough to be heard by the maid-servants without, cried: "Down on your other knee! Declare you have acted against Lord Ferrers. Your time is come – you must die." Then suddenly drawing a pistol from his pocket, which was loaded, he presented it and immediately fired. The ball entered the body of the unfortunate man, but he rose up, entreating that no further violence might be done to him; and the female servants at that time coming to the door, being alarmed by the report, his lordship quitted the room. A messenger was immediately dispatched for Mr Kirkland, a surgeon, who lived at Ashby-de-la-Zouch; and Johnson being put to bed, his lordship went to him and asked him how he felt. He answered that he was dying, and desired that his family might be sent for. Miss Johnson soon after arrived, and Lord Ferrers immediately followed her into the room where her father lay. He then pulled down the clothes and applied a pledget, dipped in arquebusade water, to the wound, and soon after left him.

From this time it appears that his lordship applied himself to his favourite amusement – drinking – until he became exceedingly violent (for at the time of the commission of the murder he is reported to have been sober), and on the arrival of Mr Kirkland he told him that he had shot Johnson, but believed he was more frightened than hurt; that he had intended to shoot him dead, for that he was a villain, and deserved to die; "but", said he, "now that I have spared his life, I desire you would do what you can for him." His lordship at the same time desired that he would not suffer him to be seized, and declared that if anyone should attempt it he would shoot him. Mr Kirkland told him that he should not be seized, and directly went to the wounded man. He found the ball had lodged in the body; at which his lordship expressed great surprise, declaring that he had tried that pistol a few days before and that it then carried a ball through a deal board nearly an inch and a half thick. Mr Kirkland then went downstairs to prepare some dressings, and my lord soon after left the room. From this time, in proportion as the liquor which he continued to drink took

effect, his passions became more tumultuous, and the transient fit of compassion, mixed with fear for himself, which had excited him, gave way to starts of rage and the predominance of malice. He went up into the room where Johnson was dying and pulled him by the wig, calling him a villain, and threatening to shoot him through the head; and the last time he went to him he was with the greatest difficulty prevented from tearing the clothes off the bed, that he might strike him.

A proposal was made to him in the evening by Mrs Clifford that Mr Johnson should be removed to his own house; but he replied: "He shall not be removed; I will keep him here to plague the villain." He afterwards spoke to Miss Johnson about her father, and told her that if he died he would take care of her and of the family, provided they did not prosecute.

When his lordship went to bed, which was between eleven and twelve, he told Mr Kirkland that he knew he could, if he would, set the affair in such a light as to prevent his being seized, desiring that he might see him before he went away in the morning, and declaring that he would rise at any hour.

Mr Kirkland, however, was very solicitous to get Mr Johnson removed, and, as soon as the Earl had gone, he set about carrying his object into effect. He in consequence went to Lount and, having fitted up an easy-chair with poles, by way of a sedan, and procured a guard, returned at about two o'clock and carried Mr Johnson to his house, where he expired at about nine o'clock on the following morning.

To Catch an Earl

The neighbours now began to take measures to secure the murderer, and a few of them, having armed themselves, set out for Stanton; and as they entered the yard they saw his lordship, partly undressed, going towards the stable, as if to take out a horse. One of them, named Springthorpe, then advancing towards his lordship with a pistol in his hand, required him to surrender; but the latter putting his hand towards his pocket, his assailant, imagining that he was feeling for some weapon of offence, stopped short, and allowed him to escape into the house. A great concourse of people by this time had come to the spot, and they cried out loudly that the Earl should come forth. Two hours elapsed, however, before anything was seen of him, and then he came to a garret window and called out: "How is Johnson?" He was answered that he was dead. But he said it was a lie, and desired that the people should disperse; and then he gave orders that they should be let in and furnished with victuals and drink, and finally he went away from the window, swearing that no man should take him. The mob still remained on the spot, and in about two hours the Earl was descried by a collier, named Curtis, walking on the bowling-green, armed with a blunderbuss, a brace of pistols and a dagger. Curtis, however, so far from being intimidated by his bold appearance, walked up to him; and his lordship, struck with the resolution he displayed, immediately surrendered himself, and gave up his arms, but directly afterwards declared that he had killed the villain, and gloried in the act. He was instantly conveyed in custody to a public-house at Ashby, kept by a man named Kinsey; and a coroner's jury having brought in a verdict of wilful murder against him, he was on the following Monday committed to the keeper of the gaol at Leicester.

Prisoner in the Tower

Being entitled, however, by his rank to be tried before his peers, he was, about a fortnight afterwards, conveyed to London, in his landau, drawn by six horses, under a strong guard; and, being before the House of Lords, he was committed to the custody of the Black Rod, and ordered to the Tower, where he arrived at about six o'clock on the evening of the 14th of February. He is reported to have behaved, during the whole journey and at his commitment, with great calmness and propriety. He was confined in the Round Tower, near the drawbridge: two wardens were constantly in the room with him, and one at the door; two sentinels were posted at the bottom of the stairs, and one upon the drawbridge, with their bayonets fixed; and from this time the gates were ordered to be shut an hour sooner than usual.

During his confinement he was moderate both in eating and drinking: his breakfast was a half-pint basin of tea, with a small spoonful of brandy in it, and a muffin; with his dinner he usually drank a pint of wine and a pint of water, and another pint of each with his supper. In general his behaviour was decent and quiet, except that he would sometimes suddenly start, tear open his waistcoat, and use other gestures, which showed that his mind was disturbed.

Mrs Clifford and the four young ladies, who had come up with him from Leicestershire, took a lodging in Tower Street, and for some time a servant was continually passing letters between them; but afterwards this correspondence was permitted only once a day.

Mrs Clifford came thrice to the Tower to see him, but was not admitted; but his children were suffered to be with him some time.

A Court of Peers

On the 16th of April, having been a prisoner in the Tower two months and two days, he was brought to his trial, which continued until the 18th, before the House of Lords, assembled for that purpose; Lord Henley, Keeper of the Great Seal, had been created Lord High Steward upon the occasion.

The murder was easily proved to have been committed; and his lordship then proceeded to enter upon his defence. He called several witnesses, the object of whose testimony was to show that the Earl was not of sound mind, but none of them proved such an insanity as made him not accountable for his conduct. His lordship managed his defence himself in such a manner as showed an uncommon understanding: he mentioned the fact of his being reduced to the necessity of attempting to prove himself a lunatic, that he might not be deemed a murderer, with the most delicate and affecting sensibility; and, when he found that his plea could not avail him, he confessed that he made it only to gratify his friends; that he was always averse to it himself; and that it had prevented what he had proposed, and what perhaps might have taken off the malignity at least of the accusation.

The Peers having in the usual form delivered their verdict, of guilty, his lordship received sentence to be hanged on Monday the 21st of April, and then to be anatomised; but in consideration of his rank, the execution of this sentence was respited till Monday, the 5th of May.

During this interval he made a will, by which he left one thousand three hundred pounds to Mr Johnson's children, one thousand pounds to each of his four natural daughters, and sixty pounds a year to Mrs Clifford for her life; but this disposition of his property, being made after his conviction, was not valid, although it was said that the same, or nearly the same, provision was afterwards made for the parties named.

In the meantime the scaffold was erected under the gallows at Tyburn, and part of it, about a yard square, was raised about eighteen inches above the rest of the floor, with a contrivance to sink down upon a signal given, in accordance with the plan then invariably adopted; the whole being covered with black baize.

First Victim of the 'New Drop'

On the morning of the 5th of May, at about nine o'clock, his lordship's body was demanded of the keeper of the Tower, by the Sheriffs of London and Middlesex, and his lordship, being informed of it, sent a message to the sheriffs, requesting that he might be permitted to be conveyed to the scaffold in his own landau, in preference to the mourning-coach which was provided for him. This being granted, his landau, drawn by six horses, immediately drew up, and he entered it, accompanied by Mr Humphries, the Chaplain of the Tower, who had been admitted to him that morning for the first time. On the carriage reaching the outer gate, the Earl was delivered up to the sheriffs, and Mr Sheriff Vaillant entered the vehicle with him, expressing his concern at having such a melancholy duty to perform; but his lordship said he was "much obliged, and took it kindly to be accompanied". The Earl was attired in a white suit, richly embroidered with silver; and when he put it on he said: "This is the suit in which I was married, and in which I will die." The procession, being now formed, moved forward slowly, the landau being preceded by a considerable body of Horse Grenadiers, and by a carriage containing Mr Sheriff Errington, and his under-sheriff, Mr Jackson, and being followed by the carriage of Mr Sheriff Vaillant, containing Mr Nichols, his under-sheriff, a mourning-coach-and-six, containing some of his lordship's friends, a hearse-and-six for the conveyance of his body to Surgeon's Hall after execution, and another body of military. The pace at which they proceeded, in consequence of the density of the mob, was so slow that his lordship was two hours and three-quarters in his landau, but during that time he appeared perfectly easy and composed, though he often expressed anxiety to have the whole affair over, saying that the apparatus of death and the passing through such crowds were worse than death itself, and that he supposed so large a mob had been collected because the people had never seen a lord hanged before*. He told the sheriff that he had written to the King to beg that he might suffer where his ancestor, the Earl of Essex, had been executed, and that he had greater hopes of obtaining that favour as he had the honour of quartering part of the same arms, and of being allied to his Majesty; but that he had refused, and the Earl thought it hard that he must die at the place appointed for the execution of common felons.

When his lordship had arrived at that part of Holborn which is near Drury Lane he said he was "thirsty, and should be glad of a glass of wine-and-water"; upon which the sheriffs, remonstrating with him, said that a stop for

* It had previously been the privilege of nobility to be beheaded.

that purpose would necessarily draw a greater crowd about him, which might possibly disturb and incommode him, yet, if his lordship still desired it, it should be done. He most readily answered: "That is true – I say no more – let us by no means stop."

When the landau advanced to the place of execution his lordship alighted from it, and ascended the scaffold with the same composure and fortitude of mind he had exhibited from the time he left the Tower. Soon after he had mounted the scaffold, Mr Humphries asked his lordship if he chose to say prayers, which he declined; but upon his asking him if he did not choose to join with him in the Lord's Prayer he readily answered he would, for he always thought it a very fine prayer. Upon which they knelt down together upon

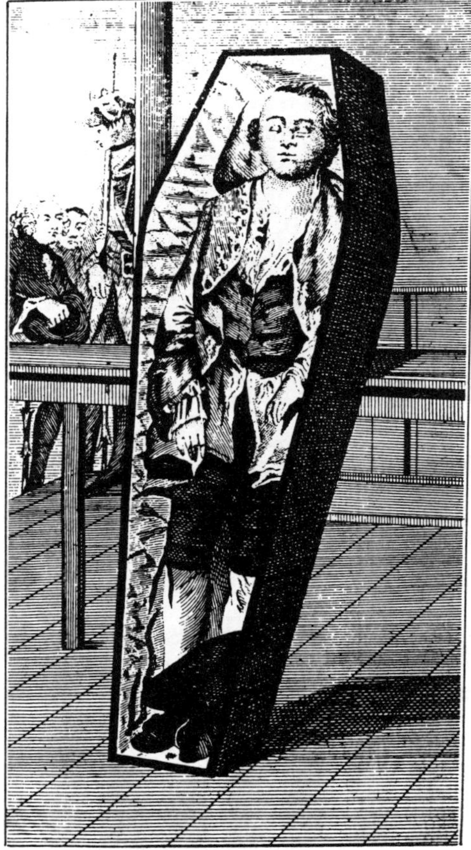

"The body was brought from Tyburn in a coffin lined with satin; his hat and the halter lay at the feet, and upon the lid was a plate with these words: 'Laurence, Earl Ferrers suffered 5.5.1760' "

two cushions covered with black baize, and his lordship, with an audible voice, very devoutly repeated the Lord's Prayer, and afterwards, with great energy, ejaculated: "Oh, God, forgive me all my errors – pardon my sins!"

His lordship, then rising, took his leave of the sheriff and the chaplain; and, after thanking them for their many civilities, presented his watch to Sheriff Vaillant, of which he desired his acceptance, and requested that his body might be buried at Breden or Stanton, in Leicestershire.

The executioner now proceeded to do his duty, to which his lordship, with great resignation, submitted. His neck-cloth being taken off, and a white cap, which he had brought in his pocket, being put upon his head, his arms secured by a black sash, and the cord put round his neck, he advanced by three steps to the elevated part of the scaffold, and, standing under the cross-beam which went over it, which was also covered with black baize, he asked the executioner: "Am I right?" Then the cap was drawn over his face, and, upon a signal given by the sheriff (for his lordship, upon being before asked, declined to give one himself), that

that part upon which he stood instantly sank down from beneath his feet, and he was launched into eternity, the 5th of May, 1760.

The accustomed time of one hour being past, the coffin was raised up, with the greatest decency, to receive the body; and, upon being deposited in the hearse, was conveyed by the sheriffs, with the same procession, to Surgeon's Hall, [see *Murder Club Guide No. 1*], to undergo the remainder of the sentence. On the evening of Thursday, the 8th of May, the body was delivered to his friends for interment.

The following verse is said to have been written by Ferrers in his apartment at the Tower:

In doubt I live, in doubt I die,
Yet undismay'd the vast abyss I'll try,
And plunge into eternity
Thro' rugged paths...

[*Based on an account in* The Malefactors Register *of 1776.*]

THE NEW DROP

Though by all literal standards the scaffold must be called the first 'drop', it is a far cry from the 'long drop' which was to ensure the (notionally) instant decease of the condemned more than a century later. The platform was not a trap-door, and was anyway only 18 inches deep. In fact, due to the rope being a new one, and unstretched, the unlucky Ferrers's feet still brushed the ground, and in true gallows style he was "despatched by the pressure of the executioner"; that is, the hangman swung on his feet to hasten the strangling.

A further bizarre anecdote not often included in accounts of the Earl Ferrers execution concerns the quarrel that broke out between the hangman and his assistant and delayed the execution: "His lordship then, by mistake, gave five guineas (to ensure a swift end) to the executioner's assistant; which was immediately demanded by the master, but the fellow refused to deliver it, and a dispute ensued which might have discomposed his lordship, had not Mr Vaillant instantly silenced them."

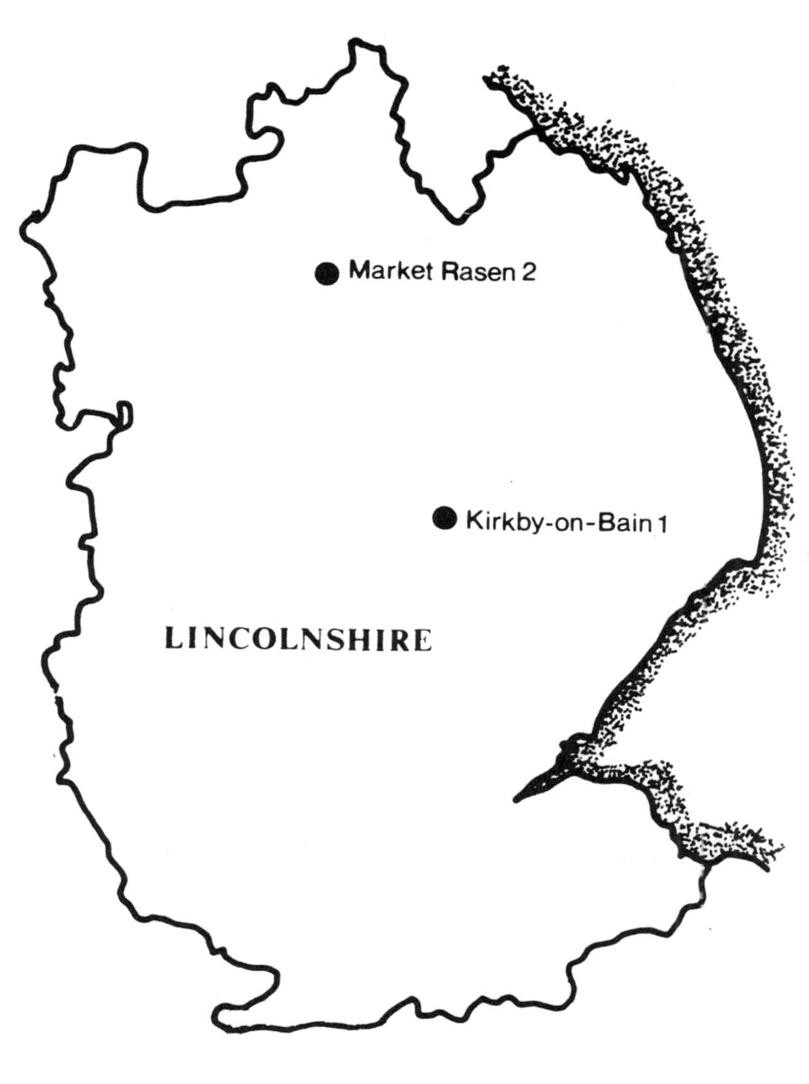

Lincolnshire

1. Ethel Lillie MAJOR 74
2. Isaac and Thomas HALLAM 75

The Dog it was that Died

The Murder of ALFRED MAJOR by his wife ETHEL LILLIE on Thursday the 24th of May 1934 at their home in Kirkby-on-Bain

It is a fact of every police officer's life that he receives his share of letters, telephone calls and visits from cranks and attention-seekers. It is very rarely that the officer will ignore such seeming red herrings, for though many police hours may be lost chasing wild geese, at least a small percentage prove, on previous experience, to be vital clues.

In the case of the death of Arthur Major the police would have been unaware that there had even been a crime to solve had it not been for an anonymous letter – the writer of which remains unknown to this day.

On 26 May 1934 Inspector Dodson of the Horncastle force received this letter:

> Sir, Have you ever heard of a wife poisoning her husband? Look further into the death (by heart failure) of Mr Major, of Kirkby-on-Bain. Why did he complain of his food tasting nasty and throw it to a neighbour's dog, which has since died? Ask the undertaker if he looked natural after death? Why did he stiffen so quickly? Why was he so jerky when dying? I myself have heard her threaten to poison him years ago. In the name of the law, I beg you to analyse the contents of his stomach. 'Fairplay'

A quick check revealed that forty-four-year-old lorry driver Arthur Major had indeed died – on the 24th of May – of what had been diagnosed as an epileptic fit. The symptoms – violent spasms and muscular contortions – had begun two days before. Dodson acted swiftly in getting a Coroner's order to prevent the funeral taking place at its appointed time on May 27th, and it must have been a uniquely disturbing experience for mourners to look on as the police removed the coffin from before their very eyes.

Meanwhile, Dodson's officers had confirmed that a wire-haired terrier belonging to the Majors' next-door neighbour Mr Maltby had died during the night of May 23rd after suffering muscular spasms. The direct cause of the unfortunate beast's untimely retreat could not elude the redoubtable Dr Roche Lynch of St Mary's Hospital, Paddington, distinguished analyst to the Home Office. Nor could the reason for Arthur Major's recent demise – both had succumbed to a fatal dose of strychnine – in Major's case, probably two doses.

So what of the wife who had been anonymously accused of the terrible crime? What of Ethel Major? An account is appropriately supplied by the Scotland Yard officer who was placed in overall charge of the case, Chief-Inspector Hugh Young:

> She impressed me as a cool and resourceful woman suffering no pangs of sorrow at the loss of her husband. In fact, she seemed quite callous about the whole affair, and even informed me that she felt "much better in health since he was gone". She began, however, by telling me that she was sure her husband had died through eating corned beef. She appeared over-eager to impress me with the fact that she had nothing to do with providing his meals, explaining that for a fortnight before her husband's death she and her young son had not slept at home but had stayed with her father.... "My husband bought his tinned beef himself," she went on, adding with great insistence: "I know that I never bought any. I hate corned beef and I think it is a waste of money to buy such rubbish." This obvious desire to dissociate herself from any provision or purchase of corned beef seemed to me rather important, because corned beef was the last meal eaten by Arthur Major before he was seized with his fatal illness on the night of 22nd May.
>
> (Hugh Young *My Forty Years at the Yard)*

Further investigation began to colour-in many of the details of the Majors' unsettled married life; for a start, they couldn't stand the sight of each other – in fact Ethel, a cantankerous, arrogant woman, was pretty much disliked throughout the neighbourhood. Arthur was also sinking financially as a result of what he saw as his wife's extravagance. It was a development worthy of note in the circumstances that Major had, the very week he died, arranged to have a notice published in the *Horncastle News* dissociating himself from all the debts accumulated by his wife – an arrangement countermanded by Mrs Major immediately her husband died. Jealousy also emerged as a potential motive. Ethel claimed to have found two letters written by Mrs Rose Kettleborough (a neighbour) to her husband; to her detriment she showed these letters to her doctor with the accompanying comment: "A man like him is not fit to live, and I will do him in."

When Chief-Inspector Young next interviewed Mrs Major she claimed: "I did not know my husband died from strychnine poisoning." "I never mentioned strychnine," the detective replied, "how did you know that?" "Oh, I'm sorry. I must have made a mistake."

When she came up for trial at Lincoln Assizes, Ethel Lillie Major was defended by Mr Norman (later Lord) Birkett. He could not have faced a more daunting task in the whole of his long career. The evidence against his client was overwhelming.

The police had proved access to the poison when they found a key in Ethel Major's purse that opened a box containing strychnine belonging to her ex-gamekeeper father. He had used the poison to exterminate vermin, and vaguely remembered having mislaid his spare key some years before. The corned beef from which Mrs Major had been at such pains to distance herself was proved to have been bought by the couple's 15-year-old son Lawrence, on his mother's instruction.

Norman Birkett would surely have been one of the first to concur with the claim made by his learned colleague for the Crown, Mr Edward O'Sullivan KC: "The case is really on the evidence unanswerable." The defence called no witnesses, and Ethel Major did not take the witness stand. When the jury filed back with their verdict after one hour, Birkett already knew that he had lost.

Mr Justice Charles passed sentence of death on the prisoner, and relayed the jury's inexplicable recommendation to mercy. This latter was not acted upon by the Home Secretary and Ethel Lillie Major was executed at Hull Prison on the 19th of December 1934.

A Dead Post-Boy*

The Murder of WILLIAM WRIGHT by ISAAC and THOMAS HALLAM around the month of January 1733 at Faldingworth Gate, Nr. Market Rasen

ISAAC and THOMAS HALLAM
Murderers and Highwaymen
Hanged in Lincolnshire upon the Spot where they Committed their Crime

Isaac and Thomas Hallam were brothers, who had long, with too much success, carried on a series of daring robberies, and perpetrated cruel murders, insomuch that Government offered a reward for their apprehension.

---

* 'Never . . . see . . . a dead postboy, did you?' inquired Sam.
'No,' rejoined Bob, 'I never did.'
'No!' rejoined Sam triumphantly. 'Nor never will; and there's another thing that no man ever sees, and that's a dead donkey.' (*Pickwick Papers*, Charles Dickens)

They were at length taken, and charged with the murder of William Wright, a youth of only eighteen years of age, who was found in a post-chaise at Faldingworth Gate, near Market Rasen, in Lincolnshire, with his head almost severed from his body, covered with the seat-cloth, and his pockets rifled. In consequence of the proclamation, extraordinary search was made after these desperate depredators, but they baffled their pursuers nearly a month. At length they were taken into custody, and committed to the gaol of the city of Lincoln.

Among their varying outrages, they, in mere wantonness, forced a post-boy to blow his horn, then told him he had sounded his own death-peal, and immediately cut his throat, as well as that of his horse, and the bodies of the man and beast were next morning found close together. From this detestable barbarity, the post-boys of Lincoln mustered with their horns on the entrance into Lincoln, and greeted them with their loudest blasts; whereupon, now stung with remorse, one of them was observed to weep.

They were convicted of the murders of William Wright and Thomas Gardner; and afterwards confessed that they committed, in company with each other, sixty-three robberies and one murder, exclusive of that for which they were condemned to die. Yet did these shocking offenders attempt to evade their punishment. They procured a case-knife, which they notched like a saw, in order to cut off their irons; and then, with a spike-nail, they began digging through the wall of their prison; but were detected. In passing to the place of execution of Isaac, which was the spot where they had murdered the post-boy, this unfortunate brother fell into violent agonies and perturbation of mind. At the gallows, there being no clergyman to attend them, he called to one of the spectators to assist him in his devotions, which the good man readily complied with, and he prayed with much fervency. Thomas was ordered to be carried farther, to the place where they had murdered Mr Wright, but on his seeing his brother turned off, and struggling with life, he shrieked out in a dreadful manner. He then was drawn to Faldingworth Gate, where he died in dreadful agonies of mind. This execution took place on the 20th of February, 1733.

Northamptonshire

1. Alfred Arthur ROUSE 78
2. Mary CLARKE and Phillip HAYNES 92
3. Thomas GORDON 93

The Blazing Car Murder

The Murder of an Unknown Man by ALFRED ARTHUR ROUSE on Wednesday November the 5th 1930 in Hardingstone Lane, Hardingstone

It was two o'clock on the morning of November the 6th 1930, and Alfred Brown and William Bailey were strolling down Hardingstone Lane on their way home after a Guy Fawkes night dance; some fifty yards ahead of them they saw something burning. Given the bonfire activity of the previous evening they were less surprised by the sight of the fire than by the sudden appearance of a man who seemed to climb out of the ditch and rush past them, remarking as he did so that "it looks as if someone has had a bonfire".

Approaching closer Brown and Bailey saw that the 'bonfire' was in reality a Morris Minor motor car ablaze. They immediately called the police, and when the fire was under control a charred body could be seen collapsed across the front seats. Burnt beyond recognition, it was taken to *The Crown* public house nearby.

The vehicle's undamaged registration plate – MU 1468 – showed the owner to be one Alfred Arthur Rouse, a thirty-six-year-old commercial traveller. And Rouse was recognised as the man seen hurrying from the conflagration by Messrs. Brown and Bailey.

When Rouse was apprehended he made a blustering attempt at an explanation of his extraordinary conduct on the morning of the sixth, a story which was to form the basis of his subsequent defence at the Northampton Assizes. A story that would be torn to shreds by Norman Birkett KC acting, unusually, for the Crown.

Alfred Arthur Rouse told the officers that he had picked up a hitch-hiker on the Great North Road just outside St Albans. He had stopped in Hardingstone Lane to answer a call of nature and asked his travelling companion to fill the car's tank with petrol from a can in the boot. When he looked back the car was ablaze: "I saw the man was inside and I tried to open the door, but could not as the car was by then a mass of flames... I did not know what to do; I saw the two men... I lost my head".

Described in Mr Justice Talbot's summing up as "a most facile liar", Rouse was found guilty of murder, and after an unsuccessful appeal was executed on March the 10th.

But why kill a perfectly innocent man and at the same time burn out your own car?

The answer lay in Rouse's personality; a personality which – unhappily as it ended – was very attractive to the ladies. Nobody ever catalogued the extent of Rouse's amours, but at least one bigamous 'wife' and two other women who had had children by him gave evidence at the trial; then there was Ivy Jenkins, a current girl-friend.

Entertaining the ladies and keeping up with the expenses of several 'homes', not to forget a couple of maintenance orders, were beginning to overstretch Rouse's modest income. His 'harem' had become a liability. A liability from which he desperately needed to escape. What if he were to disappear? *What if he was believed to have been killed?* Here then was the motive: Rouse had hoped that the body in *his* car would be taken for his own; hoped that he would be free to start life again with a new identity.

Despite his loud and earnest protestations of innocence, Rouse eventually confessed to the murder – but not before all hope of reprieve was gone, and then to the *Daily Sketch*.

Perhaps the most tragic victim of the Rouse affair was his real wife Lily May. Despite the evident heartbreak of watching her husband's mistresses parade before her in court, Mrs Rouse remained loyal to the end – even selling the contents of her home to underwrite the legal fees.

Looking down Hardingstone Lane, 1987

The Crown *at Hardingstone, where the charred remains were taken*

Est. 1848 NORTHAMPTON Town & County Est. 1848
BENEFIT BUILDING SOCIETY
FUNDS EXCEED £4,000,000
OPEN ACCOUNTS 37,000.
LARGE FUNDS AVAILABLE FOR IMMEDIATE ADVANCES at the LOW RATE OF INTEREST OF FIVE PER CENT.
Tax paid by the Society.
Calculations on Monthly Balances.
There is no better Building Society
H. PRESTON, F.C.I.S., Secretary. 85, Abington Street, Northampton.

Northampton & County Independent.

PRIZE MEDAL
The Corner House
WOOD HILL & St GILES' SQ
PORK PIES PER 1/4 LB

Vol. 25, No. 1283 (Price per Post 13/- for One Year 6/6 for Six Months, and 3/3 per Quarter) Saturday, November 15th 1930. (Registered at the G.P.O.) Twopence

[T]he Hardingstone Murder Charge. Police Seeking to Pierce a Baffling Mystery.

Alfred Brown, a young employee of Phipps' [Brew]ery, who was the first to notify the police of the tragedy.

Police and detectives renewing their search of the hedge near which the car was found in flames, following the inquest at Hardingstone. Shortly after, the discovery of a mallet was [r]eported.

ordinary garden rake, Superintendents Tebbey and ıd Inspector Lawrence making a further minute search of the ashes.

The starting point of the mystery—the charred ruins of the Morris Minor beside the road at Hardingstone.

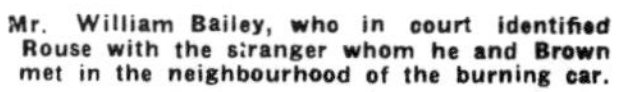

Mr. William Bailey, who in court identified Rouse with the stranger whom he and Brown met in the neighbourhood of the burning car.

Superintendent Brumby, of the Northampton Divisional Police, the officer in charge of the local investigations into the mystery.

'artling developments rewarded the investigations of the Northampton Divisional the mystery of the blazing car discovered at Hardingstone last week. The in- ·ournment of the inquest at Hardingstone on Saturday was the first definite ıt a serious charge was pending. At Angel Lane Police Station that evening ır Rouse, the owner of the burnt car, was charged with the murder of the unknown charred remains were found among the wreckage. A curious crowd watched the rch made by the Divisional Police after the inquest of the ashes of the car and the nearby hedgerows. Their search produced a dramatic development soon after in the reported discovery of a mallet near the scene of the tragedy. Public interest in the mystery was intensified on Monday by the knowledge that Sir Bernard Spilsbury, the Home Office pathologist, had been summoned to make a further examination of the charred remains, and in the afternoon hundreds were turned away from the packed court-room when Rouse appeared before Mr. F. H. Thornton, J.P., and was again remanded.

"Northampton Independent" Photos

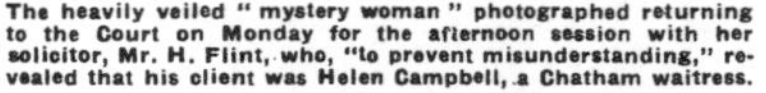

The heavily veiled "mystery woman" photographed returning to the Court on Monday for the afternoon session with her solicitor, Mr. H. Flint, who, "to prevent misunderstanding," revealed that his client was Helen Campbell, a Chatham waitress.

For The Defence. Mr. Finnemore (barrister) and Mr. H. E. Sellars, of Messrs. Darnell and Price, who will open their defence of Alfred Rouse before Justice Talbot at the Northamptonshire Assizes on January 16th.

Two sections of the eager queues which formed outside the Divisional Police Court on Monday and Tuesday, oblivious of rain and fog. Women were, as usual, well in the majority, and some sacrificed two whole days in order to hear the evidence.

Dramatic revelations by Sir Bernard Spilsbury, the famous Home Office pathologist, and Dr. Eric Shaw, honorary physician and pathologist of the Northampton Hospital, as to how the victim of the Hardingstone tragedy may have met his death marked the resumed hearing at the Northampton Divisional Police Court on Monday and Tuesday of the murder charge against Alfred Arthur Rouse.

Evidence of an exhaustive examination of the remains of the burnt car was given by Colonel Cuthbert Buckle, C.B.E., a London fire assessor, who enumerated many circumstances tending to show that the fire had not originated in the engine. Practically the whole of his evidence supported his deduction that there had been fierce fire under the body of the car, but not under the engine.

The Cause of Death.

Sir Bernard Spilsbury on Monday afternoon briefly summarised the condition of the body, of which a detailed description was given by Dr. Shaw, and stated in reply to Mr. Paling (prosecuting) that death was caused by shock due to burns. The fragments of clothing found on the body smelt distinctly of petrol. He had examined the two hairs found on the mallet and was able to say definitely that one was human, brown in colour, and was crushed and broken at one end.

No Evidence of Injury During Life.

The small size of jaw and teeth pointed to the individual having small features, and he formed the opinion that the lower jaw was rather deep and that the chin was projecting rather than receding. The nose was probably fairly prominent and certainly not snub in type, and the whole face was rather long, whilst the spread of the lower jaw indicated it was not a very narrow face. From the condition of the air passages and the lungs he deduced that the deceased had followed an occupation such as coal mining, and that he had continued to breath for some time after the fire started. There was no evidence on the body of injuries caused during life.

After two full days' hearing, Rouse was committed for trial at the Northamptonshire Assizes on January 16.

When the charge was read to him at the close of Tuesday's hearing, Rouse made the following statement:—

"I am quite innocent of this charge. I have made my statement, that's all. In any case, not being a wealthy man, whether I am found guilty or not, my all is taken."

10 THE NORTHAMPTON AND COUNTY INDEPENDENT December 6th, 1930.

Mrs. Rouse Takes Employment as Saleswoman in a Northampton Shop.

Exclusive "Independent" Picture Yesterday.

Mrs. Rouse, wife of Alfred Arthur Rouse, the central figure in the Hardingstone blazing car case, has accepted a post as a shop saleswoman in Northampton, and began work yesterday (Thursday) morning. The shop where Mrs. Rouse is engaged is that of Messrs. Harold Plews, Ltd. (Hopwoods, Trevor Lewis and H. Plews Incorporated), whose recently reconstructed shop is in Bridge Street, Northampton.

In an interview after her first hour's work, during which the "Independent" was able to secure exclusive facilities to obtain the photograph on right, Mrs. Rouse talked to our representative of her plans. A well-built woman of medium height, with a wealth of deep auburn hair and, one would imagine, a normally bright and cheerful disposition, she was well and tastefully dressed and wore a string of graduated beads.

She is obviously a very courageous woman, and despite the ordeal through which she must inevitably be passing, chose to chat for a while upon all manner of minor local topics, including the plays appearing at the theatres and the amenities of Northampton generally.

"To Help My Husband's Defence."

"I have taken this job," she said at length, "for two reasons—to help contribute to my husband's defence fund and also to keep myself, for I am not ashamed to confess that I am carrying on with practically nothing. No, I have had no experience of selling, but I think I shall soon fall into it when I can master the various prices. After all, I think a cheerful face and an obliging manner are the main things," added this remarkable woman with a smile.

In response to further queries, Mrs. Rouse continued, "I like Northampton so much that if it is at all possible I shall stay and live here."

A customer entered at that moment and proceeded to select a box of handkerchiefs, unaware that she was being served by probably the most-talked-of and certainly one of the bravest women in England.

Mrs. Rouse selling a pair of silk stockings.

6 THE NORTHAMPTON AND COUNTY INDEPENDENT. January 31st, 1931.

The Trial Of Alfred Arthur Rouse At Northampton.

Blazing Car Case Provides Most Baffling Mystery in Local History.

Impressions of a Memorable Hearing.

By The "Independent" Special Representative.

The learned Judge,
Sir George John Talbot, Kt.

Alfred Arthur Rouse, the accused. A recent photograph with Miss "Paddy" Jenkins.

The gutted wreck from which the case has taken its name.

As the scene of one of the most celebrated trials of the decade, Northampton has been the centre of interest of the whole country since the beginning of the week. Pictures of the grim Assize Court building in which the drama is being enacted have been circulated throughout the country through the medium of the national Press, and Northampton is acquiring a notoriety which it has not merited, considering that neither of the principal figures in the drama—Alfred Arthur Rouse, who stands charged with the murder, and the unidentified victim of the tragedy—has any established connection with Northampton.

scrupulously pressed and brushed. He wore a stiff white collar and club tie of brown and silver grey. His moustache was severely clipped, and in every way he looked the smart young "commercial" about to make a business call. No one could have looked less like a prisoner in the dock.

A GREAT ORDEAL.

Towards the close of the day, however, the prisoner's will and courage seemed to flag

There were several other witnesses, and it came as no surprise to see Rouse drooping towards the end of the day, which had demanded the utmost of all concerned—judge, counsel and jury.

Two sad loyal figures there were in court who had everyone's sympathy. Mrs. Rouse, who has sat through so many patient hours in the old court with its wonderfully moulded ceiling, and Mr. Rouse, sen., the prisoner's grey-headed father, who sat by her side.

The intense interest which the case has aroused is partly attributable to the mystery which surrounds the victim, and in his charge to the Grand Jury on Friday, Mr. Justice Talbot remarked upon " the very unusual and certainly surprising fact that it had been absolutely impossible to say who was the man whom the accused is said to have murdered." It is believed that there has not been a parallel case for 200 years.

One of the most marked features of " The Blazing Car Trial " has been the widespread tendency on the part of a certain section of the populace to treat it as a public entertainment, with the result that large crowds have thronged the entrance of the Court each day long before the trial opened and the police have frequently been hard pressed in repelling the rushes to gain unauthorised entrance to the Court. Women have been the worst offenders in this respect.

The significant incidents during the progress of the trial are vividly summarised in the accompanying impressions of an Independent correspondent who has been present throughout the trial.

When Alfred Arthur Rouse faced Mr. Justice Talbot at the opening of the fight for his life against a charge of murder at Northamptonshire Assizes on Monday he was in every way the self-possessed. confident young business man whose smart unruffled appearance has so deeply impressed all who have watched him since he was first charged with the killing of the unfortunate unknown whose charred remains were lifted out of Rouse's burned-out car in the early hours of the morning of November 6th.

Rouse looked very handsome indeed in his lounge suit of a pleasant brown, which was and at times he looked haggard and distressed, turning at last for relief to one of the warders, who passed him a white tablet and a glass of water. Soon, however, Rouse's head was sinking on to his hand again. Occasionally he glanced at the clock or ran his hand over his thick dark hair, brushed straight back from his forehead

The ordeal which had changed the debonair young business man into the tired, worn-out prisoner was no light one. For over two hours he had listened while Mr. Norman Birkett, K.C., had outlined the case for the prosecution in an unemotional but powerful address which made but one passing reference to one of the women with whom the prisoner is alleged to have been intimate and to the admission of whose evidence the defence took such strong exception in the earlier stages of the proceedings.

TOUCHING LOYALTY.

After that the prisoner heard the two young Hardingstone men, Brown and Bailey, tell of their dramatic meeting with him in Hardingstone lane shortly before two o'clock in the morning, and he heard how Police-Sergeant Harris found the mallet on the grass verge fourteen yards in front of the car.

An interesting figure at the barrister's table was that of Mr. W. A. Attenborough, who forms a link with another historic murder trial at Northampton, for Mr. Attenborough was counsel for MacRae when that prisoner was tried in the same court nearly forty years ago.

Mr. Attenborough, who was called to the Bar fifty-six years ago, carries his age wonderfully well. Among other things he has been an M.P. and a cornet soloist.

Apart from the counsel actually concerned in the case Mr. Attenborough was the only member of the Bar at the large baize-covered table on which rested the attache case which Rouse is said to have taken with him after the burning of the car, and other exhibits such as the burst and distorted petrol can.

WOMEN JURORS REJECTED.

Great interest was taken in the opening of the trial, and shortly after half-past seven on Monday morning a queue began to gather outside the court. The first to arrive were a middle-aged man and woman, and they had their reward for they obtained entry to the court for the first session.

About fifty members of the public are admitted to each session, and those disappointed on Monday were but a few of hundreds who on subsequent days had to content themselves in watching the witnesses, counsel and other celebrities arrive in court.

Something of drama came early in the proceedings, for the defence challenged the two women jurors whose names were taken out of the ballot box, and two male jurors were sworn in their place, the result being that Rouse is being tried by an all-male jury.

When it became known that there was still some room available after ticket holders had gained admission and that a certain number of the public had gained admission, a crowd made a concerted rush for the entrance, where, as seen, they were only prevented from entering by the attendant police.

Mr. Norman Birkett, K.C., the famous counsel briefed by the Crown for the prosecution. Scrupulous fairness has been the keynote of his procedure throughout.

Mr. D. L. Finnemore, instructed by Messrs. Darnell and Price, appeared for the defence. He discharged his duties with brilliant ability.

January 31st, 1931. THE NORTHAMPTON AND COUNTY INDEPENDENT. 7

Miss Nellie Tucker avoids the curiosity of passers-by as she leaves her hotel in Northampton.

Rouse pleaded not guilty in a low but firm voice. Mr. Norman Birkett, who has for his junior Mr. Richard Elwes, a member of the family whose associations with Northamptonshire are so well known, opened the case for the prosecution.

Mrs. Rouse, the wife of the accused, was present at court through most of the proceedings.

" 'My car, my identification numbers, a dead body, and I—I alone—seen on the road.' So he might have thought, and it may be that you will think that any original plan had certainly miscarried."

During the short pause which followed the close of Mr. Birkett's powerful address and the calling of the first witness Rouse spoke cheerfully to one of his warders. He had little room in the dock, closely hemmed in as he was by a warder on either side, while to the back of him sat the Governor and doctor of Bedford Gaol and a third warder.

A HUMAN INCIDENT.

The presence of the prison Governor in the dock with Rouse provided an amusing human incident after lunch, for the Governor was a

Miss Helen Campbell, who has become known as the "mystery woman" in the case.

examination from Mr. D. L. Finnemore, said that the body of the unknown man was lying face downwards across the front seats, with his face in the driver's seat. One leg was doubled up under the body and the other was stretched out, extending a little way outside the car.

Public interest in the trial was unabated on Tuesday and there was again a queue outside the court long before the resumption. This time the police allowed the members of the public to enter four at a time, four men and four women alternately, for women had complained of the bustling to which they had been subjected in previous rushes when the court was opened.

ROUSE STILL BUOYANT.

In the gallery were several clergy, including the Rev. E. G. P. M. Kingdom, formerly of St. Sepulchre's, Northampton, and now of Kettering.

Col. Cuthbert Buckle, who gave evidence of a highly technical nature concerning the cause of motor fires. His investigations, he said, indicated that the fire was not started accidentally.

Mr. Bird, who has contributed in no small measure to the elucidation of the facts in the case by having undertaken a very comprehensive personal investigation of any and every clue which might lead to the establishment of the identity of the victim.

Rouse again looked fit and well when he entered the dock, but after lunch he looked worn and tired once more—a tremendous contrast to the buoyant manner in which he had left the dock before the interval, when he had a smile for the young women who pressed

Again and again the prisoner looked at the clock, ticking out the slow, dreary minutes that take the trial to its inevitable conclusion—vindication of the prisoner's innocence or. . . .

ROUSE'S STATEMENT.

Inspector James Lawrence, who gave evidence on Tuesday morning, said in cross-examination that when Rouse was making his statement at Hammersmith Police Station he did not appear to witness to be telling the truth. Asked why he came to this conclusion witness said the prisoner would correct himself three or four times before he allowed Detective-Sergeant Skelley to put down what he said.

Mr. Alfred Brown, the young employee of Messrs. Phipps' Brewery, who was the first to inform the police of the tragedy on November 6th; and (below) Mr. William Bailey, who shared with Brown the tragic discovery, while returning from a dance in the early hours of the morning.

Mr. A. P. Marshall, joint counsel for the defence with Mr. Finnemore.

Mr. A. J. Darnell, of the firm of Darnell and Price, the Northampton solicitors acting for the accused.

THE PROSECUTION OPENS.

"It is no part of the duty of the prosecution to supply a motive," he told the jury. "The springs of human conduct are many times beyond all human divining and hidden far from that region where the human eye can see or the human mind can extend. You may think there never could be an adequate motive for murder. . . . . You may think that the facts and the circumstances in this case point to the conclusion that, for some reason, the prisoner desired the charred remains of that unknown man to be taken for his, and that when he emerged out of that hedge at that hour of the morning and was seen by two young men, the plan or design may have miscarried.

Mr. Richard Elwes, junior counsel to Mr. Norman Birkett, for whom his eminent senior evidently entertains the highest regard. At one stage in the proceedings Mr. Elwes had occasion to remind his senior of a small matter. Mr. Birkett immediately turned, and placing his hand affectionately on Mr. Elwes' shoulder, remarked "As my learned young friend reminds me, etc., etc."

Dr. Eric Shaw, hon. pathologist to the Northampton General Hospital, who thrilled the court with a comprehensive if necessarily gruesome, description of the results of his examination of the charred remains found in the car.

little late in returning from lunch and when he re-entered the dock Rouse leaned over and shut the dock door for him.

At the afternoon session at which this incident occurred Alfred Brown and William Bailey, the young Hardingstone men, described how they met Rouse in Hardingstone lane at ten minutes to two in the morning. They were surprised to see a well-dressed man come out of the ditch at that time of the morning, they said. He called out to them "It looks as though someone has got a bonfire up there," but what they found was a blazing car with the flames leaping twice a man's height into the air.

"EQUALITY OF THE SEXES."

Other witnesses on Monday were P.C. Copping, of Hardingstone, P.C. Valentine, of Northampton, and P.S. Harris, of Collingtree. P.C. Copping, who came in for a lengthy cross-

Dr. Hervey Wyatt and Dr. A. T. Telling, both of whom contributed to the medical evidence of the case.

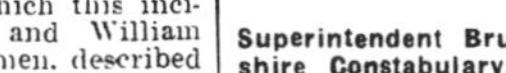

Superintendent Brumby, of the Northamptonshire Constabulary, has ably directed police investigations from the first and received from Rouse at Hammersmith on November 7th a statement which was the subject of prolonged cross-examination on Tuesday.

forward to see him step backwards down the steep stairs from the dock. At one stage of the proceedings he appealed to the prison doctor and was given smelling salts, some white tablets and water.

Mr. A. P. Price and Mr. Sellars of the firm of Messrs. Darnell and Price.

"There was no need, in my opinion, if he was telling the truth, to correct anything," said the witness, who stated later that the corrections were to bring the statement round to look as favourable to prisoner as possible.

Answering the Judge the inspector said he did not think the dead man could get into the position in which he was found.

Mr. William Bailey.

Those members of the public who hoped to hear something of human interest must have been disappointed at having to listen for three hours to the technical evidence of Colonel Cuthbert Buckle, C.B.E., an expert on fires. But Colonel Buckle's evidence was brilliantly given, and it forms a most important part of the case for the prosecution. It seemed amazing that any man could deduce so much from the charred and fused wreckage which

(continued on page 10.)

THE NORTHAMPTON AND COUNTY INDEPENDENT.

Rouse Trial Contd.—Prisoner in the Box.

Colonel Buckle was called upon to inspect. The car, he said, was destroyed by an intense fire which was fed for a definite period of time.

Mr. Ray, a London journalist, who was alleged to have remarked to Supt. Brumby on the morning of November 6th at the scene of the fire that there were marks of a car having reversed on the grass. The Superintendent, however, said he had no recollection of the remark.

Mr. Henry Flint, solicitor, who is watching the case on behalf of Miss Helen Campbell, who has come to be described as the "mystery" woman in the case.

"THOUGHT IT WAS A HUMAN HAIR."

The expert on cars and fires was followed into the box by another expert witness. Dr. Eric Shaw, pathologist of Northampton and Kettering Hospitals, who told how terribly charred was the body of the unknown man, and said that he thought that one of the hairs he took from the head of the mallet found by P.S. Harris was a human hair.

Within an hour of the resumption after lunch the case for the prosecution was closed.

Mr. Donald Finnemore submitted that the case was not sufficiently strong to go to the jury for consideration, and urged that the evidence was as consistent with the fire having been caused accidentally as with anything else. Here, also, one was faced with the extraordinary circumstance that the victim appeared to be a man quite unknown, with no quarrel or grudge existing between him and the prisoner.

JUDGE'S RULING.

The Judge said it was quite proper for the defence to go to the jury on the footing that there was no case to answer, but for him to give a ruling on the matter of law was an impossible contention.

Mr. Finnemore then said that in that case he proposed to call evidence, and went on to address the jury.

Up to this point it had been a gloomy day for Rouse. Outside the skies were overcast and the court itself, lacking the brightening gleams of sunshine that streamed in on Monday and Tuesday, was dull and forbidding. The prisoner sat through the morning and early afternoon with none of the smiles one often surprises upon his features.

Mr. Finnemore's fine speech to the jury obviously heartened him, however, and for once he left the dock looking more cheerful than when he entered.

ROUSE SEES NELLIE TUCKER.

One of the witnesses who attracted special attention was Miss Nellie Tucker. An attractive girl, she simply gave the time at which Rouse last saw her in London and the period for which she had known him.

Prisoner's eyes scarcely left her while she was in the box. When they did, he buried his head in his hands.

PRISONER TELLS HIS STORY.

The great moment of the trial arrived on Thursday morning when Alfred Rouse was called to the box at 11.35 as the first witness for the defence. This had been rumoured in advance and a huge crowd swarmed round the doors of the court before they were opened for the afternoon session and overflowed into the road. Additional police had to be stationed on the doors to resist the attempts of the crowd to force their way into the court.

Rouse was, as usual, perfecly groomed, but his demeanour was more serious than hitherto. He had a smile, however, for his wife, who occupied her usual seat beside the dock and was accompanied by a friend.

Mr. Finnemore spoke for over an hour during the morning session, laying emphasis upon the fact that the medical testimony supported the prisoner's story in many particulars. He laid particular stress upon the divergence of the police witnesses' evidence on certain points.

There was a stir in court when, at the close of his speech he called the prisoner to the witness-box. Rouse entered the box between the two warders and seemed perfectly composed as he took the oath. He appeared slightly ill at ease during the opening questions put to him by Mr. A. B. Marshall (defending) upon his age and war record, but he rapidly regained his composure.

THE PASSENGER.

He left home on business, he said, on November 5th and travelled about thirty miles round about London. He left again about nine p.m. and had just passed Tally Ho! Corner when a man put up his hand and asked for a lift. He replied that he was bound for the Midlands and the man said that was where he wanted to go. For the sake of companionship he agreed to take him. By the small light on the dashboard he saw that his passenger was respectably dressed. He wore a mackintosh of light texture. He could not say what was the colour of his eyes or of his hair. "One man would not look at another man's eyes to see the colour," he explained. "He was about my own build, but perhaps not so 'meaty.'"

Near Northampton he pulled up at his passenger's suggestion for a doze, but first he got out of the car to see how much petrol he had. He took the petrol can from the back of the car and unscrewed the cap. He did not remember using the mallet, but he thought he might have used the handle. He decided to leave the passenger to fill the tank and after partially unscrewing the cap he put the can back in the driving seat.

ROUSE BREAKS DOWN.

Rouse then described how the man had asked him for a "smoke" and after a moment's hesitation he threw him a cigar. The passenger said he had a match, so he left him and went down the road about two hundred yards.

A few moments later he saw the reflection of a light.

"I stood up to have a look," he said, "and took a couple of steps forward. Then I saw quite plainly a huge flame which I took to be my car. I took it my car was in flames. For a moment or so I looked. I could not understand it. It was the last thing in the world I thought of happening."

After describing the scene Rouse broke down. His voice failed and he brushed his hand across his eyes. He was given a glass of water and the Judge ordered that he should be given a seat. "I'm all right, sir," said Rouse, "I would rather stand."

He went on to describe how he ran panic-stricken for help. "I lost my head entirely," he said, explaining how he had passed Brown and Bailey on his way to the main road, bent on getting help.

His next clear recollection was of being on a lorry. He could not recall what he had said. Finally, after he had described his visit to Wales, Mr. Marshall asked:

January 31st, 1931

"Did you, in fact, do any harm or hurt to the man you picked up as a passenger?"

Rouse: "I have never done what I consider any harm to anybody."

ALMOST INCOHERENT.

Rouse was in the box for little over four hours, and for over three hours of this he was subjected to a searching cross-examination by Mr. Birkett. Rouse admitted that he told lies to many people about his car. He admitted he had been close to Scotland Yard when he was in London and could have told the police about the horror before he went to Wales. "But," he said, "I wanted my breakfast and meant to go to Wales before I saw the police."

Towards the close of his cross-examination Rouse became almost incoherent as he denied that he had stunned his passenger and thrown him into the car. He was exhausted when he returned to the dock on Thursday afternoon and drank a cordial with obvious gratitude.

It should have been added beneath the photographs of Messrs. Darnell and Price on page 7 that they are acting in conjunction with Mr. Lee Roberts for the defence.

STILL IN HARNESS

Shoe Union Secretary's New Sphere.

Mr. E. L. Poulton, for many years one of the outstanding figures of the footwear industry in his capacity of Secretary of the Boot and

THE NORTHAMPTON AND COUNTY INDEPENDENT.

The Final Scene of a Memorable Trial.

Alfred Arthur Rouse Condemned To Death.

Awaiting the Verdict. So dense was the crowd that barriers had to be erected the whole length of the pavement fronting the Assize Court. (Inset is a photograph of Rouse from a recent snapshot.

By the verdict of the jury Alfred Arthur Rouse has been adjudged a murderer, and by his own confession he is a libertine whose unrestrained lust has condemned three illegitimate children to pay part of the price of his sins.

He is, however, a man of courage, and in the closing moments of the memorable trial at Northampton Assizes last week he won one's admiration by the way in which he received the verdict of "Guilty." Pale he was and his eyes were fixed in a glassy stare whilst the knuckles stood out white in the hands which gripped the front of the dock.

His courage was unquenchable, however, and at no period of the trial had he shown to better advantage.

ROUSE IN TEARS.

The day which closed with the sentence of death had been a memorable one. It opened in an atmosphere of dread expectancy, and Mr. Donald Finnemore attained heights of moving oratory when he addressed the jury. When he begged them to blame any omissions of defence upon him and not the prisoner, Rouse buried his head in his hands and wept.

Rouse took heart from his advocate's speech, but Mr. Norman Birkett's incisive sentences and eloquent hands brought him to gloom again. He heartened once again when Mr. Justice Talbot told the jury that no motive had been adduced, "but," added his Lordship, "there are certain obvious improbabilities in the account he gives."

From that point Rouse drooped. Lines seamed his face, deeper and deeper, and in the next hour he seemed to age ten years.

The Judge's summing-up was a model of fairness, but Rouse seemed to realise that doom was at hand, and with admirable courage he pulled himself together for the last few dramatic moments.

THE JURY RETURN.

After the summing-up the jury had lunch and then inspected a Morris Minor, similar to the one burned in Hardingstone lane. Twenty-five minutes afterwards they were filing into court, with faces solemn and grave, to announce the verdict designed to send a man to the gallows.

The atmosphere of the crowded court into which they filed was of tense and grim foreboding, which deepened as those who were waiting realised the significance of the expression on the faces of the jurors.

Asked if he had anything to say why judgment of death should not be passed upon him, Rouse said in low but firm, clear tones, "Only that I am innocent, sir."

His Lordship was obviously distressed when he passed sentence of death upon this man, but half his own age, and his voice could scarcely have reached the man in the dock.

WOMEN'S EMOTION.

Rouse passed from view, his courage undimmed, but for a moment the whole court remained still—not a movement, not a sound. Then a rustle and the court was alive again.

Helen Campbell and Nellie Tucker, two of the mothers of Rouse's children, were led weeping from the court, and other women sobbed in sympathy.

Outside thousands had gathered to hear the verdict and sentence, and the news spread like wildfire. Within ten minutes, however, the crowded road without the court had been cleared and with it the most mysterious and thrilling chapter in local criminal history.

TWENTY-FOUR UNCLAIMED BODIES IN FIVE YEARS.

The practice of sending unclaimed bodies of persons who die in workhouses to medical schools for the use of students of anatomy was mentioned at a recent meeting of the Northamptonshire Public Assistance Committee when it was revealed that Wellingborough Guardians in the past five years had sent twenty-four such bodies to the School of Anatomy at Cambridge.

A circular letter from the Minister of Health urged the Public Assistance Committees not to abandon this practice, as it was of vital importance that the increasing numbers of medical students should have every facility for perfecting their surgical knowledge. The Minister pointed out that the prevailing system of supplying the requirements of the medical colleges without offence to the living, and that ultimately the bodies employed for research work and instruction were buried in the customary manner.

The Poor Law Institution Sub-Committee recommended the Public Assistance Committee to comply with the Minister's suggestions.—

THE NORTHAMPTON AND COUNTY INDEPENDENT. February 7th, 1931.

Rural Dean on Death Penalty.

Is there Justification in Human Morality ?

Following immediately upon the condemnation of Alfred Arthur Rouse at the Assize Court on Saturday, a striking reference to the justification of the death penalty, advancing a new and interesting line of thought upon this much-discussed subject, was made in the course of his sermon by the Rural Dean, the Rev. J. Trevor Lewis, M.A., at All Saints' Church on Sunday. Mr. Lewis said:—

What justification is there in human morality for the death penalty? "None," says the literalist, "the command 'Thou shalt not kill' is absolute. If your country is invaded you must not repel the invader; if a brutal murder is committed the murderer must not be condemned to death." He would even say that the judge who sentences such a one repeats the very crime he would condemn.

One hears such a proposition gravely argued in debating circles by men who evidently feel their arguments are unanswerable. Somehow the literalist is always unanswerable until you take him literally; until you look at the letter then invariably you will find that inconsistency which comes from not going far enough.

For, in the base letter, the command says nothing of HUMAN life. Therefore we must never kill a sheep for food or a snake for safety; you must drop your gun when a tiger springs at you and, further still, you cannot walk, for assuredly you will kill some insect or creeping thing.

So the command is reduced to an absurdity.

Ultimately you must translate the naked prohibition this way: "Thou shalt not take human life without sufficient cause." The principle which lies at the root is really that reverence for man which recognises his kinship with God, which perceives the Divine Image within him.

It is this which makes human life sacred

(continued at foot of previous column)

(continued from next column)

and different from any other life, and herein lies the justification for the dread penalty of death. Other offences we may punish by lesser sentences, but he who forgets that his fellow-man is more than a brute, who ignores this kinship with God, he must be sent away to meet God. No human court can adequately punish such a one; he must be sent, and sent swiftly, before the only tribunal really competent to deal with his case.

The death penalty is not a deterrent or in any sense a punishment. It is really the assertion of man's kinship with God, his real greatness and absolute value.

The ultimate security for human life lies in reverence for human nature, and that reverence proceeds from the truth "In the Image of God made He man."

A Copy of Verses

The Murder of Mr CLARKE by his Wife MARY, and Servant PHILLIP HAYNES

A Copy of Verses,

ON THE UNFORTUNATE MAN AND WOMAN

Phillip Haynes,

AND

Mary Clarke,

Who was Executed at Northampton March 10, 1821

FOR THE

Wilful Murder of John Clarke,

Husband to the latter at the parish of Charwelton, Northamptonshire.

Good people all of each degree,
Give ear unto my tragedy,
Which I am going to unfold,
It is as true as e'er was told.

At Charwelton Northamptonshire,
A wealthy farmer lived there,
One Mr. Clarke he had a wife,
But lived a most unhappy life.

His wicked wife we understand,
Connected got with her servant man.
One Phillip Haynes that was his name
From Adstone, Northamptonshire, he came.

Their intimacy it got so,
That all her secrets let him know,
Persuading him day after day,
To take her husbands life away.

Then this unfortunate Phillip Haynes,
For carnal lust and cursed gains.
Soon yielded to her cruel will,
Her husband Mr. Clarke to kill.

Then unto Brackley he did steer,
Into a shop he entered there,
He bought a gun, powder and shot,
To execute the cruel plot.

To Mary Clarke he did return,
Who's heart with cruelty did burn,
And told her he had obeyed her rules,
For he had got the fatal tools.

To scheming then they did proceed,
The safest place to do the deed,
Says Haynes I'll go into the barn,
For there no one can me discern.

Or where I am no one can tell,
Says Mary Clarke that's very well,
For there in secret you can stay,
Amongst the barley night and day.

Until that you have done the deed,
I'll bring you every thing you need,
So back and forward Haynes did go,
Unto the barn as you shall know.

From February the 8th day,
Until the 10th Haynes there did stay,
When Mr Clarke without regard,
Then came into the hay rick yard.

Then straight npon the rick he got,
When from the barn Haynes at him shot,
Which gave to Clarke his mortal wound,
And brought him soon unto the ground

And as upon the ground he lay,
I'm done, I'm done, Clarke he did say,
When cruel Haynes heard him say so
He knew he'd gave the fatal blow.

Then this vile murderer he did creep,
Into the barley mow so deep,
Thinking to get out of the snare,
But soon he was discovered there.

Then he confessed the cruel deed,
And to Northampton sent with speed,
So now we'll leave him there to mourn
And unto Mary Clarke return.

Who in short time she taken were,
And lodg'd with Haynes to take a share
For their sad act of cruelty,
while blood for vengeance loud doth cry

At the assizes they were brought,
To answer for their cruel fault,
The Jury soon did guilty cry,
And they were both condemned to die.

And on the 10th of March they were,
Brought up the awful fate to share,
That day upon the gallows tree,
They suffered for their cruelty,

Now let their fate a warning be,
To all of high and low degree,
Be constant to your bosom friend,
Then God will bless you to the end.

T. Bloomer, Printer, 42, Edgbaston Street, Birmingham,

Honour thy Father and thy Mother

The Killing of an Unnamed Police Constable by THOMAS GORDON in the County of Northamptonshire and his Execution for the Crime on August the 17th 1789

Mr Gordon, the father of this wretched youth, was a surgeon and apothecary in London, from whence he removed his family into Northamptonshire.

Mr Gordon continued to practise in the country, and soon became envied, and obnoxious to his neighbours, being considered as an intruder, from not being a native of the county. The consequence of this was frequent quarrels; and at length a justice's warrant was obtained against him, on a pretended charge of assault.

The constable went to Mr Gordon's house, in order to apprehend him, but the wife and the son told the officer that he was not at home. This was not the case, and the constable knew he was in the house: he, however, went away, but soon returned with some neighbours, who tried to make a forcible entry. The mother and son opposed them, and the latter was armed with a gun. The populace threw stones at the windows, when the mother, in an unlucky moment, bade her son fire; he did so, and killed the constable on the spot.

Both mother and son were tried, and found guilty of this horrid murder; but Baron Thompson, who presided on the bench, observing that the mother was indicted as an accessory before the fact, and the evidence turning out that she was a principal, had doubts whether she was properly convicted, and therefore reserved the case for the opinion of the twelve judges, who, upon solemn argument, confirmed the sentence against the son, but at the same time adjudged the indictment against the mother to be bad; and the poor youth received the sentence of death. He was, however, three times reprieved; from which he hoped, and the world flattered him with an opinion, that his pardon would ultimately follow.

While cheered with this idea, an order came for his execution.

He was scarcely nineteen years of age, and died for an act which, at the time of its commission, he considered to be a defence of his father and an act of obedience to his mother.

He was executed at Northampton on the 17th of August, 1789.

(*The Newgate Calendar*)

NORTHAMPTON ASSIZE COURT

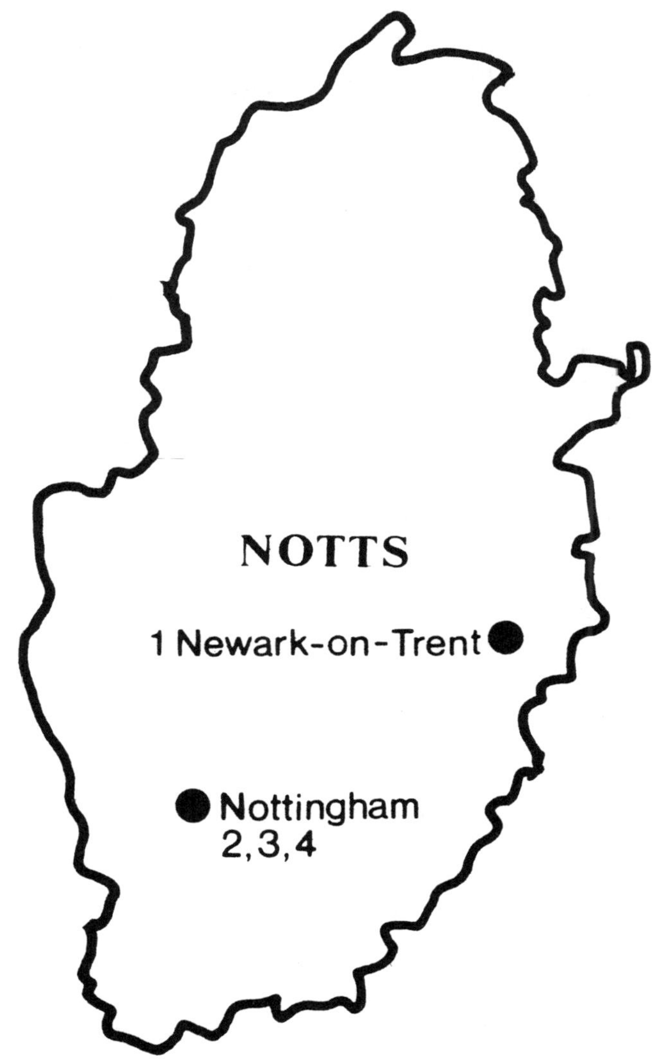

Nottinghamshire

1. Frederick NODDER 96
2. James BRODIE 99
3. Dorothea WADDINGHAM 99
4. Herbert Leonard MILLS 103

The Man Who Said Nothing

The Murder of MONA LILIAN TINSLEY by FREDERICK NODDER

on Tuesday the 5th of January 1937 at 'Peacehaven', Hayton, near Newark

The unpleasant looking man who stood in the dock of the Victoria Courts, Birmingham, had been charged in the name of Frederick Nodder. A brutish, squalid drunk, Nodder's crime was as unspeakable as the man himself, and the jury had listened to its details with undisguised distaste.

Nodder had deserted his wife some years previously, and had gone to Sheffield where he lodged with a Mr and Mrs Grimes. For no honest reason he had adopted the name Hudson and claimed to be a car mechanic, though his intemperate habits resulted in his being for the most part unemployable. After a year with the Grimeses, in 1935, Frederick Nodder took lodgings with Mrs Grimes's sister, Mrs Tinsley, at 11 Thoresby Avenue, Newark, where for some unaccountable reason he was a popular figure with the many Tinsley children to whom he became 'Uncle Fred'.

Before long Nodder, alias Hudson, was on the move again; this time as sole occupant of an isolated semi-detached near Hayton; a house inappropriately named 'Peacehaven'. Once there, Nodder seemed to have broken all contact with the Tinsleys. That is, until the 5th of January 1937. In the late afternoon of this chilly Tuesday, shortly after 10-year-old Mona Tinsley had left her school in Guildhall Street, Newark, she was seen at the bus station near the Robin Hood Hotel in the company of Frederick Nodder. According to his own statement, Mona had asked Uncle Fred to take her to visit her aunt (Mrs Grimes) and new baby cousin in Sheffield. He had persuaded Mona to spend the night at 'Peacehaven', and the following evening Nodder took his young charge by bus from East Retford to Worksop and then put her on another bus to travel alone to Sheffield.

Little Mona Tinsley was never seen alive again. When he was confronted by the police on his return to 'Peacehaven' (Mona's anxious parents had quite naturally already reported her absence from home), Nodder had at first denied any recent contact with the Tinsley family; in a second statement he gave the story outlined above which was to constitute his defence. During the 9th and 10th of March Frederick Nodder stood before Mr Justice Swift at the Birmingham Assizes accused of abducting Mona Tinsley.

The prosecution was conducted by Mr Norman Birkett KC, and despite an enthusiastic plea on his behalf by defence attorney Mr Maurice Healy KC, Nodder's case was not to be believed. In a subsequent reference to the prisoner's reluctance to take the witness stand, Mr Justice Swift in his summing up said: "Nobody knows what has become of that little girl... Whatever happened to her, how she fared, who looked after her, where she slept, there is one person in this court who knows, and he is silent – he is silent. He says nothing to you at all... He sits there and never tells you a word." In passing sentence he added: "What you did with that little girl, what became of her, only you know. It may be that time will reveal the dreadful secret you carry in your breast."

And so it was to prove.

Despite the continuing painstaking search undertaken by the police over succeeding months, no trace was found of Mona Tinsley – alive or dead. 'Peacehaven', which had been in as indescribably squalid a state as its occupant, was virtually taken apart brick by brick, stick by stick; the garden was completely dug over, and the area for miles around combed by an army of police officers. Cesspools were opened up, and the five-mile stretch of the Chesterfield Canal where it ran close to Nodder's home was drained. The river Idle was dragged several times.

NEWARK BOROUGH POLICE

Telephone No. 26

CHIEF CONSTABLE'S OFFICE,
TOWN HALL,
NEWARK-ON-TRENT.
11th JANUARY, 1937

MISSING FROM HER HOME

at 11, Thoresby Avenue, Newark-on-Trent, since Tuesday, 5th January, 1937, MONA LILIAN TINSLEY. age 10 years (rather short for age), dark hair, (bobbed with fringe), rosy cheeks, four prominent teeth at front. Dress, when last seen, light blue woollen jumper suit, brown double breasted tweed coat (frayed at bottom of sleeves), black Wellington boots, no hat, white half hose, dark blue knickers, white liberty bodice, white cotton underskirt, woollen combinations. was carrying a brown or grey handbag which contained a birthday card with figure "10" thereon. It has been established that this girl was seen at Hayton Smeath, near Retford, Notts. at about mid-day on Wednesday, 6th January, 1937, since when all trace of her has been lost. It has been suggested that she travelled to Sheffield on a bus leaving Retford at 6.45 p.m.

Any person who has seen this girl, or the clothing described above, since Wednesday mid-day is asked to get in touch with the nearest police officer immediately.

HARRY BARNES,
CHIEF CONSTABLE.

J. STENNETT, PRINTER, NEWARK

It was three months into Frederick Nodder's seven-year sentence, on Sunday the 6th of June, that a party of people boating on the Idle just below Bawtry saw the floating bundle which was Mona Tinsley's tiny corpse.

Mona had been strangled, but the advanced state of the body's decomposition made it impossible to state whether or not she had been sexually assaulted.

In November Nodder once again faced the full might of British Justice. Before Mr Justice Macnaghten at the Nottingham Assizes he was charged with Mona Tinsley's murder. Norman Birkett was once again retained for the Crown, and Mr Healy returned to present Nodder's defence. This time, however, the prisoner did go into the witness box. He described how after meeting Mona from the Wesleyan School in Newark, he had taken her by the 4.45pm bus to Retford, and from there to 'Peacehaven'. After supper, he claimed, Mona had been put to bed in his own double room and he had slept downstairs. On the following morning, in a moment of guilt, he had determined to send Mona on to her aunt in Sheffield. Quite why it took all day to put this plan into effect Nodder never adequately explained; after a day during which the girl had played around the house while Uncle Fred was out working in the garden, the couple set off in the blustery darkness of late evening. In evidence, Nodder told how he had given Mona two shillings and instructions on how to get to Sheffield; he also claimed to have given her a note of explanation for Mrs Grimes. He had never seen the child again, and advanced the possibility that she had been lured off the bus and murdered.

It was with no surprise that the court heard the jury's verdict of guilty; and in passing sentence of death upon him, Mr Justice Macnaghten told Nodder: "Justice has slowly but surely overtaken you."

At Lincoln Prison on the morning of Thursday the 30th of December 1937 the degenerate Frederick Nodder took his last breath of air before plummeting, unlamented, into the pit below the scaffold.

The Gift of Unseen Powers

Police, frustrated by their lack of success in finding Mona Tinsley and encouraged by her frantic parents, called on the services of Estelle Roberts, a medium. She was immediately able to tell detectives that Mona's body had been dumped in a river, though it was to be three months before the pathetic remains were found floating in the river Idle.

"The Heathen in his Blindness"*
The Murder of ROBERT SELBY HANCOCK by JAMES BRODIE on Tuesday the 24th of March 1800 near Nottingham

James Brodie, a blind man, was indicted at the assizes for the county of Nottingham for the murder of a boy named Robert Selby Hancock, who acted as his guide, on the 24th of March, 1800.

John Robinson, a warrener, said he went into his warren on Sunday [Tuesday] the 24th of March, 1800, about two o'clock in the afternoon. He saw the prisoner, as he supposed, fishing in a rivulet. On approaching him he found him lying on his belly, upon which he called out: "Hullo! What are you doing?" The prisoner said he was a blind man, and had been wandering about all night, for he had lost his guide, who was dead; that he had stayed with him till he had taken his last gasp. The warrener went with two men to seek the boy, and they found him about three miles from the place where the blind man was, covered all over with ling, or fern, as much as would fill a cart. The skull was found fractured in two places, the head covered with blood and torn at the ear, and the shoulders and arms beaten to a jelly.

The blind man had a stick, with which it was supposed he had committed the murder.

The prisoner, in his defence, said they had lost their way, and that the boy had got up into a tree, with his assistance, to see if there was any road near; that the boy fell from the tree and hurt himself very much; that just before he had tumbled over a log of wood; that, finding the boy was hurt, and could not stand, he covered him over with ling, in order to keep him from the cold; and that he stayed by him till he was dead.

Not one word of this defence was admitted by the jury, who instantly found him guilty, and execution, in the short time allowed to murderers, followed, at which time this culprit of darkness was but twenty-three years of age.

* 'From Greenland's Icy Mountains', Bishop Reginald Heber.

"The Old Nurse, Death"*
The Murder of ADA BAGULEY by 'Nurse' DOROTHEA WADDINGHAM on Tuesday, September the 10th 1935 at 32 Devon Drive, Nottingham

Dorothea Waddingham had almost as unsalubrious an entry into this world as she was to have a parting from it. She was born to a poor family who eked out an existence in the village of Hucknall, seven miles north of Nottingham. After a brief and undistinguished spell at the village school Dorothy (as she was known) spent a brief and undistinguished spell in a local factory. When she was in her early twenties she exchanged the drudgery of the factory for that of the workhouse infirmary at Burton-on-Trent, where

* *The friendly and comforting breast*
Of the old nurse, Death.
(*Echoes,* William Ernest Henley)

she was taken on as a ward maid. It was while she was at Burton that Thomas Willoughby Leech came into her life. Leech was considerably older than Dorothy – in fact, almost twice as old – and neither wealthy nor physically fit; he was indeed very poor, and a chronic invalid. Nevertheless, for matters that may for all we know have been connected with love, the couple married and set up their first home under the roof of one of Leech's sisters, at Church Gresley, not far from Burton. During their eight years of marriage Dorothy bore three children – Edwin, Alan, and little Mary who was a baby when tragedy finally struck the sickly Thomas Leech in the form of throat cancer, to which he succumbed. As a final act of unwitting generosity Thomas had provided his widow with a new partner. Ronald Sullivan was near to Dorothy's age, and when his marriage had collapsed and his family split up, his friend Tom Leech invited him to share his home, which was by now in Haydn Road, in Sherwood, Nottingham.

Now, there is a great deal of difference between a ward maid and a nurse; but for Dorothy it was but a short stretch of the imagination. Rudimentary understanding of nursing care she may have picked up, but despite her own extravagant claims, and despite the fact that she has subsequently become notorious as 'Nurse' Waddingham, she was no more entitled to that distinction than the next ward maid. Not that it prevented her from turning the Haydn Road house into a nursing-home.

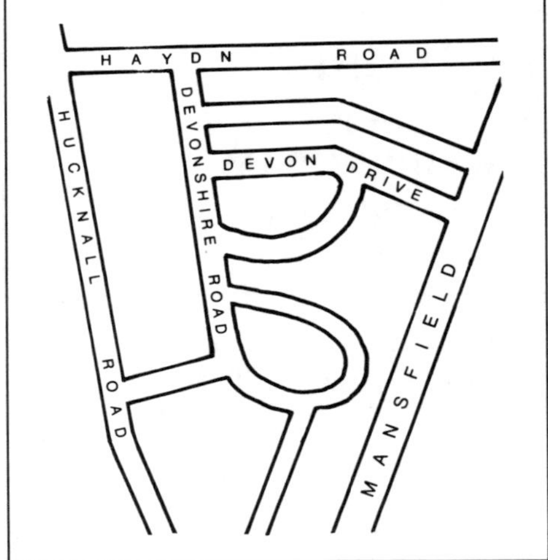

Following her husband's death, Dorothea Waddingham – now Nurse Waddingham – took a smaller house in Devon Drive, accompanied by Sullivan and the three children. Before long there was another mouth to feed in the person of baby Ronald, and it was as much as the new 'nursing home' could manage to keep those mouths satisfied.

On the afternoon of January the 5th, 1935, Dorothy was away from the house, so it was Ronald Sullivan who opened the door to Miss Blagg, dynamic secretary ('hon.') of the County Nursing Association. The Waddingham home had come to the favourable notice of the Association it seems – which probably meant that they were cheap and not too particular – and Miss Blagg wondered if it might be the suitable accommodation she sought for elderly Mrs Louisa Baguley and her paralytic daughter Ada; the former "delightful old lady" was nearing ninety, the latter somewhere around fifty.

The Baguleys were a courageous couple in their own modest way; Ada had since early womanhood suffered with what is known medically as progressive disseminated sclerosis, and popularly as 'creeping paralysis'. She had become worse as the disease had progressed over the past twenty years, and was now unable to walk or to employ her arms and hands to any very useful degree. Mr Baguley had died six years previously, and despite her own great age and frailty, her mother now devoted her time to caring for Ada the best she could. But she was beginning to realize that that best was no longer adequate, and far from being able to sustain the pressure imposed by an invalid's needs, she was feeling the want of care and attention herself.

And so a bargain was struck, pending the approval of Nurse Waddingham; and after visiting the two ladies at their present home in Burton Joyce, Dorothy accepted the rather paltry offer of thirty shillings a week each, and made ready the ground floor back room. On January 12th Mrs Baguley and Ada took up residence.

During the following six weeks the two lady 'patients' settled in comfortably to their new surroundings; and Miss Blagg was delighted to have found so pleasant a refuge for her charges. Such too was the impression of

Ada's cousin Lawrence, who was subsequently called upon to testify in court as to the great peace of mind now enjoyed by his elderly aunt and cousin.

At the end of February the house went into brief mourning for the passing of Nurse Waddingham's other patient at the time, who had died on the 26th.

Now Dorothea Waddingham was beginning to have second thoughts about the income from the Baguleys; she was frequently to be heard grumbling about the miserable reward for the huge burden of two infirm patients: "they would have to pay five guineas for no better treatment in hospital; which is really the proper place for them." In hindsight, it is a pity the ladies had not been put in a five guinea hospital, for they would certainly have had better 'treatment' than that which they were about to receive at Devon Drive. But money was not as plentiful as it might have been, and all that stood between the Baguleys and the dreaded workhouse were Ada's nest-eggs. These comprised a £500 Conversion Loan, about £120 in the bank, and a further £1,000 inherited from her father, of which the interest went to Mrs Baguley during her lifetime. What remained after her death, Ada had willed to Fred Gilbert. Gilbert, although a cousin, was also Ada's fiancé, and but for the devastating effect of her illness they might have been married long before. As it was, the closeness of even their friendship had been put under considerable strain over the years, and by now Fred's visits had all but stopped. In despair, and probably out of pique, Ada made a new will; very much at variance with the advice of her solicitor, Mr Lane. Ada proposed to settle upon Nurse Waddingham the whole of her property in return for an undertaking to look after her and her mother for the rest of their lives. As a compromise, Lane persuaded the petulant Ada Baguley that instead of handing over her property, she should simply make her will in favour of Waddingham and Sullivan, in consideration of their caring for her mother and herself during their lives. The document was signed on May the 4th.

A week later old Mrs Baguley died and was laid to rest beneath the earth of Caunton churchyard. Among the mourners, Ronald Sullivan and Ada Baguley and, reunited in sorrow, Fred Gilbert. Fred Gilbert, after all

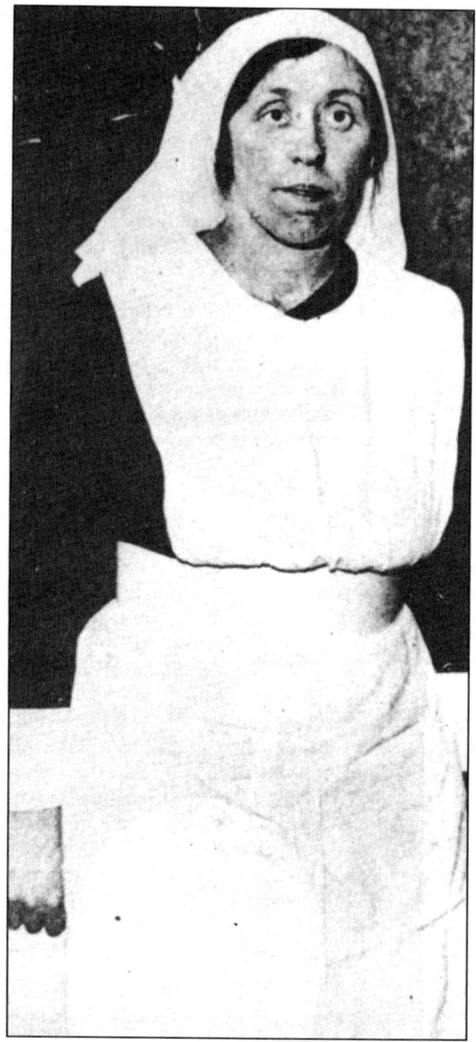

'Nurse' Dorothea Waddingham

this time; Fred pushing Ada in her wheelchair to the church! In fact, nothing of the old romance did develop, but it may have given Sullivan pause to think on the future of his recently promised inheritance.

Back at Devon Drive, life for Ada, now that her greatest companion had passed away, was a succession of unremarkable days.

One rare excitement was the visit of Mrs Briggs, a friend of the Baguley family for as long as anybody could remember. It was September the 10th, and Mrs Briggs's unexpected arrival found Ada in the garden snoozing in the last of the late summer sun. They chatted over tea, and ate some of the chocolate drops that Mrs Briggs had brought from her little shop in Alfred Street – The Black Boy Chocolate Shop. At four o'clock, after fond farewells and promises of future visits, Ada's guest left. At two o'clock the following morning Ada Baguley slipped into a coma; at nine, Sullivan phoned and left a message for Dr Manfield to attend urgently. At midday Manfield arrived. Ada was dead.

With the medical certificate reading "Death through cerebral haemorrhage due to cardio-vascular degeneration", Nurse Waddingham wasted no time in arranging for Ada's body to be cremated. Which would not be remarkable in 1988; but in 1936 less than 1 per cent of deaths received cremation, and those that did were unusual enough to be noticed. But there were other reasons why Miss Baguley's disposal attracted the attention of Dr Cyril Banks. Banks was the Crematorium referee, and in that capacity had received an extraordinary letter requesting: "It is my desire to be cremated at my death. And it is my wish to remain with Nurse (Waddingham) until I die. It is my final wish that my relatives shall not know of my death." The note purported to have been signed by Ada, but had been written by Ronald Sullivan. And it had been addressed from 32 Devon Drive, a house which, in his capacity as Medical Officer of Health for Nottingham, Dr Banks had reason to know was not, as it advertised, a "registered" nursing home, and was in contravention of the law in describing itself as such.

It was as well that Cyril Banks had his misgivings; for poor Ada Baguley had not died of cerebral haemorrhage at all. That became clear when the Nottingham City Analyst performed his post-mortem examination; after ten days' careful investigation Dr W.W. Taylor found 2.59 grains of morphine in the stomach, 0.37 grains in the spleen and kidneys, 0.14 grains in a portion of the liver, and 0.092 grains in the heart. A convincingly lethal dose of 3.192 grains. Given the speed with which the body tissues break down morphine, the celebrated Home Office analyst, Dr Roche Lynch, was able to state that the original ingestion must have been a very much greater dose than that found.

Clearly Ada Baguley had died from acute morphine poisoning; which gave rise, not surprisingly, to misgivings about the cause of her mother's sudden death. On September 30th, Mrs Baguley's body was exhumed from the churchyard and taken to Leenside mortuary, where Dr Roche Lynch was to perform the post-mortem. Casting aside the medical jargon, the conclusion was dramatically simple – Mrs Louisa Baguley had died of an excessive dose of morphine!

Somebody would have some questions to answer.

On February the 14th, 1936, Dorothea Waddingham and Ronald Sullivan were put on trial before Mr Justice Goddard (later Lord Chief Justice). In an unusual switch from his familiar role as defender, Mr Norman Birkett QC led for the Crown. On February 26th, Mr Justice Goddard instructed the jury to formally acquit Ronald Sullivan, against whom there was no evidence of complicity to murder. The following day he passed sentence of death on Dorothea Waddingham in accordance with the verdict of the jury; she was removed to Winson Green Prison, Birmingham.

Despite the recommendation to mercy, the Home Office could find no grounds on which to interfere with the course of justice, and on the morning of April 16th, 1936, Nurse Waddingham walked to the gallows.

[*See Appendix Two for a note on Morphine as a poison*]

Louisa Baguley

"How I Met Murder"*

The Murder of Mrs MABEL TATTERSHAW by HERBERT LEONARD MILLS on Friday the 3rd of August 1951 in the woods near Sherwood Vale, Nottingham

It is not often that a national newspaper gets the chance of a scoop, of a totally exclusive murder story, so it must have seemed as though Christmas had come in August when a voice came through on the *News of the World's* news-room telephone: "I've just found a woman's body. It looks like murder."

Of course it was more than the fragile co-operation between police and journalist could have withstood to have kept the law in ignorance of such a dramatic revelation, so, having ascertained the location of the public booth from which the informant had telephoned, and its number, the reporter asked the young man to wait by the box for a return call. In the meantime the Nottingham police force were alerted that there was a possible murder in their area. The *News of the World* had barely time to resume telephone contact before the police had arrived at the call-box.

The caller, it was discovered at the police station, was nineteen-year-old Herbert Leonard Mills, of Mansfield Street, Nottingham. The youth had certainly not been lying about finding a woman's body, it was there in a secluded part of the woods near Sherwood Vale; and judging by the marks of strangulation and bludgeoning, he had been right about murder. The victim was later identified as Mrs Mabel Tattershaw, aged forty-eight, who had lived at Longmead Drive.

Mills also had possession of a broken bead necklace which he claimed to have picked up at the scene of the crime, and he gave a rather hazy description of a man with a limp whom he had seen in the neighbourhood of the body.

* This was the title of Mills's story as given to Norman Rae for publication in the *News of the World.*

After giving blood samples and finger-nail parings, Leonard Mills was released to the eagerly waiting *News of the World,* where Mills seemed in his element. He expounded to crime reporter Norman Rae how he had had this idea for a sonnet – Mills had great, though as yet unfulfilled, literary ambitions – and sought romantic inspiration in the leafy glades of Sherwood. Then he found the woman's body, "very white and pale", and had taken up Shelley's 'Ode to Death' to read; he had then telephoned the newspaper. There was an obvious feyness to the story, but it seemed at least credible. In return for cash, Mills was to make several more increasingly elaborate statements to Rae.

Meanwhile the police had been probing into the background of Mabel Tattershaw, trying to find a motive for what on the face of it seemed to be a motiveless murder. Mrs Tattershaw was married to a man who worked away from home more often than not, and by him she had two daughters, one living in Nottingham, the fourteen-year-old still at home with her mother. To make her meagre ends meet, Mrs Tattershaw took in lodgers. Poverty had been unkind to Mabel, and had aged her beyond her middle years, and had taken its toll of what physical attraction she may once have claimed. Like a shabby spectre on life's periphery, she came and went, unremarked, about her humdrum existence. Who, detectives wondered, even *noticed* poor Mabel Tattershaw, let alone felt compelled to kill her?

Norman Rae, a detective of a different kind, was finding it difficult to stop Leonard Mills making statements to his newspaper – each a little more explicit than the last, and each accompanied by a similar exaggerated demand for payment.

On the 24th of August they met again at a

hotel in Nottingham, where in an episode that must be unique in British criminal history, Mills was to write for a newspaper journalist (on hotel notepaper) his complete confession to the killing of Mrs Mabel Tattershaw. With the scrupulous correctness that dignified the best of his profession, Norman Rae cautioned Mills that he must acknowledge that he made the statement of his own volition, and that "I have warned you, if it contains information material to the murder, I will take your statement and yourself to City police headquarters." For the next hour Mills wrote in silence; on the following morning Rae accompanied him to Nottingham and handed over the document to Superintendent Ellington.

At the beginning the statement contained Mills's motive: "I had always considered the possibility of a perfect murder", and at the end, his confession: "I now confess I murdered Mrs Tattershaw"; between the two, the story of a cold-blooded, pointless killing.

On August 2nd 1951 Mabel Tattershaw had gone to the Roxy Cinema in Nottingham; seated next to her was Herbert Leonard Mills. We do not know what he used as an opening gambit, but before long they were whispering together in the dark like old friends. We do know what was in the young man's mind: "Seeing the possibility of putting my theory into practice, I consented to meeting her on the morrow." To be noticed, and by a young man at that, must have thrilled Mabel for the first time in many dull years. Little surprise, then, that she kept the assignation; little surprise that she was willing to follow wherever her escort might lead. He led her into the seclusion of the woods, "she took off her coat and laid down... she said she was cold, I covered her with her own coat, and then my coat... I put on a pair of gloves..."

That he was happy with the result of his 'experiment' is clear from Mills's statement: "I was rather pleased. I think I did rather well. The strangling itself was quite easily accomplished."

But this formed only part of the evidence carefully collected and assessed by police officers in preparation for Leonard Mills's trial; there was also the medical testimony. Professor Webster, pathologist with the Home Office Laboratory in Birmingham,

Mabel Tattershaw

detailed the many other bludgeoning injuries committed on Mrs Tattershaw's body, both before and after strangulation. Further forensic evidence linked Mills with the murder by identifying hair from his head on the victim's clothing, while fibres from under her finger-nails came from the blue suit that he had worn on the afternoon of the murder.

All this made it very difficult for Mr Elwes KC to construct any kind of adequate defence at the Nottingham Assizes in the November of 1951. It was Mr Elwes's contention – on behalf of his client, for it is difficult to see how so able a counsel could have accepted his brief with anything approaching optimism – that Mills had come across the woman's body in the wood and, in an attempt to gain notoriety and money, had invented a sequence of stories which he told to the Press.

But for the jury Mills's story was just too good to be false; they concluded that it was he who had killed Mabel Tattershaw, leaving it to Mr Justice Byrne to condemn him to death. And so in December the brief moment of fame ended for Leonard Mills; on the drop at Winson Green Prison.

Shropshire

Jocelin HARWOOD 106

Too Bad for his own Good

The Murder of Sir NEHEMIAH BURROUGHS and his Family by JOCELIN HARWOOD at their home and his Execution at Shrewsbury in 1692

JOCELIN HARWOOD
Highwayman, who committed such Barbarous Crimes that his Associates gave him up to Justice
Executed in 1692

Jocelin Harwood was a degenerate plant from a good tree. His father was honest, moderately rich, and of undoubted reputation; and the greatest misfortune of his life was his having a child so unworthy of him. Jocelin was born in the year 1669, at Wateringbury, in Kent, where he was educated with all the caution necessary in such cases. When he grew towards seventeen years of age he ran away from his father, carrying off with him about sixty pounds. When he had wasted what he took from his father in luxury and wantonness he made no scruple of getting more in the same dishonest way. Being now in London, also, he had every disadvantage that a young man can have who has given way a little to the allurements of vice. His money brought him into bad company, and then that bad company persuaded him to seek for more money. He submitted at first only to pilfering and picking of pockets, which he followed for about three years, and then he resolved to move in a higher sphere, make a greater blaze in the world for a time, and receive his fate, when it came, with more honour.

The ill success of his first adventure on the highway was enough to have reformed him, and deterred him from ever attempting the like again. He had stolen a horse, bridle, saddle, holsters and pistols, with which he set out on Black Heath, and was so hardy as to order two men at once to stand and deliver. The gentlemen engaged him, shot his new horse, and had certainly taken him, if the wounds they had received in the encounter had not disabled them from exerting themselves. Harwood was terribly frightened at the bravery of his antagonists, and was glad he could get off with only the loss of a horse.

Jocelin continued to rob on the highway for about two or three years, during which time he lived in all manner of excess, passing from county to county as it suited either his pleasure or his safety.

The last and worst action of his life was committed at the house of Sir Nehemiah Burroughs, in Shropshire, where he was informed of an immense treasure in plate and money. In company with two more he went one night and broke open this house, gagging and binding all the servants as fast as they could get to their chambers. When the rest of the family was secure he went to the knight and bound him and his lady; then going to his daughters' room, one of the young ladies said to Harwood: "Pray, sir, use us civilly; which if you do, we will use you in the same manner, in case you and your companions should be taken; for I am sure we shall know you again." "Shall you so?" said the inhuman wretch. "I'll take care then, to prevent you doing any mischief." Upon this he cut them both in pieces with his hanger, and then running into the old people's room again – "What," says he, "and do you know me too?" They told him no. "Damn you," said he, "You are only a little more artful than your daughters, but I shan't trust you." Then he run them both through, and left them wallowing in their blood, seeming as well satisfied as if he had done a meritorious deed.

His companions were so astonished at the barbarity of this fellow that they stood like stocks, unable either to prevent him

in his bloody attempts, or to apprehend him for them on the place, which latter they had most mind to. But the horror continued so strong on their minds that, though they were both old offenders themselves, they could not help exposing him to justice as soon as they had left the house of this unhappy family. Being on the road, one of them by agreement shot his horse, and then they joined to bind him hand and foot, and leave him on the ground, with a piece of the knight's plate by his side, telling him it was but a just requital for his inhumanity.

The next day, an enquiry being made all over the county, he was found in the condition he had been left by his companions. He was sent under a strong guard to Shrewsbury Jail, where he behaved very audaciously. At his trial he was even so impudent as to spit in the faces of the judge and jury, and talk to them without any regard to decency. The matter of fact being plainly proved against him, he was condemned to be first hanged on the gallows till he was dead, and then to have his body hanged in chains on a gibbet for a public spectacle.* This sentence made no impression on him; so that he continued the same horrid course of oaths, profaneness and blasphemies till his death. When he was at the gallows, with a steady countenance he said that he should act the same murder again, in the same case. This was all he would say to anybody.

It is shocking to think that such a wretch should be but twenty-three years of age at the time of his death, which was in the year 1692.

* See *Murder Club Guide No.2* for a note on Hanging in Chains.

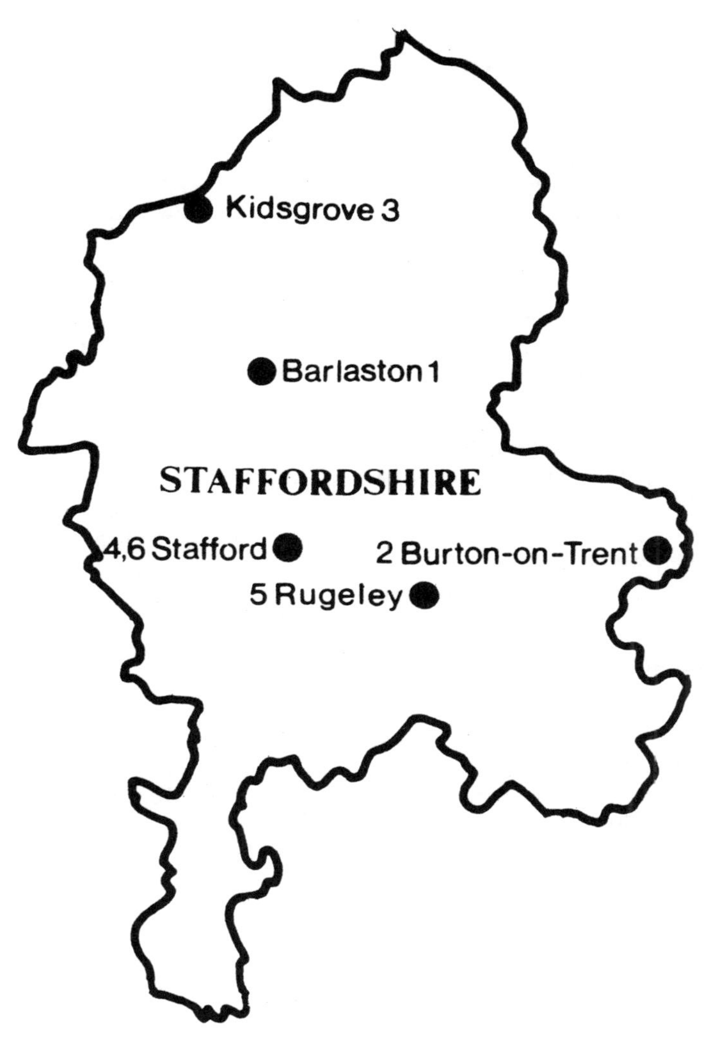

Staffordshire

1. Leslie GREEN 110
2. George CADDELL 112
3. Donald NEILSON 114
4. Joseph JONES 117
5. Dr William PALMER 119
6. George ALLEN 123

No Way Out

The Murder of ALICE WILTSHAW by LESLIE GREEN on Wednesday the 16th of July 1952 at her home 'Estoril', Station Road, Barlaston

On the unwritten register of Barlaston's socially notable residents in the early 1950s, the names Cuthbert and Alice Wiltshaw are certain to appear. Mr Wiltshaw is – predictably, for this region of Bennett's Five Towns – a wealthy and successful pottery manufacturer; he and his 62-year-old wife share the luxury of 'Estoril', a 14-room house in Station Road. The couple have lived alone since their daughters married, and they employ a couple of daily maids and a chauffeur.

On the evening of July 16th, 1952, Mr Wiltshaw returns home to find his wife dead. He had entered, as usual, by the back way, through the kitchen where he noticed that raw vegetables were floating about the tiled floor in water from their cooking-pot, and into the hallway; there lies Mrs Wiltshaw, her skull smashed, her jaw broken, and her face gashed open. There are supplementary stab wounds and gashes to other parts of the body, notably the stomach. Beside the body lies a heavy metal poker, some broken china, and a brass bowl. They are all heavily bloodstained.

This is clearly a matter for London expertise. It is not long before the representatives of Scotland Yard (in the persons of Detective Superintendent Spooner and his Detective Sergeant, Ernest Millen) are at the scene of the crime. Useful clues have already been turned up, among which the most significant seem to be the bloody footprint on the kitchen floor, and a pair of bloodstained chamois leather gloves found beneath a tree in the garden, and probably accounting for the absence of alien fingerprints in the house. On the thumb of the left glove is a small tear, and a small pearl button is missing; the button will be found underneath the body of Mrs Wiltshaw.

The disappearance of £3000 worth of jewellery and a number of other significantly valuable items indicate robbery as the immediate motive. A less explicable loss is an old RAF raincoat which Mr Wiltshaw kept against the inclement weather when gardening: he could identify it by three cigarette burns. It is now missing from the hall cupboard.

The way that Reginald Spooner has reconstructed the crime in his own mind leaves him with one certainty – that whoever robbed and murdered Mrs Wiltshaw had first-hand knowledge of the layout of the house.

Friends, neighbours, trades-people: all are seen and questioned. One of Spooner's imaginative ideas has been to set the children of the local school a special essay: write about anything that you saw unusual on the way home on July 16th; it was Millen's job to check this extra homework for clues.

Former staff employed at the house have been traced, and one by one eliminated from the inquiry. All except one; all except Leslie Green. Green had until comparatively recently held the position of chauffeur to the

Wiltshaws. A disagreement over Green's adopting the car for his pesonal use had led to his dismissal two months previously. Subsequently, Green's wife told police, he had worked as a delivery driver and as a labourer. Money had been tight, and Leslie had walked out on her some time since. Immediately a police search is mounted for Green, and his picture is decorating the front page of most of the popular press. As it will turn out, it was pressure from his own girl-friend that forced Leslie Green into the Longton police station "to clear himself".

The account of his movements that Green gives to DS Millen has all the appearance of a carefully constructed alibi: Green claims that on the day of the murder he was in Stafford. Since deserting the marital home he has had an affair with a nurse in Leeds, and now wants a separation from his wife; he was on his way to discuss it with her when he stopped off at Stafford. During the day he had wined and lunched in the company of four other men at the Station Hotel and, after indulging rather too much, he slept off his excess in a park opposite the hotel. When he woke, he collected his suitcase from the station and returned to the hotel. He remembers having a brief conversation with the manager at 5.45pm. After dinner he caught a train leaving Stafford at seven o'clock bound for Leeds. Arriving in that city after midnight, he booked himself into the Metropole Hotel on the way to meet his girl at the nursing home where she worked. In fact she was already in bed, and Green entertained one of her friends to a late supper instead.

Now that they come to check out Green's alibi, it becomes clear that although in broad outline it stands up to scrutiny, the times attributed to the sequence of activities is often at variance with the recollections of witnesses. Spooner is convinced that somewhere in that seemingly crowded afternoon, Leslie Green made the trip to Barlaston and back. If he had caught the 5.10 from Stafford he would have had fifteen minutes to commit the crime before returning on the 6.05. Which just coincided with the unverifiable time that Green claims he was snoozing in the park.

BARLASTON VILLA MURDER TRIAL

ESLIE GREEN IN THE BOX YESTERDAY

RE THAN 40 PROSECUTION WITNESSES CALLED

UIETLY THAT HIS COUNSEL HAD TO REBUKE HIM ON SEVERAL OCCA-
E HE COULD NOT BE HEARD, LESLIE GREEN, 29-YEAR-OLD UNEMPLOYED
F NO FIXED ADDRESS, DENIED FROM THE WITNESS BOX AT STAFFORD-
TE YESTERDAY (WEDNESDAY) AFTERNOON THAT HE KILLED MRS.
WILTSHAW AT HER HOME, "ESTORIL," BARLASTON, ON JULY 16th.

Green went into the box on the third day of the trial, after more than 40 prosecution witnesses had been called. A married man, he is alleged to have been seen in Leeds within eight hours of the crime, and to have had in his possession part of £3,000 of jewellery which was stolen from the Wiltshaw home. Two rings, it is said, were given by him to a nurse to whom he had become engaged a few weeks previously.

IS
ED
SH

Stafford-to-Cannock Road near Brocton was blocked for a

The trial is being heard by Mr. Justice Stable and a jury of ten men and two women. Green is represented by Mr. G. G. Baker, Q.C., and Mr. G. T. Meredith. The Crown case is being conducted by Mr. F. Ryder Richardson, Q.C., and

where the murderer had finished her off in a dreadful and gruesome manner.

After the police had arrived, Mr. Wiltshaw and the doctor went out of the house, presumably for air. On a garden path, which would

Meanwhile Sergeant Millen is working on a pet theory of his own. Convinced that the missing RAF coat holds the answer, he has engaged the help of an old friend in the Railway Police, Harry Grimley. Grimley's task is to come up with the coat somewhere along the train route between Stafford and Holyhead, passing through Barlaston. It was a hunch that paid a handsome reward. Days later the bloodstained coat is traced to Holyhead lost property desk after a porter clearing the train had found it on the Stafford-Holyhead run.

As the days pass the detectives become more and more confident of building a watertight case against Leslie Green, a man, they now know, with four convictions for theft. A significant breakthrough comes when Reg Spooner interviews the girl-friend from Leeds, and hears for the first time about two rings. The two rings that Green had given her on July 16th – the day of the murder. Rings, it turns out, that had been pulled from Mrs Wiltshaw's dead fingers only hours before they were given.

In a preposterous attempt at bluff, Green now adds to his previous statement the fact that during his sojourn at the Metropole, Leeds, he had met two crooks with the burlesque names of Lorenzo and Charlie, who had sold him the rings for £15. These rings, the gift to his lady-friend, had been promptly given back to him when that lady read a description of the jewellery missing from the Wiltshaw house. Green claims he threw them into Leeds's muddy river Aire.

All it needs now is to fill in a few chinks to make the case watertight; to parcel up Leslie Green for delivery to the courts. One piece is added by the manager of the Station Hotel; he clearly remembered that though Green arrived in the morning without it, he returned to the hotel in the evening carrying a blue RAF raincoat. And then, to make quite sure, Reg Spooner returns to his first two clues. Leslie Green is invited to try on the pair of gloves found at the scene of the crime; to nobody's surprise the cut in the left thumb of the glove corresponds exactly with a recently healed cut on Green's thumb. Nor is it a great surprise to find that his rubber-soled shoe proves a perfect match for the bloody print in Mrs Wiltshaw's kitchen. Finally, a minute search is undertaken of the flat and surrounding area of a friend of Green's girl-friend where the couple are known to have stayed on the night after the murder. Police find, behind a loose brick in the coal-house, two rings.

Never was such a complete case brought against a killer. For three relentless days the damning evidence is paraded before the jury at Stafford Assizes; two days before Christmas, 1952, Leslie Green stands on the drop at Stafford Gaol.

Horrid Murder

The Apocryphal Story of the Murder of Miss PRICE by GEORGE CADDELL close to the Town of Burton in the latter part of the Nineteenth Century

A theme common in catchpennies (as indeed in real life) this broadsheet helps to highlight the widespread sexual exploitation of women in the last century. The story of the landowner, or one of his male progeny, taking advantage of females of humbler breeding, treating them as chattels of less value than livestock, is a common one. Equally common is the inevitable rejection in the event of the wretched girl becoming pregnant; and by no means rare is the callous killing of the 'embarassment', and sometimes of its mother too.*

* Perhaps the archetype of the story is the celebrated case of William Corder, son of a wealthy Suffolk farmer who, in 1827, having seduced and given a child to Maria Martin, daughter of the neighbourhood mole-catcher, promised marriage, but instead murdered her and buried the body in the Red Barn at Polstead [see *Murder Club Guide No. 6*].

There is another version of this sheet, also published by Catnach in London, printed from the same type but using a cut (ie. woodcut) depicting the young 'gentleman' actually *cutting* his sweetheart's throat with a knife not – as in the example here, strangling her.

[*see Appendix Three for a general discussion of Broadsheets*]

HORRID MURDER,

Committed by a young Man on a young Woman.

George Caddell became acquainted with Miss Price and a degree of intimacy subsisted between them, and Miss Price, degraded as she was by the unfortunate step she had taken, still thought herself an equal match for one of Mr. Caddell's rank of life. As pregnancy was shortly the result of their intimacy, she repeatedly urged him to marry her, but he resisted her importunities for a considerable time. At length she heard of his paying his addresses to Miss Dean, and threatened, in case of his non-compliance, to put an end to all his prospects with that young lady, by discovering everything that had passed between them. Hereupon he formed a horrid resolution of murdering her, for he could neither bear the thought of forfeiting the esteem of a woman who he loved, nor of marrying one who had been as condescending to another as to himself. So he called on Miss Price on a Saturday and requesting her to walk with him in the fields on the following day, in order to arrange a plan for their intended marriage. Miss Price met him at the time appointed, on the road leading to Burton, at a house known by the name of "The Nag's Head." Having accompanied her supposed lover into the fields, and walked about till towards evening, they sat down under a hedge, where, after a little conversation, Caddell suddenly pulled out a knife and cut her throat, and made his escape, but not before he had waited till she was dead. In the distraction of his mind he left behind him the knife with which he had perpetrated the deed, and his case of instruments. On the following morning, Miss Price being found murdered in the field, great numbers went to take a view of the body, among whom was the woman of the house where she lodged, who recollected that she said she was going to walk with Mr. Caddell, on which the instruments were examined and sworn to have belonged to him. He was accordingly taken into custody.

J. Catnach, Printer, Monmouth Court.

The Black Panther

The Murders of LESLEY WHITTLE, DONALD SKEPPER, DEREK ASTIN, and SIDNEY GREYLAND by DONALD NEILSON

on various dates in 1974 and 1975 at locations in the Midlands and North of England

By November 1974 the mystery man had notched up some twenty robberies in seven years with a combined haul of over £20,000. Worst still, the elusive thief had killed three times and left several other victims seriously wounded. The *modus operandi* was almost invariable: armed with a shotgun the intruder chose the early hours of the morning to drill through window frames to release the catches, rouse the still-sleeping occupants, mainly of sub-post offices, and demand the keys to the safe. His working uniform was always the same: black plimsolls, army camouflage suit, white gloves, and the black hood which earned him his sobriquet of 'The Black Panther'.

The first to die had been Donald Skepper. On the 15th of February 1974 the youngest son of this sub-postmaster woke with a start to find himself looking down both barrels of the shotgun held by a man demanding keys to the safe. When the intruder failed to find them where the boy had indicated, he entered the parents' bedroom with the same demand. With more courage than forethought Donald Skepper shouted "Let's get him", and was immediately shot.

On the 6th of September in the same year sub-postmaster Derek Astin tackled an intruder in his post office at Higher Baxenden, near Accrington; he was shot dead in front of his wife and two children.

The intense activity on the part of the Yorkshire constabulary obliged the Panther to transfer his activities to a different location, and mid-November found him in Langley, Worcestershire. Here he shot Sidney Grayland, bludgeoned his wife Margaret, fracturing her skull, and stole £800 from the cash box.

It was less than two months later that the Black Panther committed the crime that was to move the nation and make him Britain's most wanted man.

'Beech Croft' was the family home of the Whittles in the village of Highley in Shropshire. On the morning of Tuesday the 14th of January 1975, Mrs Dorothy Whittle was alarmed to find her daughter missing from the house; seventeen-year-old Lesley had simply disappeared. In her place was a number of messages pressed out of red Dymo-tape which left the family in no doubt that Lesley had been kidnapped. The ransom demand was £50,000 and the conditions graphically clear: "No police.... You are on a time limit. If police or tricks, Death". Nevertheless, Lesley's brother Ronald made immediate contact with the West Mercia police force.

Despite the quite obvious need for the police involvement to be kept secret, news of the kidnapping and of the ransom demand was 'leaked' to a freelance journalist who, with a callous disregard for Lesley Whittle's safety that characterises the worst elements of his profession, sold this information to a Birmingham newspaper and to the BBC; the latter went so far as to interrupt programmes to broadcast the newsflash.

On the same night, an incident took place which provided the Scotland Yard team which had been called in with their first major clues. Gerald Smith was a security officer at the Freightliner container depot at Dudley, and while on a routine patrol had observed a man loitering around the perimeter fence. So strange was the man's behaviour when approached that Smith decided to call the police. Turning his back, the next thing he was aware of was the loud report of a gun and a searing pain in his buttocks; the attacker then emptied the remaining five bullets into the unfortunate watchman and disappeared. Remarkably, Gerald Smith was able to crawl to a telephone and alert the police.

Subsequently, ballistics experts were able to confirm, by matching the tell-tale ejection marks left like 'fingerprints' on the spent cartridges, that they came from the same gun that had been used in two earlier crimes – crimes known to have been the handiwork of the Black Panther. When investigating officers traced the green Morris 1300 saloon car that had been seen parked at the Freightliner depot they were rewarded with further vital pointers to the identity of the man who had added kidnapping to robbery and murder. Among the items recovered from the car was a number of Dymo-tape messages, quite clearly pieces of a ransom trail and identical to those left at the Whittle home. A cassette recorder contained a taped message from Lesley Whittle to her mother. Soon Gerald Smith's description of his assailant had been transformed into a portrait drawing that was to become one of the best-known faces in the country and was carried by the television networks as well as by the Press and cinemas.

Just before midnight on January 16th Ronald Whittle received a telephone call from a man claiming to be Lesley's captor. Following a trail marked by further Dymo-tape messages, Ronald arrived at Bathpool Park near the town of Kidsgrove, Staffordshire. Here the kidnapper was supposed to respond to Ronald Whittle's flashing car headlights with a torch. In the event there was no contact and Lesley's brother and his 'undercover' police escort were left once again helpless and frustrated.

For reasons best known to themselves, the police took more than a fortnight to get around to a detailed search of Bathpool Park, by which time the developments had received sufficient publicity to prompt a local headmaster to remember that one of his pupils had handed him a strip of Dymo-tape bearing the message 'Drop Suitcase into Hole' which he had found in the park a couple of days after the kidnapping. Another significant clue was a torch found by another schoolboy wedged in the grille of a ventilating shaft to the sewage system that runs beneath Bathpool Park.

Encouraged by these clues, police and tracker dogs began to search the underground culverts; it was during this operation that the naked body of Lesley Whittle was found at the bottom of one of the ventilating shafts. Around her neck was a noose of wire attached to the iron ladder. It was to be almost a year, though, before the Black Panther was captured.

On the night of December 11th 1975, Pcs Stuart Mackenzie and Tony White were on a routine Panda car patrol in the Nottinghamshire village of Mansfield Woodhouse. Seeing a small, shambling man carrying a black holdall the two officers decided to investigate; the suspect in his turn produced a sawn-off shotgun and forced White and Mackenzie back into the car. Taking the front passenger seat, and with his gun stuck in Pc Mackenzie's ribs, the man issued only one instruction – "Drive!"

With a cool professionalism, the more remarkable under the circumstances, the two officers, using a combination of verbal and visual signals (via the rear-view mirror), conspired to disarm and capture the man holding them at gunpoint. Jamming his foot on the brake at a T-junction Mackenzie sufficiently surprised the gunman for White to lunge at the gun now pointed away from his companion. In the struggle which followed the car became a riot of smoke and noise as the shotgun exploded into action and, despite injuries to White's hand from pellets and Mackenzie's eardrums which had been perforated by the explosion, they hung on to their former captor. With assistance from a member of the public who was queueing for fish and chips where the car had stopped, the two officers were able to subdue their prisoner and make an arrest. Although they did not know it yet, Pcs White and Mackenzie – with a little public-spirited help – had just terminated the career of the Black Panther.

The Black Panther; born near Bradford in 1936 and christened Donald Nappey, he had subsequently changed his name to Neilson to avoid the association with babies' underwear. This was a characteristic gesture of a man who, after being conscripted for National Service with the British forces in Cyprus, became obsessed by the techniques of 'survival' and of guerrilla warfare.

When the police searched his home at Grangefield Avenue, Thornaby, Bradford, they found all the evidence they needed to bring four charges of murder against Neilson. For these he was to receive life sentences; for kidnapping he was condemned to sixty-one years' imprisonment.

Gerald Smith died in March 1976 as a result of his confrontation with Neilson; but the laws of England allow a person only a year and a day in which to die if a charge of murder is to be brought.

A police officer wearing the costume of the Black Panther

Better than the Workhouse

The Murder of EDMUND CLARKE by his Father-in-Law, JOSEPH JONES on Saturday the 1st of December 1906 at their home in Quarry Bank, Nr. Stafford

We can never know quite how childhood images and experiences will affect a person in later life, though there can be no doubt as to the formative power that these events have. Events that have almost certainly turned some men – and women too – into savage killers.

When Little Joe Jones walked home from play through the streets of Pensnett village in the middle years of the last century he had to pass the front door of an old man's cottage, not far along the street from his own. On one particular day Joe was surprised to see two burly, uniformed men emerge from the door of this cottage dragging the frail old man between them and pushing him roughly into the back of a horse-and-cart. Joe never saw his grandfather again; and he never forgot the last pathetic look on that loved face as it was carted off to the Wordsley workhouse.

In later life Joseph Jones learned that his grandfather had survived only a brief four weeks in the feared institution, and it hardened a childhood resolve – that they would never, ever, take him into the workhouse.

In time the small son of a poor but happy family grew into a strong young man, popular and well respected both among his community, and among his colleagues at the steelworks – that blossoming token of the industrialization brought about by Mr Watt's improvements to the steam engine, and the mighty Industrial Revolution that was its result. Soon the young man was married, to a homely local girl, and the couple bought a modest house at Quarry Bank, a few miles from his childhood home. In 1880, both joy and sorrow struck at once, when Joe's beloved wife died soon after the birth of their baby daughter.

Joseph Jones grew into middle age, and young Ethel into womanhood. Joe never remarried, though this was not for want of opportunity; he preferred instead to devote all his love and care to the child left so cruelly motherless.

When she was eighteen years old, Ethel Jones started the family cycle over again; she began to see young Edmund Clarke, a chain-maker by trade, and a most pleasant and obliging fellow by everyone's account. The couple married after three years' courtship, and Joseph showed his ultimate approval of the match by inviting the young couple to share his house at Quarry Bank.

For four years, there could have been no happier family in the county; old Joseph took pride in his job, and spent his leisure in modest social drinking and placing the occasional bet; he clearly revelled in the pleasure and comfort of having his own dear daughter under his roof, and the bonus of a 'son', a quiet, hard-working young man, whose greatest vice was his Saturday game of football, and whose Sundays were spent as a chorister and teacher in the local church Sunday-school.

It was in the autumn of 1905 that tragedy hit the happy home at Quarry Bank. Old Joe lost his job at the steel-mill; and Joe was a proud man, an independent man, not the man to idle around and let his family look after him. True, he had made some provision, but with more time on his hands the drinking and the gambling increased; they began to take over all the hours that once were occupied in gainful labour. And they took over all of Joe's savings.

This may have been when Joseph Jones was first transported back fifty years, to the street outside his grandfather's cottage. The Spectre of the Workhouse had crept behind his eyes and into his mind.

Joseph Jones

Perhaps with more generosity than good sense, Edmund came to the rescue and offered to buy their communal home from his father-in-law, so that perhaps life would settle once more into its old pattern. But by now the old man was hopelessly addicted to drink, and what money did not find its way into the tap-room till was spent in obsessive gambling. Till once again Joe Jones was penniless. Once again the Spectre of the Workhouse haunted his drunken days and invaded his sleepless nights. Now he was a lodger in the house he once proudly called his own; now he relied on hand-outs from his son-in-law to pay for his beer. The Spectre grew larger, occupying more and more of his drink-crazed brain. Too late did Edmund try to curb the old man's lust for alcohol, too late began to refuse him the drink that was destroying both body and mind; for refusal now merely brought down wrath, and abuse, and spine-chilling threats of violence.

At six o'clock on Saturday evening, December the 1st 1906, Edmund Clarke returned home weary from his customary football match, and stretched out to doze peacefully on the sofa; Ethel meanwhile popped out to finish the family shopping. Old Joseph was out – probably trying to drink dry a local ale-house.

Eight o'clock had passed before Ethel returned, and Joe had clearly come home ahead of her, and was sitting in his chair beside the sofa on which Edmund still lay.

It is impossible to guess at the feeling of sheer horror that racked Ethel Clarke as she gazed on what two hours before had been her loving, beloved, husband. It was a horror that tore from her heart such screams as the neighbours had never before in their lives been cursed to hear. And when they gathered at the door in response they beheld what had driven poor Ethel out of her mind in one terrifying instant of realization.

There on the couch, quite still where his wife had left him, lay Edmund Clarke; in a room that swam with blood – blood dripping from the walls, blood coagulating in pools on the floor, blood like a crimson dye soaked into the fabrics and the sofa and washed about the body of the late Edmund Clarke. It was Edmund's blood, of course, though how much of it had come from the savage blows that had crushed his skull to reveal his brain, and how much from the gash which had all but severed his head from his neck, was of no importance to anybody. Least of all to old Joseph Jones; Joe simply got up from his chair, went out the door, and took the short walk to Brierly Hill police station.

The bloody poker, and the similarly stained pair of cut-throat razors which had so barbarously cut short young Edmund's life were quickly recovered by detectives, and marked for presentation at Joseph Jones's trial; Jones himself was confined in Birmingham's Winson Green Prison.

The trial took place the following March – 1907 – at the Stafford Assizes; it barely occupied a day's sitting, and Joseph Jones was sent to the death cell at Stafford Gaol to await his execution there in three weeks. During this time he was a perfectly behaved, if taciturn, prisoner, and when Henry Pierrepoint arrived to conduct the hanging, Jones seemed almost pleased by the sight of the gallows. Pierrepoint it was who recorded Joseph Jones's last words: "This is a damned sight better than the workhouse!"

The Fatal Consequences of Gambling

The Murder of JOHN PARSONS COOK by WILLIAM PALMER on Thursday the 22nd of November 1855 at Rugeley

Born in 1824 of what used to be termed 'bad stock', Palmer took readily to petty crime at an early age. By seventeen he had already been dismissed from one apprenticeship with a druggist (for embezzlement), and subsequently had to flee from another after "grossly abusing his Master's hospitality" (Palmer was running a private abortion service, not least to cope with his own prodigious output). However, it says something for his innate intelligence that he eventually qualified as a doctor – at St Bartholomew's Hospital, in London.

Notwithstanding his unruly past, Palmer set himself up in a modest practice in his birthplace of Rugeley, Staffordshire, and got married. However, it seems that as a leopard is said to have no control over its coat, so William Palmer found it impossible to settle down to a life of domesticity and honest toil. At home there was constant marital friction – not the least cause of which was the bastard child that he had given one of the servant girls. His business began to suffer – almost certainly on account of his preference for the race-track, horses and gambling over medicine.

To finance his ever-increasing gaming debts, Palmer ensured the decease of his mother-in-law, which in turn ensured his inheritance of her fortune. As his debts and racing stable losses increased, so his family decreased. His wife Annie, who had been insured for £13,000, died mysteriously; his brother Walter, insured for a similar sum, quickly followed. And along the line four of Palmer's children had also died, plus an uncle, and several of his more pressing creditors.

None of these 'windfalls' ever did more than satisfy, in the smallest part, Palmer's financial needs, and by 1855 he was not only in deep debt but in the claws of the moneylenders. Then in November of that year Palmer visited Shrewsbury Races with a gambling companion called John Parsons Cook. Cook won; Palmer, not unusually, lost. Cook's celebration party, however, proved to be Palmer's golden opportunity.

Cook was taken suddenly ill. Palmer generously offered to collect his winnings – and used them to pay off his own debts. Meanwhile John Cook, back at the Talbot Arms Hotel, was not responding well to the treatment administered by his 'friend' the doctor. In fact, by November 21st he was dead.

The suspicious nature of Cook's stepfather proved the undoing of Palmer, the worthy man insisting on an autopsy for John; an autopsy that was to reveal the traces of antimony that put William Palmer first in the dock of the Old Bailey in London before Lord Campbell, and then on the scaffold at Stafford Gaol, before an audience of fifty thousand.

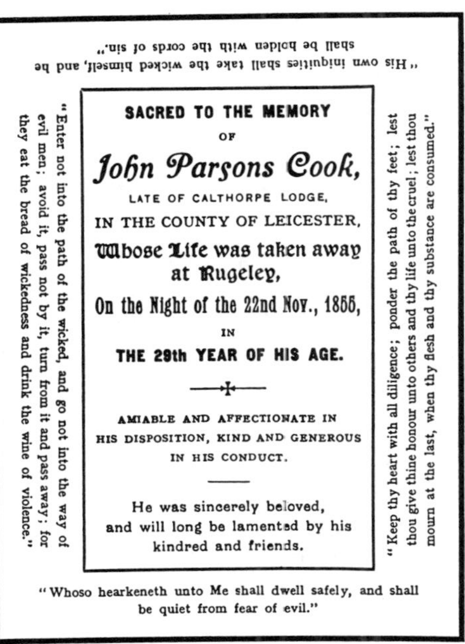
"His own iniquities shall take the wicked himself, and he shall be holden with the cords of his sin."

"Enter not into the path of the wicked, and go not into the way of evil men; avoid it, pass not by it, turn from it and pass away; for they eat the bread of wickedness and drink the wine of violence."

SACRED TO THE MEMORY
OF
John Parsons Cook,
LATE OF CALTHORPE LODGE,
IN THE COUNTY OF LEICESTER,
Whose Life was taken away
at Rugeley,
On the Night of the 22nd Nov., 1855,
IN
THE 29th YEAR OF HIS AGE.

AMIABLE AND AFFECTIONATE IN
HIS DISPOSITION, KIND AND GENEROUS
IN HIS CONDUCT.

He was sincerely beloved,
and will long be lamented by his
kindred and friends.

"Keep thy heart with all diligence; ponder the path of thy feet; lest thou give thine honour unto others and thy life unto the cruel; lest thou mourn at the last, when thy flesh and thy substance are consumed."

"Whoso hearkeneth unto Me shall dwell safely, and shall be quiet from fear of evil."

£200 REWARD

Whereas, on the 26th day of December last, a RACE HORSE in the stables of Mr John Scott, at Whitewall-house, near Malton, in the East Riding of the county of York, was wilfully and maliciously POISONED by the administration of arsenic.

A reward of £200 will be paid by Mr Scott to any person or persons who shall deliver the guilty parties; or if the party who actually administered the poison will furnish Mr Scott with such information as shall lead to the apprehension of the persons who incited or procured him to administer the poison, the reward shall be paid to him, and an application will be made to the Secretary of State to obtain her Majesty's pardon for any person giving such information.

Whitewall-house, Malton
February 14th 1856

The text of a poster issued by trainer Mr John Scott regarding a horse that had been 'nobbled' by William Palmer and James Cook

---

THE SENTENCE

"William Palmer, after a long and impartial trial you have been convicted by a jury of your country of the crime of wilful murder. In that verdict my two learned brothers, who have so anxiously watched this trial, and myself entirely concur, and we consider the conviction altogether satisfactory. The case is attended with such circumstances of aggravation that I will not dare touch upon them. Whether this be the first and only offence of this sort which you have committed is certainly known only to God and your own conscience. It is seldom that such a familiarity with the means of death should be shown without long experience; but for this offence, of which you have been found guilty, your life is forfeited. You must prepare to die; and I trust that, as you can expect no mercy in this world, you will, by a repentance of your crimes, seek to obtain mercy from Almighty God. The Act of Parliament on which you have been tried, and under which you have been brought to the bar of this court, at your own request, gives leave to this court to direct that the sentence under such circumstances shall be executed either within the jurisdiction of the Central Criminal Court or in the county where the offence was committed. We think that for the sake of example the sentence ought to be executed in the county of Stafford. I hope that that terrible example will deter others from committing such atrocious crimes; and that it will be seen, whatever art, or caution, or experience may accomplish, that such an offence will surely be detected and punished. However destructive poison may be, it is so ordained by Providence, for the safety of its creatures, that there are means of detecting and punishing those who administer it. I again implore you to repent, and to prepare for the awful charge which awaits you. I will not seek to harrow up your feelings by an enumeration of the circumstances of this foul murder; but I will content myself now by passing upon you the sentence of the law which is: that you be taken from hence to the gaol of Newgate, and be thence removed to the gaol of the county of Stafford, being the county in which the offence for which you stand convicted was committed, and that you be taken thence to the place of execution, and be there hanged by the neck until you be dead, and that your body be afterwards buried within the precincts of the prison in which you shall have been last confined after your conviction, and may the Good Lord of Heaven have mercy on your soul."

ILLUSTRATED AND UNABRIDGED EDITION

OF

The  Times

REPORT

OF THE

TRIAL OF WILLIAM PALMER,

FOR POISONING JOHN PARSONS COOK,

AT RUGELEY.

THE TALBOT ARMS, RUGELEY, THE SCENE OF COOK'S DEATH.

FROM THE SHORT-HAND NOTES TAKEN IN THE CENTRAL CRIMINAL COURT FROM DAY TO DAY.

LONDON: WARD AND LOCK, 158, FLEET STREET.

1856.

THE FATAL CONSEQUENCES OF GAMBLING.

A SERMON

PREACHED IN ST. MARY'S CHURCH, HULL,

ON SUNDAY EVENING, JUNE 22, 1856:

SUGGESTED BY THE

HISTORY AND END OF WILLIAM PALMER, OF RUGELEY:

Who was Executed at Stafford, June 14, 1856,

FOR THE WILFUL MURDER OF JOHN PARSONS COOK.

BY THE REV. JOHN SCOTT, M.A.

INCUMBENT.

"BE SURE YOUR SIN WILL FIND YOU OUT."—Num. xxxii. 23.

"HE THAT WALKETH WITH WISE MEN SHALL BE WISE: BUT A COMPANION OF FOOLS SHALL BE DESTROYED."—Prov. xiii. 20.

HULL:
PRINTED AND SOLD BY J. PULLEYN,
20, SILVER-STREET;
SEELEY, JACKSON, & HALLIDAY, 54, FLEET-STREET, LONDON.

A SERMON PREACHED IN ST MARY'S CHURCH, HULL BY THE REV. JOHN SCOTT

(AN EXTRACT)

He [Palmer] was the known seducer of one, whose affections he had unhappily won, and whom he afterwards basely deserted. He lived a life of what is commonly called the man of pleasure; reckless of the misery which his accursed course might inflict on the victims of his brutal lust and their distressed parents. And here let me add, that whatever the world may think, or say of such matters, there is no sin whatever, more strongly reprobated in God's book: there is none which God more palpably visits with the living brands of His righteous displeasure in this world: none which He will more signally punish in the next... Shew me the man who begins as a seducer, and I care not what be his rank or station, or influence, it would never surprise me to learn that he had ended as a MURDERER. None can count the murders and suicides which spring from this one source alone! While the tears which flow from the eyes of the seduced, degraded and deserted, and from their unhappy relatives and friends, might swell the broadest river in the world...

But yet there is one more crime, a master-crime, which occupies the throne and fills the chief place of pre-eminence on all such occasions, and that is GAMBLING – gambling – under the name and disguise of betting, and involving in many cases every imaginable form or shape of overreaching, deception, covetousness, villainy, if not open robbery...

The race-course and its unvarying concomitants open up to view 'a field of iniquity' which it is impossible adequately to picture. A scene in which Satan revels, and which is lit up by the very light kindled in Hell. For blasphemy, the most impious, and daring: for oaths, and curses, and imprecations, the most varied and profane: for revellings and drunkenness, terminating at nightfall in abominable and most unbridled licentiousness: for variance the most discordant: for envyings the most venomous: for wrath the most malignant and intense: for strifes the most bitter and unceasing: for hatred the most heartfelt and abiding; the race-course is the most perfect scene, the most prolific source... And more than this: the race-course is crowded by the very dregs – the scum and refuse – of society: by masses of thieves and prostitutes, and prize-fighters and idlers of every shape: by all the undetected and detected classes, for whom minor modes of gambling are largely provided in the low loathsome booths which surround the field of action. Great God! what scenes Thine eyes behold on such occasions! How unbounded Thy forbearance! How marvellous and matchless Thy long-suffering! – Wert Thou not merciful beyond conception, who should ever leave such a scene, save to stand at once speechless and confounded before Thy judgement seat... Such was the chosen sphere in which the wretched Palmer revelled.

Victim of the Night-Mare

The Murder by GEORGE ALLEN of his Wife and Three Children on Monday the 12th of January 1807 and his subsequent Execution at Stafford Gaol

Insanity probably caused the horrid deed to be committed which we are now going to relate. It appeared in evidence on the trial that George Allen had previously thereto been subject to epileptic fits, but that on the Sunday preceding the day he committed the murder he was considerably better*.

At eight o'clock on the evening of the 12th of January, 1807, he retired to rest, and when his wife followed him up, in the course of an hour, she found him sitting upright in bed, smoking his pipe, which was his usual custom. In another bed, in the same room, lay three of his infant children asleep, the eldest boy, about ten years old, the second a girl about six, and another boy about three. When his wife got into bed, with an infant at her breast, he asked her what other man she had in the house with her. To which she replied that no man had been there but himself. He insisted to the contrary, and his wife continued to assert her innocence. He then jumped out of bed and went downstairs, and she, from an impluse of fear, followed him. She met him on the stairs and asked him what he had been doing in such a hurry. In answer he ordered her to get upstairs again. He then went to the bed where his children were and turned down the clothes. On her endeavouring to hold him he told her to let him alone, or he would serve her with the same sauce, and immediately attempted to cut her throat, in which he partly succeeded, and also wounded her right breast; but a handkerchief she wore about her head and neck prevented the wound from being fatal. She then extricated herself (having a babe in her arms all the time, which she preserved unhurt), and jumped, or rather fell, downstairs. Before she had well got up, one of the children (the girl) fell at her feet, with her head almost cut off, which he had murdered and thrown after her. The woman opened the door and screamed out that her husband was cutting off their children's heads. A neighbour soon came to her assistance, and when a light was procured the monster was found standing in the middle of the house-place with a razor in his hand. When asked what he had been doing, he replied coolly: "Nothing yet: I have only killed three of them!" On their going upstairs a most dreadful spectacle presented itself: the head of one of the boys was very nearly severed from his body, and the bellies of both were partly cut and partly ripped open, and the bowels torn completely out and thrown on the floor. Allen made no attempt to escape, and was taken without resistance. He said that it was his intention to have murdered his wife and all her children, and then to have put an end to himself. He professed his intention also to have murdered an old woman who lay bedridden in the same house. An inquest was held on the bodies of the three children, before Mr Hand, coroner of Uttoxeter, when he confessed his guilt but without expressing any contrition. In answer to other interrogations he promised to confess something that had lain heavy on his mind; and Mr Hand, supposing it might relate to a crime he had heretofore committed, caused him to be examined in the presence of other gentlemen, when he told an incoherent story of a ghost, in the shape of a horse, having, about four years ago, enticed him into a stable, where it drew blood from him, and then flew into the sky. With respect to the murder of his children, he observed to the coroner, with apparent unconcern, that he supposed it was as bad a case as he had ever heard of.

The horrid circumstances of these murders were fully proved, and he was convicted, and suffered the final sentence of the law.

---

* See Appendix Four for a note on Epilepsy, Murder and the Homicide Bill.

Untitled aquatint by Francisco de Goya

Warwickshire

1. The Killing of Charles Walton 126
2. John DONELLAN 129

The Devil's Work

The Killing of CHARLES WALTON by an Unknown Assassin on Wednesday February the 14th 1945 in a field outside Lower Quinton

The calendar proclaims many brief oases in the otherwise monotonous flow of time; days when there is an opportunity to celebrate – or not, as we choose: Christmas, Easter, a number of Bank Holidays, Jewish New Year, Muslim New Year, and the First Day of Ramadan to name a few. In addition there are some more personal dates – birthdays, anniversaries, and a few gratuitous occasions on which shopkeepers can fill their tills between the major festivals – Mother's Day, Father's Day... And St Valentine's Day, February the 14th, the day for sending hearts and flowers; lovers' day. In fact the likelihood of St Valentine ever existing was considered to be so remote that his name was removed from the Calendar of Saints long ago. What survives – the sending of 'valentines' – has nothing to do with the saint anyway, but became confused with the Roman fertility festival of Lupercalia when, on February the 15th, the priests ran around the city waving goatskin thongs; a blow from the thong was said to be a sure cure for infertility in women.

Just an innocent relic of older, more pagan rites, St Valentine's Day has nothing really to do with the mysterious death of Charles Walton – except that it took place on the 14th of February. But other, blacker, pagan ceremonies might well have been very closely connected.

Charles Walton lived with his niece Edith in the medieval village of Lower Quinton, between Chipping Norton and Stratford-on-Avon. Although he was seventy-four and crippled with rheumatism, Walton exhibited a fierce independence and still earned his own scant living as a hedge-cutter. On Wednesday February 14th 1945, he left his cottage at nine in the morning as he had done for most of his insular life – slash-hook in hand, double-pronged hayfork over his shoulder, a shambling figure hobbling up Meon Hill to attend to the hedges bordering Alfred Potter's farm about a mile from the Walton home.

When Charlie had not arrived home by six o'clock, Edith Walton began to worry – the old man was never later than four, and with his legs as bad as they were she feared he might have had a fall. Summoning company in the person of neighbour Harry Beasley they hiked up the hill to Potter's farm, The Firs. Potter thought that he had seen Charlie Walton earlier in the day – it had been way across the fields, but the figure had been cutting hedges on his land so it could hardly have been anyone else. By torchlight, Potter, Beasley and Edith Walton picked their way over the fields to the lower slopes of the hill where farmer Potter had caught a sight of the hedger.

Quite suddenly, out of the darkness, the flashlight picked out the figure of a man. One look was enough for Potter, and protecting Miss Walton from the sight before them, he hurried her back home and called the police. Beasley was left the unappetizing responsibility of standing guard over a corpse in the middle of a dark field.

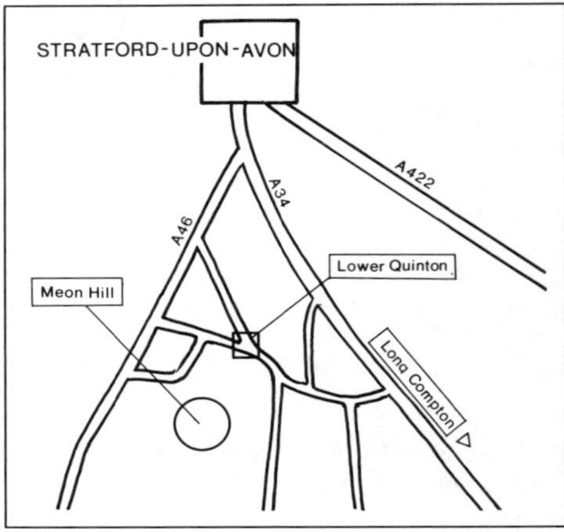

When the police arrived at the scene later they could fully appreciate the revulsion felt by Alfred Potter. Walton had been impaled by his own hay-fork, the two prongs of which had been driven with such force through his neck that they had penetrated six inches into the ground beneath; on his cheeks, throat and body the sign of the cross had been etched with his slash-hook. Close to his body lay the old man's walking stick, bloody from the blows it had dealt to its owner's head.

With commendable foresight the Warwickshire police asked for assistance from Scotland Yard, and were rewarded by the presence of Detective Superintendent Robert Fabian – famous throughout the country simply as 'Fabian of the Yard'.

At first Fabian and his assistant, Detective-Sergeant Albert Webb; acted on the assumption that this was an ordinary murder – if particularly brutal and seemingly motiveless. Understandable war-time xenophobia resulted in the close scrutiny of the several thousand enemy prisoners of war incarcerated in the camp two miles away at Long Marston. But however many deaths they may have been responsible for on the field of battle, the pathetic rag-bag of Italians, Slavs and Germans were apparently innocent of the death of Charlie Walton.

But events were now, in the parlance of Hollywood, about to take a dramatic turn. Robert Fabian recalled the opening scene:

Charles Walton

> I climbed Meon Hill, a bleak and lonely spot, to examine the scene of the crime for myself. A black dog, a retriever, sat on a nearby wall for a moment. then it

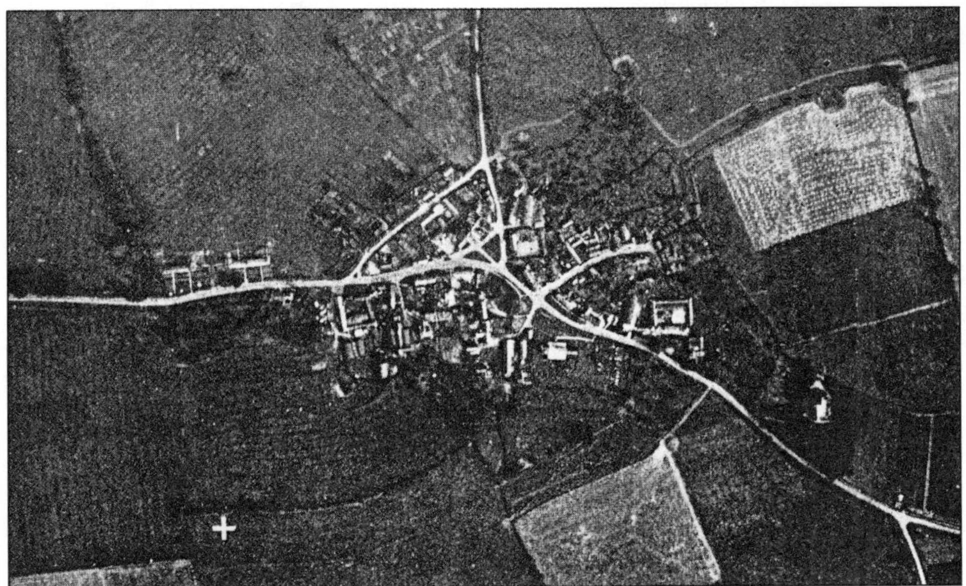

> trotted past me. I did not look at it again. Shortly afterwards a farm boy came along.
> "Looking for your dog?" I asked him.
> "What dog?"
> "A black dog..."
> The lad didn't wait to hear any more. He fled down the hill.
> Instantly, word spread through the village that I had seen the Ghost.

Now read this passage from an obscure book entitled *Folk Lore, Old Customs and Superstitions in Shakespeare Land* written by an equally obscure Warwick parson named J. Harvey Bloom in 1930:

> At Alveston a plough lad named Charles Walton met a dog on his way home nine times in successive evenings. He told both the shepherd and the carter with whom he worked, and was laughed at for his pains. On the ninth encounter a headless lady rushed past him in a silk dress, and on the next day he heard of his sister's death.

Charles Walton! The same Charlie Walton!

Regardless of his own feelings at the time about country superstitions this was clearly a line of inquiry that Fabian could not ignore; especially after Detective-Superintendent Alec Spooner of the Warwickshire C.I.D. drew his attention to another piece of local lore. In his work *Warwickshire,* Clive Holland related the circumstances of a murder which took place in the nearby village of Long Compton in 1875. In this case a simple-minded youth, John Haywood, slew an old woman named Ann Turner whom he was convinced was one of a coven of witches meeting at Long Compton. At his trial, Haywood declared: "Her was a proper witch, I pinned her to the ground [with a hay-fork!] before slashing her throat with a bill-hook in the form of a cross." Long Compton was reputedly still an important centre of witchcraft.

Whether or not the urbane detectives from Scotland Yard believed in the continued existence of the Warwickshire Witches, it was plain that the inhabitants of Lower Quinton were taking no chances; and not a word would they utter, not a gesture would they now make towards helping the inquiry. It was, they declared, best left alone; best left to rest – particularly when the body of a black dog was found hanging from a tree close to where Charles Walton had been murdered.

Alfred Potter

In the end, even the experience and determination of one of the country's finest detectives found that it had met its match in the stubborn silence of Lower Quinton, and Detective-Superintendent Fabian and Detective-Sergeant Webb retreated to London, and less spooky investigations.

Charlie Walton was buried in the quiet graveyard attached to the village's picturesque Saxon-Norman church. Life resumed its normal pattern.

In retrospect, though, Robert Fabian discovered that there was a clear warning to be taken from the Mystery of Lower Quinton:

> I advise anybody who is tempted at any time to venture into Black Magic, witchcraft, Satanism – call it what you will – to remember Charles Walton and to think of his death, which was so clearly the ghastly climax of a pagan rite. There is no stronger argument for keeping as far away as possible from the villains with their swords, incense and mumbo-jumbo. It is prudence on which your future peace of mind and even your life could depend.

Close to Long Compton stands the group of stones known as the Whispering Knights. Witch legend explains that a pagan king was told that if he and his knights climbed the hill to the point where they overlooked Long Compton church, the crown of all England would be his. But he reckoned without the notorious witch Mother Shipton:

She stood upon Long Compton hill
And glared upon the vale.
Ere to-morrow's height,
I'll blast the might
Of King and men in mail.
I spy them in the burra,
But me they cannot spy;
The King before,
The men two score,
I'll blast them with mine eye.
They shall not reach the hill-top,
Long Com. they ne'er shall see,
For with that sight
Is gain'd the right
Old England's king to be.
Here on the windy headland
I'll freeze them all to stones,
My cruel spell,
And trick of Hell,
Shall turn to flint their bones.
All round the ruddy flare
They sit and sip and sing,
"To-morrow we
Long Com. shall see
And crown great England's king."
They leave to you her den hard by,
Their vain burst heard with glee.
And clutching in her shrivelled hand
She stirred the deadly pottage
And muttered horribly.

"Throw physic to the dogs"*

The Murder of Sir THEODOSIUS EDWARD BOUGHTON by his Brother-in-Law, JOHN DONELLAN on Tuesday the 27th of February 1781 at their home Lawton Hall, Nr. Warwick

Son of a colonel in the Army, John Donellan attained the rank of Captain in the same service, enjoying a distinguished career, and despite wounds was reported to be instrumental in the taking of Mazulapatam. Nevertheless, some underhand dealings with the native merchants had earned him a court martial and cashierment. Subsequent manoeuvring obtained him a certificate from the War Office declaring that he had "behaved in the East Indies like a gallant officer" – which was sufficient to put him on a pension of half-pay with the 39th Regiment, and enough for him to take to himself a bride, in the person of a Miss Boughton. The marriage took place in June 1777. Less than four years later, on Friday the 30th of March 1781, Donellan stood before the Warwick Assize on the charge of the wilful murder of his brother-in-law, Sir Theodosius Edward Allesley Boughton, Bart.

* William Shakespeare, *Macbeth,* iii.37.

Mr Powell, apothecary of Rugby, deposed that on Tuesday morning, the 27th of February [1781], he was sent for to Lawton Hall, and on his arrival there, at a little before nine o'clock, Captain Donellan conducted him to the apartment of Sir Theodosius. On entering, he perceived that the baronet was dead; and on examining the body he concluded that it was about an hour since life had fled. He had some conversation with Captain Donellan with regard to the deceased, and he was told by him that he had "died in convulsions".

The mother of the deceased, Lady Boughton, testified that Sir Theodosius had been twenty years old on the previous August 3rd. On his coming of age [then twenty-one] he would have been entitled to above two thousand pounds a year, and in the event of his dying a minor, the greater part of his fortune was to descend to his sister, the wife of Mr Donellan. It was known among the family on the evening of Monday the 26th, that Theodosius was to take his physic the next morning. He used to put this medicine in the dressing-room. He happened once to omit to take it; upon which Mr Donellan said: "Why don't you set it in your outer room? – then you would not so soon forget it." After this he several times put the medicine upon his shelf over the chimney-piece in his outer room. On the evening of Monday, the 26th, about six o'clock, Sir Theodosius went out fishing attended only by one servant, Samuel Frost. Both Lady Boughton and her daughter, Mrs Donellan, took a walk in the garden, and were there over an hour. To the best of her recollection, she had seen nothing of Mr Donellan after dinner till about seven o'clock, when he came out of the house door in the garden, and told them that he had been to see them fishing, and that he would have persuaded Theodosius to come in, lest he should take cold, but he could not. Sir Theodosius came home a little after nine, apparently very well; he went up into his own room soon after, and then to bed. He requested her to call him the next morning and give him his physic.

She accordingly went into his room about seven in the morning, when he appeared to be very well. She asked him where the bottle was, and he replied: "It stands there upon the shelf"; the label read 'Purging draught for Sir Theodosius Boughton'. As he was taking it, the lad observed that it smelled and tasted very nauseous; upon which his mother had said:"I think it smells very strongly like bitter almonds." He then remarked that he thought he should not be able to keep the medicine in his stomach. At this point in the trial a bottle was handed to Lady Boughton containing the genuine draught prescribed and she was asked if it smelled like the medicine her son took that morning; she replied that it did not. She was then requested to smell another containing the draught with the addition of laurel-water; this, she said, smelled like the medicine that she had given to her son. Lady Boughton then continued her evidence. Two minutes after Sir Theodosius had taken the draught, he "struggled very much. He made a prodigious rattling in his stomach, and guggling." These symptoms lasted about ten minutes, and he then seemed as if he was going to sleep, or inclined to doze; and seeing him more composed, she went out of the room. Returning in about five minutes she found him with his eyes fixed upwards, his teeth clenched, and foam running out of his mouth. Lady Boughton immediately summoned a servant and ordered him to fetch Mr Powell.

Less than five minutes later, in answer to her request, Mr Donellan came into the room where Lady Boughton sat with her sick son, and demanded: "What do you want?" She answered that she wished to inform him of the terrible thing that had just happened; that it was such an unthinkable thing that the doctor should have sent such a medicine, for if a dog had taken it it would surely have died; indeed, she doubted that her son would live. Donellan then asked where the physic bottle was, upon which she showed him the two draughts. Taking up one of the bottles he asked "Is this it?" and when she confirmed that fact, he instantly washed the bottle and emptied it into some dirty water that was in a washhand-basin. The startled woman demanded "What are you at? You should not meddle with those bottles". Upon which he snatched up the other and rinsed it also, then put his finger to it and tasted it. She repeated that he ought not to have interfered with the bottles, and he replied that he did it merely to taste. At this point two servants entered the room, Sarah Blundell and Catherine Amos, and Donellan desired the former to remove the bottles and the basin and dispose of them. Lady Boughton, however, took back the bottles from her and, setting them down, forbad that they should be further touched. But no sooner had her back been turned on some trifling errand than the prisoner once again instructed the servant to remove the bottles, which she did. When she entered the parlour some little time later, unobserved by Mr and Mrs Donellan, her Ladyship heard the former telling his wife that her mother had noticed him washing the bottles and that it was a good thing that he had thought to say he was only tasting from them.

Dr Rattray, of Coventry, described the external appearance of the deceased's body, and reported on the post-mortem dissection. He was asked whether, having heard the evidence of the two previous witnesses, he could form a conclusion as to the cause of death, independent of his own clinical observations. Witness answered that he was of the opinion, from the symptoms that followed the taking of the draught, that it was poison, and the certain cause of death. Being passed the bottle containing the draught, Dr Rattray ventured the opinion that it was a noxious distillation of laurel leaves, called laurel-water.* He amplified this notion with details of several controlled experiments on animals indicating the lethal nature of the poison; he added that the quantity of laurel-water contained in that bottle was sufficient to cause the death of any human being. Mr Wilmer and Dr Parsons, Professor of Anatomy at Oxford, confirmed these findings.

Next to take the stand was John Darbyshire, a former inmate of Warwick Gaol for debt. He testified that he had shared a cell with the prisoner for about five weeks, and that during that time the subject of Sir Theodosius's death had arisen on several occasions. On one, the witness demanded of Donellan: "For God's sake, Captain, who could do it?" The prisoner replied that it was none of his doing, and that his guess was that the responsibility lay with "Sir Theodosius himself, Lady Boughton, the footman, and the apothecary." Darbyshire responded that he thought it extremely unlikely that the deceased had done the deed himself, and "the apothecary could hardly do it – he would lose a good patient; the footman could have no interest in it; and it is unnatural to suppose that Lady Boughton would do it." The Captain had repeated that her Ladyship was a most covetous woman, and was quite capable of such skulduggery, and several times reiterated his own innocence.

This comprised the chief evidence for the prosecution, and the prisoner's defence seemed to rely solely on a flat denial, supported by a number of testimonies to his honour and integrity; none of which impressed the jury, who found him guilty as charged.

At seven o'clock on the following day, the 2nd of April, 1781, John Donellan was borne to the place of execution in Warwick, in a mourning-coach followed by a hearse and the Sheriff's officers in deep mourning. As he went on the condemned man frequently put his head out of the coach, desiring the prayers of the people around him.

Alighting from the coach at the fatal spot, Donellan ascended a few steps of the ladder and prayed for a considerable time; next, in an audible tone of voice, he addressed the spectators to this effect: that as he was then going to appear before God, to Whom all deceit was known, he solemnly declared he was innocent of the crime for which he was to suffer; that he had drawn up a vindication of himself, which he hoped the world would believe, for it was of more consequence to him to speak truth than falsehood, and he had no doubt but that time would reveal the many mysteries that had arisen at his trial.

* See Appendix Two for a note on Laurel-Water as a poison.

After praying fervently for some time he let his handkerchief fall – a signal agreed upon between him and the executioner – and was launched into eternity. When the body had hung the usual time it was put into a black coffin and conveyed to the Town Hall to be dissected.

[*This account has been compiled from contemporary reports.*]

West Midlands

1. Abraham THORNTON 134
2. David PAGETT 158
3. Frederick William OAKLEY 161
4. Stanley Eric HOBDAY 162

The Primrose and the Wretch

The Rape and Murder of MARY ASHFORD by ABRAHAM THORNTON in the early morning of May the 27th 1817 in the Fields at Penn's Mill Lane, Nr. Erdington

Abraham Thornton was a 25-year-old bricklayer, son of a prosperous builder at Castle Bromwich. In August 1817, he stood indicted at the Warwick Summer Assizes for the rape and murder of Mary Ashford, held locally to be the unsullied flower of country maidenhood.

From the evidence, it appears that on May 26th, 1817 – it was a Whit Monday – Mary attended a special dance held at Daniel Clarke's tavern, *The Three Tuns* (or *Tyburn House),* in the hamlet of Tyburn. At seven o'clock in the evening, she called on her friend Hannah Cox who, with her mother Mrs Butler, lived at Erdington. Here, Mary

changed from her everyday clothes into the party finery which she had left with Mrs Butler earlier in the day; after which the two girls set off for the pub, arriving at around 7.40pm just as the dancing had commenced. No sooner had Mary entered the room than

she became the object of Abraham Thornton's lustful attentions, and despite an appearance described by one witness as "brutal and repulsive", Mary responded to his flattery.

Hannah Cox left the festivities at around eleven o'clock with her fiancé Benjamin Carter, while her friend was still engaged with Thornton. The four met up again on the bridge by the tavern and together walked along the Chester Road towards Erdington. At one stage Ben Carter decided that he had not made merry enough, and returned to *The Three Tuns* dance; further on, Mary announced that she intended spending the night at her grandfather's cottage which stood on the corner of Bell Lane (now Orphanage Road) and Chester Road, and so Hannah returned alone to her home in Erdington, leaving Thornton, she supposed, to escort Mary to her grandfather's. This was at midnight, and in fact Mary spent the next several hours in young Thornton's company

before she went knocking on Hannah Cox's door at about four in the morning. Mary claimed that she had left her escort some hours before, and had been at her grandfather's house; she was on her way back to her uncle's at Langley Heath, and wanted to change into her everyday clothes before setting out. This done, Mary took leave of

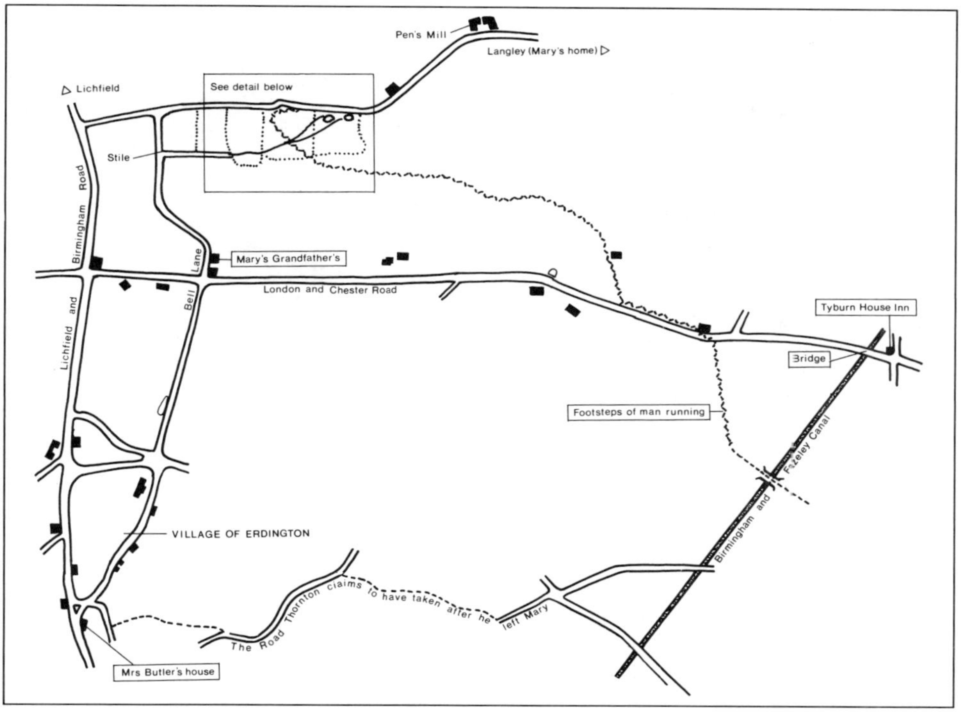

Pen's Mill
Langley (Mary's home)
Lichfield
See detail below
Stile
Birmingham Road
Lichfield and
Bell Lane
Mary's Grandfather's
London and Chester Road
Tyburn House Inn
Bridge
Footsteps of man running
Birmingham and Fazeley Canal
VILLAGE OF ERDINGTON
The Road Thornton claims to have taken after he left Mary
Mrs Butler's house

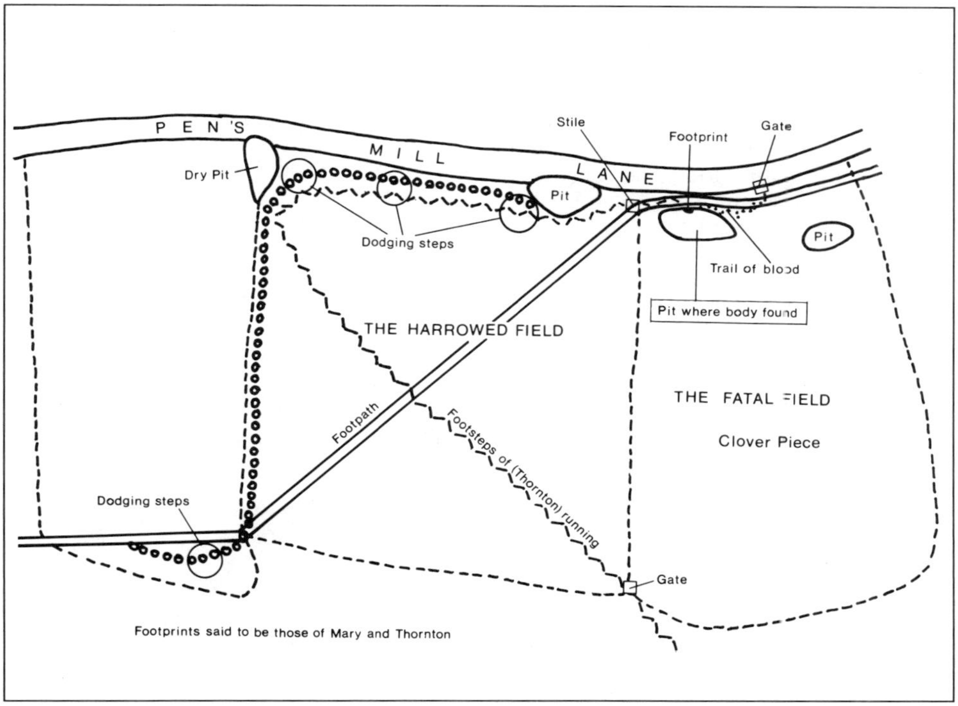

PEN'S MILL LANE
Stile
Footprint
Gate
Dry Pit
Pit
Dodging steps
Trail of blood
Pit
Pit where body found
THE HARROWED FIELD
THE FATAL FIELD
Clover Piece
Footpath
Footsteps of (Thornton) running
Dodging steps
Gate
Footprints said to be those of Mary and Thornton

her friend and passed along the route home that took her through the secluded Bell Lane, where she was seen by, and greeted, several early-rising farm labourers. A little further on, Mary entered Penns Mill Lane (now Penns Lane), taking a short cut across the fields, in one of which there was a deep water-filled pit.

When George Jackson, a road mender, came upon a blood-stained bonnet and pair of shoes by the pit near Penns Mill Lane, he immediately raised the alarm; soon a crowd had gathered to witness the dragging of the pit, and the consequent discovery of the battered body of Mary Ashford.

A contemporary account describes the state of the ground immediately surrounding the scene of the murder which gave eloquent clues to the girl's last tragic struggle:

> The circumstances proved in evidence were that the footsteps of a man and a woman were traced from the path through a harrowed field, through which [Mary's] way home to Langley lay. the marks were at first regular, but afterwards, exhibited proofs of the persons whose footfalls they represented running and struggling; and at length they led to a spot where a distinct impression of a human figure and a large quantity of coagulated blood were discovered, and on this spot the marks of a man's knees and toes were also distinguishable. From thence the man's footprints only were seen, and accompanying blood marks were distinctly traced for a considerable space towards the pit; and it appeared plainly as if a man had walked along the footway carrying a body, from which the blood dropped. At the edge of the pit, the shoes, bonnet, and bundle of the deceased were found; but only one footstep could be seen there, and that was a man's. It was deeply impressed, and seemed to be that of a man who thrust one foot forward to heave something into the pit.

The finger of suspicion was at once pointed at young Abraham Thornton – partly by dint of his reputation, and partly by his very obviously lecherous approaches of the previous evening. Mr Bedford, a magistrate of Birches Green, thus sent the landlord of *The Three Tuns,* Daniel Clark, to fetch Thornton

in for questioning. During this interrogation, the youth admitted his nocturnal involvement with Mary, but swore that it was by her total consent.

Most of the subsequent legal investigation was concerned with the verification of alibis – notably Thornton's – which proved no easy matter in the year 1817, when clocks were scarce, and ones that kept good time rarer.

The trial took place in the County Hall at Warwick on August the 8th before Mr Justice Holroyd. Mr Nathanial Gooding Clarke, KC, presented the case for the Crown, and Messrs William Reader and Henry Revell Reynold conducted Thornton's defence:

> The prisoner declined to say anything in his defence, stating that he would leave everything to his counsel, who called several witnesses to the fact of his having arrived home at an hour which rendered it very improbable, if not impossible, that he could have committed the murder, and have traversed the distance from the fatal spot to the places in which he was seen, in the very short time that appeared to have elapsed; but it was acknowledged that there was a consider-

able variation in the different village clocks; and the case was involved in so much difficulty, from the nature of the defence, although the case for the prosecution seemed unanswerable, that the judge's charge to the jury occupied no less than two hours. "It were better", he said, in conclusion, "that the murderer, with all the weight of his crime upon his head, should escape punishment, than that another person should suffer death without being guilty"; and this consideration weighed so powerfully with the jury that, to the surprise of all who had taken an interest in this awful case, they returned a verdict of not guilty, which the prisoner received with a smile of approbation.

Next morning Abraham Thornton, free again, returned to Castle Bromwich. However, such was the public, official, and newspaper outrage at the verdict, that it was but weeks before a method was found to take Abraham Thornton once again before a court. This was achieved by means of the rarely invoked law allowing the next of kin, or 'heir-at-law', of the deceased to issue a private writ of appeal; in this case it was taken out in the name of William Ashford, Mary's elder brother, and served by the Sheriff of Warwick.

On November 5th, 1817, Thornton was escorted by Mr Tatnall, Keeper of Warwick Goal, to appear at Westminster Hall, London, before the Court of the King's Bench. And here legal history was to be made.

Not to be outwitted, Thornton's advisers had also been doing a little homework with the ancient law books, and came up with the archaic right of the appellee (Thornton) to challenge William Ashford (the appellant) to Trial by Battle [see Appendix Five] – a process forgotten since the time of Charles I. It was clear that, in any form of physical combat, the frail, slow-witted Ashford would be no match for the burly, aggressive Thornton. After seemingly endless legal wrangling – throughout which time Thornton was held in the Marshalsea Prison – the Lord Chief Justice decided that Abraham Thornton *was* entitled to his 'trial by battle', and that as the appellant had refused to accept the challenge, the appellee must be set free.

Free he may have been, but such was the loathing in which he was held in his native county, that Abraham Thornton emigrated to America. His notional 'adversary', William Ashford, died in 1867 in Birmingham.

Mary Ashford's body was buried in Sutton Coldfield churchyard on June 1st, 1817, beneath the inscription:

As a warning to Female Virtue and a
humble monument to Female Chastity
this stone marks the grave of
MARY ASHFORD
who in the 20th year of her age
having incautiously repaired to a scene of
amusement
without proper protection
was brutally violated and murdered
on the 27th May, 1817

Lovely and chaste as the primrose pale
Rifled of virgin sweetness by the gale,
Mary! the wretch who thee remorseless slew
Avenging wrath, which sleeps not, will pursue.
For though the deed of blood be veiled in night
Will not the judge of all the earth do right?
Fair blighted flower! The muse that weeps thy doom
Rears o'er thy sleeping from this warning tomb.

THE MYSTERIOUS MURDER

OR,

What's the Clock?

A MELO DRAMA

IN THREE ACTS

Founded on a Tale too True

WRITTEN BY G.L.

DRAMATIS PERSONAE

MEN

Mr THORNTREE – An Independent Gentleman
Abraham THORNTREE – His Son, and the Supposed Murderer
Sir George MITTIMUS – Baronet
Mr PARSONS – Counsel for the Crown Mr REYNARD – Counsel for the Prisoner
Mr QUIBBLE – Attorney
Mr BOLUS – Surgeon
Jacob TURNOUT – Constable
Daniel TAPSTER – Landlord
Mr WEBB – Gentleman
Turnkey, Keeper, etc
Milkman, Labourer
Jury, Evidences for and against the Prisoner, etc.

WOMEN

Maria ASHFIELD – The Victim
Hannah FOX – Her Friend
Mrs THORNTREE
etc.

ACT I Scene 1
A Turnpike Road

Enter Maria Ashfield and Hannah Fox]

Maria: Well, Hannah, you see I'm soon returned from Market. 'Tis not yet 5 o'clock; I've been as good as my promise.

Hannah: That you generally are; but there was no fear when you were going to a dance; yet I think you are not very partial to dancing neither; perhaps, Maria, you expect to meet with a fresh sweetheart? Indeed, you are so springly and good-natured that you cause everyone to love and –

Mar: Have done with this nonsense, and let's make haste to your mother's; you know I left some clothes there? for I wish to change my dress before going to the dance. Come, come, I long to be there.

Han: Nay, but stay a moment; why in such a hurry? We shall be in quite time enough! Ah! Maria, had I half your spirits, I would give the world if it were possible. Pray tell me how you have acquired so lively a disposition.

Mar: Ha! ha! ha! why Hannah, you are going to be like the men, to flatter me. Women, you know, love a little flattery; I'm a giddy, thoughtless girl, and to tell you the truth, I do intend to have a fresh lover – that is, if I can; but really, I'm so whimsical –

Han: Indeed you are, about sweethearts.

Mar: I have never yet seen the man I could sincerely love; all men are alike to me, at present. I can't say but I am a little pleased with their attentions, but as soon as away, I laugh and forget them; like a child that is very pleased with its toys for a while, and then throw them aside for others.

Han: Ah, you giddy brain! but you'll be caught some time, and pay for all. But come, you have not yet told me how it is you are always cheerful and happy.

Mar: You know that I enjoy a good state of health; when I awake in the morning, I thank God for keeping me in the night; I rise early, and with pleasure do my little work; I let nothing vex me; I mind no-one's business but my own; I strive to do my duty to my uncle, and make him happy and comfortable. In this way I cheerfully pass my days; and when I go to bed, I lay my head on my pillow, with happiness, and in peace with the world.

Han: I thank you for the pleasing description of your time, and will strive to imitate you. I have got something to tell you, but you must be as mute as death; do you know that Robert wants us to be married!

Mar: Ha! ha! ha!

Han: What makes you laugh?

Mar: Ha! ha! ha! I knew that last week.

Han: I'll plague him for this! he'll want to dance with me tonight, but I won't!

Mar: Well, do as you like; but if we stand here chattering. I think neither of us will. Come, I can stop no longer now; tomorrow we'll find something to plague him. [*exeunt*

ACT I Scene 2
A Tavern

Young Thorntree and Company discovered Drinking]

Thorntree: I think Mr Tweedle don't intend coming tonight, 'tis past six o'clock now. If it be agreeable, gentlemen, we'll have a song.

Landlord: Right; and Mr Thorntree, if he pleases, shall sing it.

Thorn: You know I am no singer, but I will do my best [*sings*

Sons of mirth my call attend,
Would you cheerful moments spend,
Then behold your chief in me,
For my name's Festivity.

Sportive joys to me belong,
Sprightly dances, lively song;
Ever happy, full of glee,
Such am I, Festivity.

Is your mind oppress'd with care,
I can chase away despair:
None can long unhappy be,
Blest with blithe Festivity.

Now the toast goes cheerful round,
Jocund pleasures now abound;
While the catch and merry glee,
Still support Festivity.

Momus' pow'rs to me pertain,
Mirth and wit attend my train;
Such the joys that wait on me,
Then enjoy Festivity.

Company: Bravo! Bravo! – a sentiment if you please!

Thorn: "May the pleasures of an Evening bear the reflection of a Morning."

Enter Tweedle]

Tweedle: I should have come before now, gentlemen, but someone played me an unlucky trick, by putting some grease on my strings.

All: Ha! ha! ha!
Thorn: A dev'lish good joke, Mr Tweedle! but come, those who are for the dance will walk this way.
Enter Maria and Hannah]
Mar: Better late than never; has the dance begun?
Thorn (aside): A charming girl is that! What a shape! How springhtly she looks! – Come ladies and gentlemen, come forward, into the dancing room. [*exeunt Company*
Land: I couldn't help noticing young Thorntree, when Maria came in, he seemed confus'd.
Re-enter Young Thorntree]
Thorntree (takes the landlord aside): I say, landlord, what genteel girl is that in the straw bonnet and white gown?
Land: Don't you know? 'Tis old Ashfield's daughter!
Thorn: What old Ashfield the game-keeper?
Land: The same – there is not a more virtuous girl in the country, nor one more beloved by all who know her, rich or poor.
Thorn: Has she not a sister named Ann, that is out of service?
Land: Yes.
Thorn: I know her well, and have been intimate with her several times; and if I can not with this girl tonight, I lose my life. I'll go and engage her for a partner, if I'm not too late; this will make us better acquainted.
[*exit*

Land: What a mad-headed devil that is for the wenches! how he boasts of his amours with them! he's a fool as well as a rogue; but he has met his match this time, she'll take care of herself, or I'm much mistaken. [*Bell rings*] Coming! coming!
Company: We will, landlord, if it's agreeable.
Land: Perfectly so! Please walk this way, gentlemen. [*exeunt*

ACT I Scene 3
A Room

Company dancing; during which Young Thorntree is seen paying particular attention to Maria. After the Dance, he takes her aside]
Landlord: Ladies and Gentlemen, there's some cold ham and fowls on the table if you choose a little refreshment.
[*Company withdraw; Thorntree and Maria come forward*
Thorn: Do, for Heaven's sake, stop a moment!
Mar: Hush, we shall be noticed. [*runs from him*
Thorn: If I had tonight ten thousand lives, I'd lose them to enjoy her! [*exit*

ACT I Scene 4
A Turnpike Road

Enter Hannah Fox and Robert Baker]

Robert: What makes you in such a hurry tonight? Why you've left all the Company.

Hannah: I don't like the company at all; and as for Maria I'm sorry to hear she's dancing with that Thorntree; he is the one I don't like. I wish you'd go and persuade her to come home, and I'll wait for you here.

Rob: To tell you the truth, I don't like him myself; I think him a very disagreeable fellow.

Han: He is, to me, very disagreeable, but go, I'll be sure to wait [*Rob exits*] I hope Maria will come with him; she's so innocent herself, she cannot suspect anyone. I should not wonder but he makes love to her, and Maria I dare say will be pleas'd with it; he is a man of property, but he has such strong passions for women that makes him rather dangerous for some young women to be with; but Maria will take care of herself; for never was there one more virtuous; I am sure she'd sooner lose her life than her innocence. Here she comes.

Enter Thorntree, Robert, and Maria]

Mar: What makes you wish to go so soon tonight, Hannah?

Han: I think it's high time; will you go with me and sleep at my mother's?

Rob [*whispering to Hannah*]: Mr Thorntree wishes to go home with her.

Mar: No, I think I'll go to my uncle's.

Han: Well, then we'll bid you goodnight, as you will have company; you'll call tomorrow for your clothes?

Mar: Yes; good night [*exit Han and Rob*]. Now, Sir, let us make haste; I'm afraid my uncle will be gone to bed; besides, Sir, you know we are strangers!

Thorn: Do not be alarmed! I'll see you safe [*takes her hand*] You're a charming girl! Tell me, are you engaged? I love you to adoration!

Mar: Do not attempt to impose upon me, Mr Thorntree; for how can I believe those vows, which you have, no doubt, so often administered to the shrine of beauty.

Thorn: Nay, then, I swear by Heaven! You're the only girl that ever seriously took my fancy! Your appearance, your manner, all convince me you were born to fill a higher station in life than your present one. [*Aside*]. If she takes this 'twill do – Let us sit down on this stile.

Mar: Do let us go; indeed, I must not stay; what would my friends think if they knew I was out with you (being a stranger) till this time of night? But I trust that whilst I am under your care, as an unprotected female, I have nothing to fear.

Thorn: No, on my honour, you have not; accurs'd be him that would take any unmanly advantage of an innocent girl's virtue! [*Aside*]. How enchanting she looks!

Mar: I must acknowledge I am acting very imprudent, but my heart is innocent; my reputation is all I have to depend on, and I should not wish it sullied. Were my friends to find it out that I was with you at such a time, I am afraid – see, there's someone coming; I feel quite ashamed [*turns head, confused*].

A Labourer crosses the Stage]

Labourer: Good morning Mr Thorntree.

Thorn: Good morning, Sir [*aside*] Damn that fellow's impudence. Don't be alarmed! You need not be ashamed; you know it's the wake, and you have been at the dance, no notice will be taken.

Mar: Indeed, Mr Thorntree, you are quite mistaken; a girl, like me, who has nothing but her character for her safeguard, ought to be very cautious how she acts; for, when once that has gone, ruin inevitably must follow.

Thorn [*aside*]: What a sensible girl!

Mar: If men would but consider, that in the gratification of a few moments of sensual pleasure, they often leave the object of their lust to years of sorrow and misery, they certainly could not be capable of committing so base an action.

Thorn: Don't give over! I could listen for ever to your sensible remarks.

Mar: Thank you, Sir; As I have staid so long, I will not offer to go to my uncle's, but will return to my friend Hannah's for my clothes; twill save me the trouble of coming from home again.

Thorn [*aside*]: To change her dress! I must not put my intentions into force now; she's too much on her guard; I'll wait her return from her friend's.

Mar: What are you thinking of, Mr Thorntree, so seriously?

Thorn: I was thinking that, as your friend may, perhaps, think it rather strange for you to be out at this time of night, you had better say you slept at your grandfather's, and that I left you a long time since.

Mar: I'm not accustomed to tell untruths, but perhaps, at this time, it may be pardon'd, should it ever be found out.

Thorn: I will just see you within sight of the house, then bid you good morning, and go home to take a few hours rest.

Mar: That will be the best. I may rely on your secrecy?

Thorn: You may. Come we shall soon be there [*takes her hand, kisses it*]. Excuse me. [*Aside*]. This will do! [*exeunt*

Enter a Countryman]

Countryman [*Looks around him*]: Well, if I didn't think I heard somebody talking hereabouts, and I'm sure I can't see anyone! It appeared as if it was some man and woman – Sweethearts I suppose! So they were afraid of being seen! Ah, poor souls! When they've been married as long as Margery and me has been, they'll have something else to do than stop out till this time o' the morning courting. Od drabbit it! how anxious some people are, and what a deal o' trouble they're at to get married! as for me, I shouldn't care what I did to get unmarried. These curs'd hard times, make women so crabb'd and ill-temper'd, they're like Magpies – chatter, chatter, chatter! their tongues go like the old larum of our old clock. I can't help thinking of old Margery whenever I goes to the mill; for when the hopper's full o' corn, all goes on smoothly enough, but when short, then there's such a grating noise – just the same with my wife; for ecod! if I bring her home plenty of money, then it's "What will you have for supper, my dear?" But when there's no cash, then she begins: "Bean't you ashamed, you rascal! to starve your children? I was well off before I knew you!" But if she knew what I'm thinking of now, she'd sing a rare psalm in my ears! If I don't get home as it is, I shall catch it. [*exit singing*

ACT I Scene 5
The Inside of a Cottage

Maria and Hannah discovered; Maria changing her clothes]

Han: So you slept at your grandfather's?

Mar: Yes; I thought I would not go to my uncle's, as I had got to come here for my clothes this morning.

Han: Well, how long did Thorntree stop with you?

Mar: A good while, but he said he would go home and have a few hours sleep.

Han: And how do you like him? I suppose he was making love to you?

Mar: Why, to tell you the truth he was; but 'twas only joking; you know he's a man of property, and I a poor girl; he can never think anything of me, he knows better, but What's the Clock?

Han: By ours it's nearly five, but it is a great deal too fast.

Mar: Do lend me a comb, Hannah, a moment; I think I look so much like a rake; my uncle may, perhaps, think I've been up all night. [*Combs her hair*]. There; now I think I'll be off. [*Takes her bundle*]. Will you come down to our house today?

Han: Yes, I think I shall.

Mar: Well, they're up at my uncle's before now. Good morning Hannah.

Han: Good morning. [*exit*

ACT I Scene 6
Turnpike Road

Enter Thorntree, musing]

Thorn: What am I going to do? to ruin a poor innocent, virtuous girl! Pshaw! What's that to me? – She's such an enchanting girl, I must not let her slip through my fingers; I see I shall be compelled to use violence, she's so refined in her ideas; my former conquests, to this, will be nothing! But if she should swear a rape against me? – Ah! that must not be! – I will lose my life to effect my purpose. Yet I must act with caution, and secure my own safety, if possible. – She will tell her friend she slept at her grandfather's, and that I left her some time since. This will throw some Mys'try on the deed! – The dead tell no tales! – That pit of water! – ah! What a dreadful thought! – If I can do without, well; if not it must be so! What a damn'd thing is this? Had I better not leave her and go home? Better abandon my design? Hell and the Devil! What? Turn coward at last? and let a poor timorous girl as this overcome me? No! I have got through many a damn'd scrape, and I ought to be twice damn'd if I don't get through this! But I see her at a distance; I must watch the road she takes; I will go back, and draw her farther from the houses. How sprightly she walks! But I'll soon crop her bloom! If I am not mistaken, I see a waggoner, he must not see me, if he does, all's lost; I will retire behind the hedges. [*retires*

Enter Maria with a bundle]

Mar: I think I escap'd the jokes of Hannah pretty well; if ever I am found out, I shall never hear the last on't. What a simpleton I was! I cannot think what could possess me to stop with him. As for his promises, I don't suppose they're at all sincere. I'm a fool to think anything about him. How I must derogate from truth. I don't like it! My uncle will question me where I have been. I must tell him either at my friend Fox's or else at my grandfather's – I think I shall not so soon be found out if I say at my friend's – thus it is seen, by asserting one falsehood, how we are led on, step by step, to frame others in support of it. Yet, I've done no harm, neither; only the appearance! – Well, I'm young and thoughtless; but as time advances shall learn better. 'Twas very well he left me as he did, or we should have been seen by farmer Aston's boy [*sees Thorntree at a distance*]. Good God! if he isn't here! I don't like this! I'll run back; yet if I do, all will be found out! I must get out of his way; I can beat him at running, I know; I'll return to the stile. [*runs off*

Re-enter Thorntree]

Thorn: She shuns me; sure, she must suspect me? I have gone too far to retreat; she shan't escape. [*follows her*

ACT I Scene 7
A Field

Enter Maria, almost out of breath, pursued by Thorntree; after various turns round the stage, he seizes her by the arm]

Thorn: By Heaven! you shall not escape!

Mar: Oh! Mr Thorntree! do let me go; do not injure me [*she struggles and breaks from him; he again catches her, and carries her off the stage*]

ACT I Scene 8
A Turnpike Road

Enter a Milkman; puts down his cans]

Milkman: What a wearisome life this is; here I am forced, morning and night, to come five miles, tugging and toiling – for what? a mere subsistence; whilst thousands are now in bed; passing away their time, like drones in a hive; living upon the industry of others. It is well for many of them that they were born with a silver spoon in their mouths, or they would not have had ingenuity enough to have got iron ones to eat with; but must have been contented with wooden spoons, like myself. Well, I must e'en plod on through life's dreary road! I often wish for death, and yet if he was to come, I should be like the old man in the Fable, who called for him, and when he came, said he only wanted to be helped on with his load. Somehow, we all wish to live as long as we can; and as we can't all be rich, I must be content to carry you a little longer. [*Takes up his cans*] Heigh-ho! [*exit*

ACT I Scene 9
A Field – in which is seen a Pit and at a distance, a Mill

Maria discovered lying on a Bank senseless; her apparel in a disordered state, etc. Young Thorntree is taking off her shoes and bonnet; after which he takes the Body in his arms]

Thorn: By Heaven! she breathes! [*looks around him*]. I tremble. Sure I heard footsteps; No; 'twas but my fancy. [*Carries the Body off stage*] [*Re-enters*]. Thus have I made security doubly sure! [*Takes up the bonnet and bundle*] These must be placed near the pit [*Places them on one side of the stage*]. I must now be off, cross the fields, and get to the turnpike road. [*runs off*

END OF THE FIRST ACT

ACT II Scene 1
A Tavern

Family at breakfast]

Landlord: I don't remember having a more comfortable night since we came to this house than we had last night; the company were very numerous.
Mrs Tapster: Did you observe what attention Thorntree paid to Maria Ashfield?
Land: Hang him, he did; but he's such a devil for the wenches, you never know when he's sincere: I suppose he went home with her?
Mrs Tap: Most likely! And would tell her many a fine tale.

Enter a Gentleman in haste]

Gent: Oh, horror! horror! What a deed! What a diabolical act!
[*The Family rise, alarmed*
Land: What's the matter, Sir?
Gent: What a sight! Sure no one ever witness'd a scene so melancholy and heart-rending!
Land: Pray, sir, what's the matter?
Gent: Maria Ashfield is found murdered.
All: Murdered!
Gent: Yes, by some unknown monster in human form; first violated, then thrown into a pit of water.
Land: Is anyone suspected?
Gent: Young Thorntree is; as he was dancing with her last night; and I think there ought to be some inquiry made after him.
Land: Can you tell us any particulars of the sad story?
Gent: I could, Landlord, but am in haste to give directions about the body. Do, for God's sake, use every means to see young Thorntree immediately; and I will send for a constable.
[*exit*
Land: Good God! poor Maria! but last night, never was there one more cheerful and happy! now a mangled corpse, by one who ought to have protected thee! Was it for this, thou subtle deceiver, thou paid such uncommon attention to her person? – Satan like! But I will immediately pursue thee, thou smooth tongu'd villain; Thou artful devil! and bring thee to that punishment thy crimes have long deserved.

I'll seek an ancient custom to make good
To Britons bound by law, have 'blood for blood'

[*exit*

ACT II Scene 2
A Room at Mr Thorntree's

Young Thorntree changing his clothes]

Young Thorn: So far, so good; all's yet safe; she'll soon be discovered; and suspicion, of course, will fall on me. Let me see; I left her at four o'clock; she stopped about fifteen minutes at her friend's; the deed was done by five; by crossing the fields I gain'd about twenty minutes; and when I met Mr Fallow he said 'twas only half past four by their clock, which certainly must be too slow, as it was past five by my watch at the time – and I know that is right by the church. But no matter; 'tis in my favour. But if the clock be found out late? Then I'm lost! Well, I don't care! I can but die once. It was a bloody deed to be sure, how tenderly she begged me to spare her innocence and her life. But what could I do? Had I sav'd hers, I must have forfeited my own.* Though I can't think what could possess me! These mad fits will certainly be my ruin! But if I can escape this –

Enter a servant]

Serv: Mr Tapster wishes to see you.
Y. Thorn [*aside*]: Mr Tapster! Sure she can't be found yet. Tell him to come in [*exit Serv.*] I can't think what he wants.

---

*At this time Rape was a capital offence.

Enter Landlord]

Land: Good morning, Sir.
Y. Thorn: Good morning, Sir. To what am I indebted for this early visit?
Land: I am the messenger of ill news; Maria Ashfield is murdered.
Y. Thorn [*confused*]: Murdered! Why, I was with her till four o'clock this morning.
Land: Well, then, I'll thank you to come and clear yourself.
Y. Thorn: Certainly Mr Tapster, I will; [*rings*] I'll just leave word with the servant where I am going as my father is not at home. I think we shall have uncommon good hay harvest this year.
Land [*aside*]: There's a hardened villain! – Yes, I think we shall.

Enter Servant]

Y. Thorn: Should my father come in my absence, tell him I am gone with Mr Tapster for a short time; I shall soon return. [*exeunt*

ACT II Scene 3
A Room at Mr Quibble's

Quibble discovered reading a newspaper; over a bottle]

Quibble: Were it not for these Crim Cons, Scandal etc. what would become of half the lawyers of this country I do not know. Let me see [*reads*] "Damages to the Paintiff £5000; a swingeing sum for the lawyers and counsels out of it" [*drinks*] "The Lawyer's Harvest, the increase of Crim Cons", thats a good toast. What a happy thing it is that all people aren't of one mind! Lawyers and Counsellors might then give up business, or turn bankrupts. I think I made pretty well of my last job; when I shall have such another, God knows! I must confess there was no mighty matter of honour in it; honour nowadays is out of the question. But what asses some people are; rather than suffer a little injury they run to the lawyers: very good for me, truly! but they, perhaps, ruin or destroy the peace and happiness of their Families for ever.

Enter Servant]

Serv: Mr Thorntree, Sir, is below; and wishes to see you immediately.
Quib [*rises*]: Mr Thorntree! ah, there's another job; that scape-grace son of his is one of my best friends! Yet I'm always afraid of losing him, for some time or another he will (in spite of fate) take a trip to South Wales, or else Tyburn, Tell Mr Thorntree to come up [*Exit Servant*] Of all the hardened rascals I ever sav'd from the gallows, this young mad fellow is the worst.

Enter Mr Thorntree]

Quib: Ah! Mr Thorntree, good Morning; Pray, Sir, take a seat; what's the matter? You seem alarm'd.
Mr Thorn: Alarm'd Sir! Oh, I am wretched! This unfortunate son of mine will one day or another bring my grey hairs down with sorrow to the grave.
Quib: Come, come, Mr Thorntree, compose yourself; we've got him through many a scrape. But what misfortune has occurred?
Mr Thorn: My son, – Ah! I'm asham'd to say the word; it almost makes me shudder; he, he is, I fear, a Murderer!

Quib: What? Committed a Murder; [*aside*] I fear'd as much; this is a rare job!
Mr Thorn: Oh, Mr Quibble, for God's sake, tell me what can be done! my fortune, nay, my all, is at your service! Save, oh save him from an ignominious death!
Quib: Well, well, let me know something of the matter; compose yourself, or I can make neither head nor tail of it. [*Aside*] I'm afraid this will be my last job; I must make him pay well.
Mr Thorn: All I know of the matter at present is, last night he was at a dance, and did not return till this morning, between five and six o'clock; the young woman he was dancing with is found violated and thrown in a pit of water, and he was the last person seen with her.
Quib [*aside*]: Violated, and thrown in a pit of water! 'tis worse than I expected: Oh, the rascal!
Mr Thorn: Oh speak! speak! Your silence distracts me.

Quib: Why before anything can be done I must know a few particulars; in the first place, who is the young woman?

Mr Thorn: The daughter of Old Ashfield.

Quib: That's in our favour, she was poor.

Mr Thorn: Yes – but she bore a good character, and has many friends: Did you but hear how much she is lamented? I am afraid my son will be killed by the enraged people.

Quib: Pshaw! 'twill be but a nine days' wonder; as for her friends, 'tis a nothing; there may be, Mr Thorntree, one or two busy bodies put themselves forward; there always will be; but when money's wanted, then it either drops thro' or they sneak away, with: "Why its a great pity that such a villain should escape, but what have I to do with it, more than another? What's the business of every one is no one's." So all will drop in time.

Mr Thorn: It may be so sometimes; but it will not be so this. But what can be done?

Quib: We must act with caution; you may depend, most men may be bought, some way or another, give them but their price. A poor man must be bought accordingly; we must prove an alibi; that is, we must prove him some distance from the place at the time.

Mr Thorn: I'm afraid that's impossible; he has acknowledged to have had an improper connexion with her.

Quib: Oh, that's soon got over; 'twas with her own consent, you know. The dead don't come again to tell tales.

Mr Thorn: But they say there's much of violence on her arms.

Quib: The devil there is! Well, have a good heart! We must get him through it. But where is he?

Mr Thorn: In custody at the public house; but I hear he is going off to the dungeon; you had better go and see him immediately.

Quib: In the meantime, we must first find out the names of those who saw him. I'm afraid this will be a very expensive job.

Mr Thorn: Expensive! Oh, don't mention that! I don't mind what it costs if we can get him off! 'Tis impossible for anyone to judge what I feel, except they were in my situation, as a father. What a disgrace to our family! as for my poor wife, it will be too much for her! If he has committed the murder (and I am afraid he has) public justice demands his life. But can a public feel a father's anguish of mind? No! There are but few instances of parents giving their children up to justice from motives of honour. Those times are past. If it would please Providence to take him from me without suffering a public and shameful death, I should be happy! Though he is my only son, was he but a corpse at my feet now [*weeps*]. I could press him with pleasure to my bosom! I must return to my wife, and give her that hope and consolation I so much want myself; exert yourself, Mr Quibble, this once! Spare nothing! You shall not go unrewarded! Good morning, Sir. [*exit*

Quib: Good morning Mr Thorntree. So 'tis as I expected – I must see him – we must act very cautiously – I dare say the villain's no more alarmed than if nothing had happened; he deserves to suffer; but what shall I get by that? very little; if he escapes, a great deal. But what will the world say? damn the world! the disgrace will fall on him. Surely a man ought to live by his business. The Laws of England are good; no other country in the world can boast of such, were they abided by; but that's impossible; for when a new law is made, we immediately sit down to find out all its imperfections and errors. This enables us to take both sides of the question, either for the plaintiff or defendant; and we often get more by pointing out the faults of the law than supporting a good cause. But I must see this scape-grace immediately. It will be a rare job, the best I've had yet! [*exit*

ACT II Scene 4
A Room in the Dungeon

Young Thornton discovered at Dinner]

Thorn: Well, I think I've made a tolerable good dinner considering; I wonder how the twelve wiseacres are going on? They thought to frighten me by my touching a dead body*, but they've got a wrong one for that. – Quibble's a clever fellow; were it not for such as him,

---

* See *Murder Club Guide No. 2* for a note on Touching the Corpse.

many beside myself would have made their exit under the gallows. Well, we can but once die! If *rhino* can save me I'm sure to get through, as my old dad will stretch a point, I know, to save the family from disgrace.

Enter Jacob Turnout with Wine]

Well, Jacob, you don't hear anything yet? Come, take a glass of wine!

Jacob [*drinks*]: No; I could not get the least intelligence, after those three jury were put aside, they were so close after.

Thorn: That was a devil of a job to let Mr Good-will, the magistrate, overhear us.

Jacob: It was; yet Mr Quibble's a very clever fellow in such things as these.

Thorn: Aye, aye, he is; come, let's drink his health: "Mr Quibble, and may he live long in the memory of such unlucky dogs as myself."

Jacob: The aforesaid [*drinks*]. Well, I wonder Mr Quibble's not here. He promised he'd lose no time to let you know.

Thorn: What do you think will be the end of this affair?

Jacob: I am afraid it will be more serious than we are aware of; but Mr Quibble will do his best; here he comes.

Enter Quibble, gives money to Turnout, who retires]

Quib: Well, my friend, you must not be alarmed when I tell you that you are committed to the County Gaol; but never mind, I'll get you through.

Thorn: What? must I then go at last? could you not have prevented this?

Quib: No [*aside*] Nor did I wish it; – the evidence was so strong against you; I try'd for your committment to have been made out for the rape only, but it was over rul'd. Never mind! Money will make a prison comfortable.

Thorn: Ay! but to have on those curs't irons!

Quib: Oh! That's nothing! we'll soon make them easy. I'll accompany you; I know all their tricks; did you see how soonTurnout left us? *Shiners*! let a lawyer have plenty of those and he may do miracles! he can soften the stony heart; make heavy irons light; hard beds as soft as feathers; in short, he may do everything. Not like the jugglers, who cry "hocus pocus, quick and begone!" he can do all without a word; by putting his hand into his pocket, and taking it out again, all is done. But to our business; you must not withold any thing from me in this transaction: I must guard against all things that may come against you; but in order to avoid any confession, I'll suppose you guilty of whatever may be brought against you, and act accordingly; if innocent there is no harm done.

Enter Jacob Turnout]

Jacob: Gentlemen, I am desired to stop with the prisoner.
Quib: Oh, very well, [*aside*] I say you'll not let him want for anything, I'll see you shall lose nothing by it. – Well, I must leave you for the present; keep up your spirits. [*exit*
Jacob: I'm sorry, you must go off in the morning early.
Thorn: I may go inside a coach, I suppose?
Jacob: Oh yes.
Thorn: Come, take another glass of wine, I could wish to lay down a bit; for I feel quite knock'd up.
Jacob [*drinks*]: That you may do, I can lock the door; but at night I must sleep in the room with you.

[*Young Thorntree lays down*

ACT II Scene 5
A Room at Mr Thorntree's

Enter Mr Thorntree, musing, a letter in his hand]

Mr Thorn: For ever blighted are my fondest hopes! my reputation stain'd! pointed at as I pass, by the finger of scorn! My son, a prisoner! On the eve of being brought before a public tribunal on suspicion of the foulest crimes! now an associate with the most abandon'd part of society! perhaps in a short time doom'd to suffer ignominious death – dreadful thought! Oh! that I should have ever liv'd to see this day! Would it had pleased Providence to have cut short the days of his existence! I should now have been happy. Never, never more whilst I remain on this side of the grave, will this affair be obliterated from my mind; happiness is forever fled my wife, my family, and myself! What wicked daemon prompted him to commit so foul a deed? sure, the violation itself was too shocking! but then to hurry into eternity one whom it was his duty to have protected? a poor, innocent, virtuous girl, whom he'd ruined! my soul shudders at the thought! – Oh Lust! Lust! what direful mischief thy votaries commit to accomplish their brutal desires! Man! where is thy superior reason over the brute creation! they may destroy others of their kind to protect the object of their passion, but rarely take the life of the object itself. The laws, both moral and divine, will demand the life of him who takes it from another; yet, can the world blame me for using every means in my power to save my son? What will not a parent do for a child whom he loves, in this dreadful cause? Will not his anxious desire to save him lead him beyond the bounds of propriety? nay, make him, rather than lose all, take unlawful means? – But my son wishes me to see Mr Quibble immediately. However I may despise this man, necessity compels me to seek his assistance; [*looks at his watch*] I must lose no time, 'tis past ten; Mr Quibble will now be in his office.

Joy will to him, who spends in peace his days;
Evil will to him, who follows evil ways.

[*exit*

ACT II Scene 6
Lawyer Quibble's Office

Quibble writing]

Quib: Our affair goes on charming; the old boy bleeds freely; what a fortunate thing it is he's plenty of money. The reputations of families often cause the coffers of lawyers to fill, whilst theirs are almost drained; I must still keep him in the dark; Have I not a right to do the best I can for myself? I can't get honour, I must have something to supply its place; and what can do it more effectually than money? all powerful money! That's a theme that touches all hearts more or less; in fact, to say what it cannot do would puzzle wiser heads than mine; – to those I'll leave it. I have not the least doubt of getting my client through this time; there's no positive evidence against him. The Laws of England are full of mercy as well as justice; and many are acquitted by the law though they may be guilty; if there is a doubt arises, the prisoner can claim the benefit of it. No doubt, he deserves to die, and would if he were not properly looked after. I must confess our evidences are rather too bare-faced; will it not appear singular that so many should come forward to swear to a time so exact? if no deviation in their evidences, he must be acquitted. As I expect the old gentleman here every minute, I'll look over the expenses before he comes: in the first place, Premium and Travelling Expenses of Counsellor Reynard £500 *item,* Jacob Turnout £100. Zounds! this fellow's a greater rascal than myself! What? to demand £50 for getting some linen washed, and 50 more for holiding his tongue? That's a great sum! Though, by the bye, many husbands would not grudge twice that for their wives to hold theirs. For the three evidences swearing to the time £90. For Incidental Expenses £150; besides my own, which for obvious reasons I shall not put down, as the old man may give more that I could modestly require. We must be very circumspect; for there are those who would have great objections to swallow bolusses, but if made into pills they'd go down with ease. [*The bell rings*] 'Tis Mr Thorntree I dare say.

Enter Mr Thorntree]

Mr Thorn: You must excuse me coming so abruptly; but my anxiety to hear how matters are going on makes me use less ceremony.

Quib: Certainly, Sir; But I'm very sorry to inform you, the evidence is strong against us.

Mr Thorn: Alas! I fear after all he must fall victim to his passion? Oh, my son! my son!

Quib [*aside*]: Zounds! if he don't almost make me weep – Nay, Mr Thorntree, let us hope.

Mr Thorn: There is no hope for me.

Quib: Yes, there may be a great deal; though their evidence is strong we must endeavour to have stronger; A man cannot be in two places at one time.

Mr Thorn: Ah! Now you give me new life! those evidences to time – Yes, I'm like one who's drowning who catches at everything. Give me reason to hope, and I'm happy. My wife wishes to see him, as she thinks it will be the last time; if you could accompany us, 'twould be better.

Quib: To-night I expect the men, and wish to give them a little instruction. They would not take less than £30 each: I'll just read over the expenses.

Mr Thorn: Oh, never mind the expenses, I will pay it all; and whatever their demand is, I will give, were it as much more. I will go and prepare for our journey; you will go with us tomorrow morning?

Quib: Yes, Sir; Good day. [*Exit Mr Thorntree*] What an ass I must needs be? I might as well have got £5 a piece by them; I'm afraid yet these blockheads will ruin all. I don't fear them going on with a straight-forward tale, all my fears are when they are cross-examined.

Enter Servant]

Serv: The three men that were here last night are waiting to see you.

Quib: Send them in! [*exit Servant*] Zounds, what can the rascals want? they'll ruin all by coming at this time in the day! I'd almost as soon see the devil!

Enter Cowherd, Ploughshare, and Clodpole]

Quib: Ah! How d'ye do? I'm very happy to see you! I'm much obliged by your kind visit, though I must confess I did not expect you till night.

Clod: No, Sir; but we've had a bit of a confabulation; Cowherd's been to market this morning, and stopp'd at the Public to have a little ale, so your honour, the company were talking of our affair [*Quibble alarmed*] an' so there happened to be a man there that knew him; and he said, says he, yo' be one o' the evidences, bean't ye? yo' mun mind speak the truth, or yo'll be pillowed*; So d'ye see, he come an' told us, and we think, should we be found out, that £30 each ain't enough to be pillow'd for.

Quib [*aside*]: Here's a set of villains! – Ha! ha! ha! Gentlemen, I can't help laughing at you. You need not be alarm'd; you've nothing to fear while I'm with you.

Clod: That's what I said, says I, if we do look through the pillowry, we shall have good company, for Mr Quibble must be with us.

---

*ie. Pilloried.

Quib [*aside*]: A shrewd rascal this! – I beg your pardon, but we're now gone from our business; you must consider, this will be a very expensive job; I think, gentlemen, you should be content with what you have. I could have the whole village stand in the pillory for the money. But to put an end to it, I'll give you £5 a piece more out of my own pocket [*aside*] I will put £10 each in first.

Cow: I think Mr Quibble speaks like an honest man; we'd better tak' it! what say ye?

Plough: Take it to be sure! an' as we're here, I think we may as well ha' a bit of a drill, instead o' coming at night.

Quib: It will suit me as well, Gentlemen, take seats; [*they sit*] Now, my honest friends, you must remember, when you're asked any question you needn't answer directly, but think to yourselves; by that means you'll not make so many mistakes. William Cowherd.

Plough: I'm the first.

Cow: I tell you, I'm the first!

Clod: You're both wrong, I'm the first.

Quib: Gentlemen! gentlemen! it don't matter which of you is first! – William Cowherd?

Cow: Here!

Quib: Do you know the prisoner?

Cow: Yes.

Quib: When did you first see him?

Cow: Let me see . . .

Quib: Why don't you speak?

Cow: I'm thinking.

Quib [*aside*]: Blockhead! – You must not think so long.

Cow: How long must I think?

Quib: About the time you could count five; – How long have you known the prisoner?

Cow: One . . . two . . . three . . . four . . . five . . .

Quib: Pshaw! what's the fel . . . gentleman about?

Cow: About twelve months.

Quib: Do you recollect seeing the prisoner on the 29th or the 30th of May last?

Cow: Yes.

Quib: Was it morning, noon, or night?

Cow: About half past four in the morning.

Quib: Are you certain it was about that time?

Cow: Yes, I'm certain it was: I left home at half past three, an' walked to the place in an hour; so it must be exact half past four o'clock.

Quib: That's well; stick to that and we shall do. Gentlemen, I have no occasion to examine any farther; all you'll have to mind is, when you saw the prisoner; you understand me gentlemen? You may now retire.

Clod: Yes; you'll remember the £5 extra. [*exit evidences*

Quib: Damn that fellow! I'm very much obliged to him for his compliment! What I, Mr Quibble, the honestest lawyer in the whole country, stand in the pillory? Zounds! the fellow's impudence sets me in a flutter; £15 before breakfast? that will do! follow the old proverb, to – the pillory! curse the pillory! Feather your nests against winter, make hay while the sun shines. The old boy has been saving for many years, but I think his money has got wings now, and will fly away – the pillory! the pillory! [*exit*

ACT II Scene 7
A Prison Cell

Young Thorntree asleep; Enter Turnkey and Mr Thorntree]

Turnkey: There he is, fast asleep.

Mr Thorntree [*gives him money. Exit Turnkey*]: Asleep! is it possible he can sleep so sound? Alas! I fear his awful situation and this horrid place has made but little impression on his mind! [*looks around*] *What a sight to the guilty! Those chains and heavy locks and bars strike terror to my soul! And yet this victim of depravity sleeps as sound as if all were peace within. "The innocent sleep", so do the guilty!* [*points to his son*]. But how sweet is the sleep of one from that of the other? The one awakes to happiness and peace, the other to wretchedness and woe! He wakes; I will retire; perhaps I may be wrong in my conjectures.

Y. Thorn [*awakes and half rises*]*:* Heigho! another night of misery is past! Yet, upon the whole, I think I sleep very well; considering these horrid irons. Mr Quibble was right about money making them lighter; but we shall soon be separated, and perhaps I may change them for something softer to go round my neck. What a fool I am to get into so many scrapes through women! It's a rare thing my daddy's plenty of money or I should be in a sad mess. I wonder the Turnkey don't come – by the sunbeams darting through these iron bars it must be 7 o'clock. Well, if he don't chuse to let me out. I don't chuse to get up. [*Lays down again.*]

Mr Thorn [*comes forward*]*:* Abram?

Y. Thorn [*arises*]*:* Sure, I heard my father's voice?

Mr Thorn: It is your father; I trust that apathy I've now been witness to is not real – do not let me think I have given birth to a monster in human form. [*Pointing to his irons*] Do not those strike your mind with horror?

Y. Thorn: Yes, they did at first; but, you know, I'm now familiar with them; they hurt my legs a bit to be sure!

Mr Thorn: Is that all you care for them? Abram, I'm your father, and as such have done everything in my power to save you. I have neither directly or indirectly upbraided you, nor cast the least reflection on your past misconduct; nor will I now – 'twould be cruel. I hope you have suffered sufficient to bring you to a sense of your situation. The time is now come, and I consider it my duty to give you some little advice; I have made choice of the present thinking it may make a deeper impression. In a short time you must appear before a tribunal of your country. Should you be doom'd to suffer an ignominious death, to prepare you for that awful change I must leave to one who is more abler than myself – may He, whose chiefest attribute is mercy, shew you mercy!

Y. Thorn: Oh, forbear! You make me almost tremble.

Mr Thorn: Hear me. On the contrary, should you escape the justice of man, that of an Almighty and offended God you cannot escape; nor can you the censure of mankind. By the law you may be acquitted for want of evidence. But there's something so atrocious attached to your crimes that has, and ever will, render you obnoxious to society. Let me advise you to fly to Him who is able and willing to blot out your iniquities, and try to make some atonement to that family you have so much injured.

Y. Thorn: A little money will soon make up all things.

Mr Thorn: 'Tis well for the lower class of society that your sentiments are not more prevalent with the higher; though I must confess there are many like you who think any injury done to the poor may be compensated by a little money. 'Tis erroneous, a poor man possesses feelings equal to a rich one's; and we ought to be as cautious of wounding the feelings of one as the other, for by nature all are equal; 'tis virtue alone that raises us above and vice that sinks us beneath others. Yet we often see the slightest faults of the poor punish'd with severity, whilst those of a more gross nature of the rich pass unnoticed. I must leave you, as I expect your mother here; I trust her advice will make a deeper impression than my own. I will see if she is arriv'd. [*going out*

Y. Thorn: Oh, do not go! I wish not to see my mother!

Mr Thorn: Not see your mother?

Y. Thorn: No – if I suffer, she can do me no service, and if I don't, she will see me when I return home.

Mr Thorn: What do I hear? Those words are daggers to my soul! for God's sake! for the sake of common humanity! recall those unfeeling words! [*kneels*] Oh, Thou! Who can soften the most obdurate heart!...

Mrs Thorntree rushes in]

Mrs Thorn: Oh! Where's my Son? [*She sees Mr Thorntree, shrieks, and falls senseless into the arms of her son; Mr Thorntree runs to her assistance*]

Enter Turnkey and Quibble]

Turnkey: What's the matter? [*starts*] Ah! What a sight this is!

Y. Thorn: Help! help! she's dead!

Mrs Thorn [*revives*]*:* Oh, where am I? ah! now does horror shake my soul! my head is giddy; my brain is scorched; I faint... my Son! my Son! [*faints in his arms. They all weep, except Quibble who stands unmoved, watching the emotions of Young Thorntree. Curtain falls*]

END OF SECOND ACT

ACT III Scene 1
A Prison

Young Thorntree musing]
Y. Thorn: All will soon be o'er! the situation I am now placed in, to many would be dreadful; to me it has no terrors; sure, there must be some defect? If denied those tender feelings others possess, am I to blame? Yes: had I not given way (in my childhood) to those little acts of cruelty I was permitted to pursue; or had I listened to the advice of my parents, I might have escaped many evils, which the impetuosity of my passions have plung'd me in. I cannot weep; – nay, was I going to suffer tomorrow I could meet my fate with indifference. Could I repent, 'twould be now. Pity and remorse are both strangers to this bosom! – step by step, led on by cruelty and lust; – now to repent I can not.
Enter Quibble]
Quib: What? do I see my old friend in a musing mood?
Y. Thorn: Ah, Quibble, for once in my life I have felt the effects of a guilty and wounded conscience.
Quib: Pshaw! nonsense 'tis all a farce!
Y. Thorn: With all my boasted apathy of thought, I feel there is a power above.
Quib [*aside*]*:* Should he escape he may repent, then I shall lose my jobs.
Y. Thorn: Ah Quibble! I wish you and me may not find it too true, to our cost. But away with it: – where is my father and mother? I hope she is better?
Quib: Yes, when I informed her how matters stood, she became reconcil'd; and your father thought it would be best to return, as they expect we shall soon follow them. Your clothes are come, and the keeper will bring them to you. You must prepare for your trial, and it is now five o'clock and I expect it will commence at eight. As I have some things to arrange, I must leave you, and shall not see you again before the trial. Keep up your spirits, and I have no fear that you will be comfortable at home by tomorrow at this time. Good bye. Remember – don't be daunted.
[*exit*
Y. Thorn: I'm glad Quibble came; I was going into one of my melancholy fits; they come but seldom, yet too often.
Enter Keeper with clothes]
Keeper: Here's a coat and waistcoat to change yourself; I wish you good luck. Your trial is to commence at eight o'clock, what would you choose for breakfast?
Y. Thorn If I could have half a pint of wine and a little biscuit –
Keeper: You shall have it.
[*exit*
Y. Thorn [*changes his clothes*]*:* I'll keep this coat as a memento if I should return home. [*Walks about the stage*] I cut a very respectable figure, ha! ha! ha! I look something like Macheath; but where's my Polly Peachum? – Aye, there's the rub!
Enter Keeper with wine and biscuit]
Keeper: Now, sir, you'll make all the haste you can; the Hall is full of people and the judge is expected in a short time.
Y. Thorn [*takes the refreshment*]*:* Well, now I'm prepared.

Now to my fate undaunted will I be;
E'n welcome death, or welcome liberty.

ACT III Scene 2
A County Hall

Prisoner at the Bar; Judge, Jury, Counsellors, Quibble, etc., etc., discovered]
Cryer: Prisoner hold up your right hand. My Lord, a true Bill of Indictment against Abraham Thorntree; not having the fear of God in his eyes, but, instigated by the devil, to commit the dreadful crime of murder on the body of Maria Ashfield, spinster, on the 30th of May last. Are you guilty, or not guilty?
Prisoner: Not guilty!
Parsons: My Lord and Gentlemen of the Jury, it is with the deepest regret I rise to lay before you one of the most melancholy cases that ever came before a British Jury. Maria Ashfield, a young woman of irreproachable character, down to the time which terminates in her death was found, on the 30th of May last, drowned in a pit of water. On the morning of the 29th she left home to go to a neighbouring market; and on her way called on her friend Hannah Fox, and arranged with her to return soon in the evening. She left some clothes with the

other of her friend in order to change her dress on her return, to go to a dance which was to be held in the village where she resided. The deceased was not in the habit of attending dances, only at this. Previous to the commencement of the dance, the Prisoner was at the house drinking with the landlord and others. On the arrival of the deceased, her form and manner took the attention of the Prisoner; he left his company, and I do not think it is necessary to repeat the various expressions he made use of, only that which is most material: *I will have connexion with that girl* (meaning the deceased) *or lose his life.* And to accomplish this, by his insinuating manner, persuaded her to dance with him. During the dance he drew her out of the house once or twice, and press'd her to take a walk with him, which she refused, being by themselves, and strangers. Before the dance was concluded he had removed these maiden fears as far as to gain her consent to see her home. They left the dance about 12 o'clock, in company with her friend Hannah Fox. Here, Gentlemen, I cannot pass over the conduct of her friend without a little censure: She knew the Prisoner and had said she did not like him and her friend dancing together, and yet could accede to her going with him at that time of night. It will be unnecessary to bring forward any evidences to prove that the Prisoner was with the deceased till early on the following morning, as he confesses himself that he was with her until four o'clock. After this period we have no occular proof that the Prisoner was with her; but I shall proceed to bring forward evidences who will adduce such circumstantial proofs against him that I trust will not leave a shadow of doubt on your minds that he was not only with her, but that, after a time, he actually accomplished his diabolical intention of having connexion with her; and that he did likewise throw her into the pit of water; there cannot exist in your minds the least doubt but that she was forcibly violated: the marks on her arms are positive proofs to that effect. Could we suppose that she, whose very soul was purity itself, would willingly submit, at that time, and I may say in such a public place, to give up her virtue to an entire stranger? Common sense forbids the thought; – After the Prisoner was in custody and had been examined, he then confess'd he had had connexion with her. Gentlemen, you'll recollect the Prisoner did not make this confession until he was compell'd by the circumstance of the state of his linen.

Reynard: You have no right to influence the minds of the Jury.

Par: I beg your pardon, Sir; I have a right! Gentlemen, I say the Prisoner never confess'd till he was oblig'd by existing circumstances. That the deceased was to this period innocent of having connexion with any one I shall bring forward the evidence of a very respectable surgeon to substantiate. And that she was so weakened with loss of blood that it would have made it impossible for the deceased to have thrown herself into the pit. The first evidence I shall call is the deceased's friend Hannah Fox.

Hannah: Here!

Par: You are now to speak the truth, and nothing but the truth.

Han: The deceased and myself was brought up together, and were to the time of her death on the strictest terms of intimacy. On the return of the deceased from the market on the 29th of May, I accompanied her to a dance in the village; I did not dance myself, but saw the Prisoner there. We left about 12 o'clock, and the Prisoner said he would see her home. On the morning after, about 4 o'clock, deceased called me up, chang'd her dress, and then left me to go to her uncle's.

Rey: Did you not observe the deceased was very much confused when she came in?

Han: No, she was always lively, and did not appear to the contrary then.

Rey: Didn't you see some stains on her clothes?

Han: No; if there had been any I could not have avoided seeing them, for she chang'd her clothes in my presence; she said she slept at her grandfather's, and the prisoner had left her some time since.

Rey: You may now retire.

Par: William Lavender?

Lavender: Here!

Rey: What do yo know about this affair?

Lav: On being informed that a pair of shoes, bonnet, and a bundle was lying in the field near the house where I live, I went to the place and found the things lying near the pit, on dragging which I found the body. At a short distance I saw some blood in a heap, and a train following towards the pit for 14 or 15 yards. I could discern the impression of a man and a woman's feet in the next field: as if they had been running, struggling, and walking together. The Prisoner's and the deceased's shoes corresponded with the footsteps.

Rey: How do you know they were the Prisoner's footmarks?
Lav: Prisoner's shoes are right and left, and on the right and left side of the shoes are nails; on the right shoe there were two nails out, and the impression in the field was the same. If it was not the Prisoner, it was someone he had lent the shoes to, and returned them again.
Rey: In what situation did you find the deceased in the water?
Lav: Her head was close to the bank, and the feet from it; the face was upwards, and from the quantity of the slough, 'twas impossible she could change her position during the time she was in the water.
Rey: You may retire.
Par: Mr Webb?
Rey: What do you know concerning the Prisoner and the deceased?
Webb: On the morning of the 30th of May last, between 6 and 7 o'clock, I was informed that Maria Ashfield was found murdered. On my arrival at the place, the body had just been dragged out of the pit. I found some marks on the arms of the deceased, as if they had been violently pressed.
Rey: Did you examine the footsteps?
Webb: Yes, they exactly corresponded with the deceased and the Prisoner's shoes.
Rey: That is sufficient, Sir.
Par: Mr Bolus?
Bolus: Being a Surgeon I was sent for on the 30th of May to examine the body of the deceased who was found in a pit of water. On a strict examination, I found there were no wounds inflicted which could occasion her death. She appeared to have been violated. Up to this period I do not believe she had ever had connexion with a man.
Rey: Do you think she came to her death by drowning?
Bolus: The deceased was not dead when first thrown into the pit; but from the exceeding quantity of blood she had lost, I do not think she could possibly have survived.
Rey: Then you mean to say she was thrown into the pit?
Bolus: I do, positively, say so; but by whom I do not know.
Rey: You may retire.
Par: Daniel Tapster?
Rey: Well, what do you know, Sir?
Tapster: Hearing of the murder of Maria Ashfield I went to the Prisoner at his father's house, and desired him to come with me, as he was the last person seen in her company.
Rey: Did the Prisoner seem alarm'd when you told him of the murder?
Tap: Yes; but turned the discourse to farming; I asked him why he did not come past our house in the morning when he left Maria Ashfield, but he made no answer.
Rey: You may withdraw.
Par: The last witness I shall call for the Crown is Jacob Turnout.
Rey: Speak what you know of this affair.
Jacob: I went to apprehend the Prisoner on the 30th of May; I searched him, and found his linen in a very foul state.
Rey: Did Prisoner acknowledge before you search'd him that he had connexion with the deceased?
Jac: Yes, he did.
Quibble [*aside*]*:* What a rascal is this; with what impudence he tells a lie!
Par: Mind what you say; recollect you are on oath; the linen of the Prisoner was given to your charge – where is it?
Jac: I don't know.
Rey: You have no right to ask him any question.
Justice Mittimus: I will myself ask the question: what has become of the prisoner's linen?
Jac: I don't know. So many had it in their hands that at last it was lost.
Jus: I think you very remiss in you duty. Do you recollect any of the conversation that pass'd between you and the prisoner?
Jac: I cannot call to mind that we had any conversation concerning the deceased at all.
Jus: You may retire. Counsellor Reynard, you may now bring forward the evidence for the Prisoner.
Rey: My Lord, the first evidence I shall bring forward is William Cowherd.
Cowherd: Here!
Par: Well, who are you?
Cow: I'm a milkman; and on the morning of the 30th of May, I left home at half past three o'clock, and about half past four I saw the Prisoner by the side of the Navigation.

Par: How far might that be from where the deceased was found?
Cow: About three miles and a half.
Par: How did you know it was half past four when you saw the prisoner? Have you a watch?
Cow: No, but I ax'd a man.
Par: Remember you are on oath. You positively swear that you saw the Prisoner on the 29th of May at half past four in the morning.
Cow: No, I said on the 30th.
Quibble [*aside*]*:* This fellow's got his lesson well!
Par: You may go back.
Rey: Peter Clodpole?
Par: Who are you, Sir?
Clodpole [*bows to the court*]*:* My name's Clodpole, I was a farmer and now I be a miller.
Par: Do you recollect seeing the Prisoner on the 29th or 30th of May last?
Clod: I do; it was on the 30th of May at half past four in the morning; I was coming from the mill.
Par: How did you know it was half past four?
Clod: I ax'd.
Par: What were your motives?
Clod: I don't know; 'cause I did, that's all.
Quibble [*aside*]*:* Blockhead! he'll ruin all!
Par: You say that on the 29th you saw the Prisoner at half past four in the morning?
Clod: No, I didn't say so; let me see . . . it was on the 30th.
Par: How far was it from where you saw the Prisoner to the pit?
Clod: About three miles and a half.
Par: You may retire.
Rey: Honest miller, we thank you for your evidence.
Clod: Yo' be mighty welcome, Sir. [*retires*]
Rey: Robin Ploughshare?
Par: Well, and who are you?
Ploughshare: I be Robin Ploughshare; I be foreman to farmer Holder.
Par: Do you recollect seeing the Prisoner towards the latter end of May?
Plough: Aye! I saw him about half past four o'clock in the morning of the 30th of May.
Par: Are you sure it was half past four in the morning?
Plough: Yes; I'd ask'd Mr Holder.
Par: What were your motives for asking?
Plough: I wanted to fetch the cows.
Par: From the place where the deceased was found to that where you saw the Prisoner, how far do you think that might be?
Plough: About three miles and a half.
Par: That will do.
Rey: My Lord, I could bring forward several other respectable witnesses to prove that the Prisoner was so far distant from the place at half past four, and between that and five o'clock on the morning the murder was committed, that it would have been impossible for him to have come from the pit in so short a time.
Sir Mittimus: Gentlemen of the Jury – You have heard a fair and candid examination of the evidences for and against the Prisoner, and are now required to give your verdict. You must lay aside all that you may have heard concerning this affair, out of this place, and give your verdict according to the evidence you have heard here. Hannah Fox's deposition goes no farther than to prove that she was with her at four o'clock on the morning the murder was committed. There is one thing to be observed – she says she saw no stains on her clothes. I believe, myself, the connexion must have taken place after she left her friend's. The evidence of Lavender is more particular: that by the position she was found in, it would be impossible for the deceased to have thrown herself into the water. You are to give your opinion, whether it was or was not the Prisoner who threw the deceased into the pit. If the evidences for the Prisoner are true, you must acquit him. Mind, Gentlemen, I say if they have spoken the truth, relating to the time when she was with her friend, and the time the evidences saw the Prisoner, he could not have perpetrated the murder and be that distance from the place. Here, Gentlemen, you must judge for yourselves, and in doing so I sincerely hope you will only attend to the facts which have been here adduced, and bring in your verdict to the best of your belief; but should a doubt arise, the Prisoner must have the benefit of it, and if you do err, let it be on the side of mercy.

The Jury after a few moments consultation return their verdict]

Foreman: Not Guilty.

Young Thorntree bows to the court]

Sir Mittimus [*addressing himself to the Prisoner*]*:* You are now acquitted by a Jury of your country of the heinous crime laid to your charge. Young man, let me advise you to refrain from those ill habits and lustful passions to which it is evident your mind is too prone. I cannot pass over your conduct in this affair without some little censure – it appears evident that you used every means within your power to accomplish your views of seduction on the unfortunate young woman. I sincerely hope, however, this circumstance will operate as a warning to you in future – you may now retire.

Thorntree again bows, and exits, attended by the Turnkey, Quibble, etc., etc.]

Sir Mittimus: Gentlemen of the Jury, I thank you for the unity you have displayed, and the impartiality of your conduct throughout the trial; and I trust that in bringing your verdict *Not Guilty,* you have done your duty to God and your country. [*exeunt*

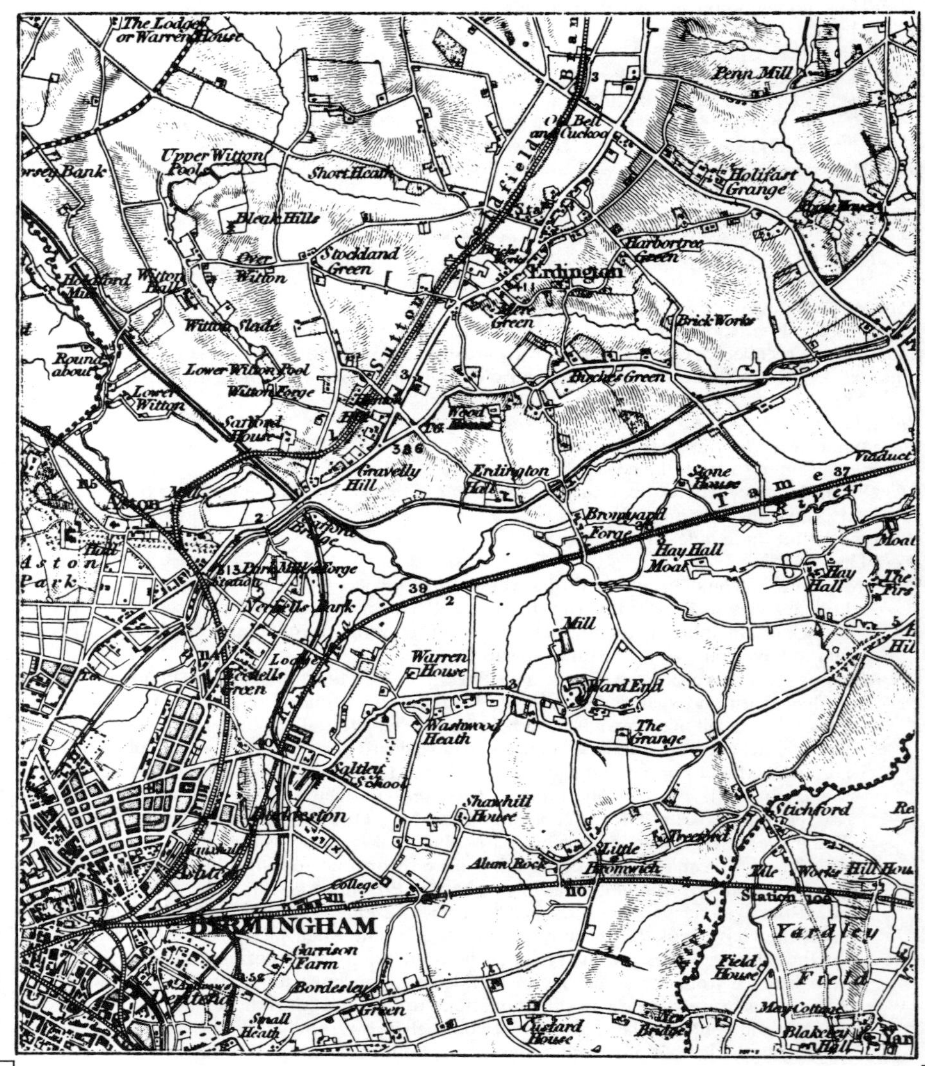

ACT III Scene 3
A Church-Yard

In which is seen a white marble monument with the following inscription]

Sacred
to the Memory of
Maria Ashfield
whose Prudence and Virtue rendered her
universally belov'd and respected,
by all who knew her.

Yet by a Monster in human form, fell victim
to Cruelty and Lust.

This monument was erected by her Friends
to perpetuate the fatal Effects
of Inordinate Passions.

On the right hand side of the monument are five young men, and on the left are five young women with flowers in their hands, dress'd suitable to the occasion. Music plays a solemn dirge during which a young man and woman go to the monument, kneel, and repeat: "Peace to her shade", *and retire to their respective places. This is done by the whole. A Chorus of Spirits is heard. The young men and women kneel on one knee*]

CHORUS

Cease, cease, fond youths and maids those tears
Maria sleeps not here;
Rewarded for her Love and Truth,
Now she reigns above your sphere.

Lo! we clear your mortal sight,
And celestial scenes display:
Clad in Robes of virgin light,
She shines in bright Eternal Day.

During the symphony of the first verse, Maria is seen to descend in radiant clouds; a crown of gold on her head, in her right hand an harp, and the fore finger of her left hand pointing towards Heaven. The music for a moment ceases; a voice from the clouds is heard: "Mortals arise!" *They rise.* "Behold the Reward of Virtue! Be silent and Adore!" *The chorus is then sung to the end, after which Maria ascends. The Music dies away at a distance. The young men and women gradually sink on one knee. The curtain slowly falls*]

F I N I S

Murder by Proxy

The Shooting of GAIL KINCHIN by Detective-Constable GERALD RICHARDS in the early morning of Thursday June the 12th 1980 at 4 Deelands Road, Rubery, Birmingham and the Trial for her Murder, and Conviction for her Manslaughter of DAVID PAGETT

Wives, mistresses and girl-friends have always featured at the top of any list of likely murder victims, and while rivalry still supports sexual role play, bleakly unaffected by a new liberalism, it is certain to stay that way. By and large, domestic killings are squalid, uninspired crimes; commonly the pathetic conclusion to years of less lethal violence.

Such was the death of Gail Kinchin, and the conviction of David Pagett for her killing. The difference was, Pagett didn't kill his mistress; she and her unborn child were shot by a policeman.

The affair started when Gail was only 15 years old and living with her mother Josie and step-father Eric Wood in Brandwood Park Road, King's Heath, Birmingham; in a council flat across the way David Pagett lived with his common-law wife Sheila. Thirty-one-year-old Pagett was a mechanic who earned his living mending washing machines, supplementing bad patches with a little petty crime; he was a flashy braggart, much given to the pleasures of women and drink. Young Gail used to baby-sit for the Pagetts while they went out on the town, and it was when he returned, full of drink, that he began to notice that maybe his babysitter was more than just the kid over the road. And youngsters being what they are, Gail responded to the unaccustomed flattery from an older person, and sat entranced by Pagett's heavily embroidered tales of heroism with the Green Jackets in Northern Ireland. At once a bond grew between them that was to destroy their two families and ultimately themselves. First, Sheila came home unexpectedly early one day and found her 'husband' on the bed with Gail; Sheila moved out, Gail moved in, so causing great emotional grief to her parents. Mrs Wood was heard to complain to neighbours: "When kids reach the age of sixteen, they think they know it all!"

So far, this story is not as unfamiliar as we might like to think; it is being told the world over, every day; grubby perhaps, but not criminal. What made this relationship so vulnerable was David Pagett himself. Already a man known to be a bully, Pagett now began to be driven by the blind belligerence that came with an increase in his need for alcohol, and his behaviour towards Gail deteriorated into violence and paranoia. Gail would be locked up in the flat for days on end while he roamed from pub to club, from girlfriend to girlfriend, coming home only for more sex and to give Gail another cautionary beating.

Inevitably, Gail became pregnant, and equally predictably, Pagett made her condition the excuse for still further indignities – often forcing her to spend nights sleeping on the draughty floor.

The unhappy girl had tried in a half-hearted way to leave several times, but by now her self-confidence had been destroyed, her spirit broken, and she allowed herself to be dragged back – usually physically – to face punishment and further degradation. On the last occasion the physical savagery was accompanied by Pagett's very believable threats against her mother's life.

But of such desperation are desperate means born, and if for no other reason than the safety of her unborn child, Gail Kinchin and her mother secretly plotted the only way they knew to rid themselves of Pagett's constant threat.

Gail Kinchin

He was sitting behind the wheel of a stolen car when police picked him up; they had been acting on an anonymous telephone call! But then the Woods made a foolish, if understandable, mistake.

Instead of waiting for Pagett's case to come to court at the end of the month, and take advantage of his almost certain imprisonment, Gail fled the flat on the afternoon of June 11th, 1980, and travelling via her mother's home, sought refuge in the house of a friend in Masefield Square, in the Northfield district.

Pagett's response was predictably brutal. Loading himself, a double-barrelled shotgun, and a pocketful of cartridges into his car, he raced across town to the home of Gail's parents, smashed his way into the house and raised his gun. In fear for his own and his wife's life at the hands of this lunatic, Eric Wood made a dash for the front door and out into the night to summon the police. It was the burning pain in his back and legs that cut his dash for freedom short as a shower of lead shot from the barrel of Pagett's gun, leaving the badly injured man to crawl to safety in a neighbouring house.

Pagett now grabbed Josie Wood by the hair and dragged her screaming, the gun to her head, into his car. Realising she was in the clutches of a madman who, for all she knew had just blasted her husband to death, it is no surprise that Mrs Wood was co-operative; there was only one thing that her captor wanted – an address!

When he reached the 'safe house' in Masefield Square, the crazed gunman grabbed Gail and kicked and punched her down the steps and into the car beside her terrified mother; now driving madly back across Birmingham to his own flat, the shotgun in readiness by his side.

By this time neighbours had alerted police to the attempted murder of Eric Wood and the abduction at gunpoint of Mrs Wood and her daughter, and a series of road blocks had been set up in the area. It was while Pagett was negotiating one of these – with his gun – that Josie Wood, with immense courage, managed to flee the car; but blind with anger and satisfied that he still had one captive, Pagett sped on seeming not to be concerned. He had Gail. He was going to teach her a lesson she would never forget!

When he reached the first-floor flat, David Pagett bolted the doors as if for a siege. And siege was what the police were preparing for at the same time, for armed police officers were at that moment surrounding the block. Inside the building were Detective Sergeant Thomas Sartain and Detective Constable Gerald Richards, both carrying police issue Smith and Wessons.

It was just after 2.15 on the morning of June the 12th when the detectives had positioned themselves outside Pagett's front door; the tense atmosphere was made more acute by the darkness imposed by the broken hall lights. Suddenly there was a rattling of locks and a dim silhouette appeared framed in the light from Pagett's doorway; in one arm he cradled the lethal shotgun, the other held Gail tightly in front of him – a human shield. Clearly feeling secure enough from the law, Pagett refused all opportunities to surrender, indeed, he took advantage of his position to force the two officers back up the stairs towards the second floor. To their horror the policemen found themselves trapped – behind was a solid wall, in front a madman with a shotgun and a pregnant hostage. Their only defence – training, experience, and a pair of .38 revolvers.

The shotgun approached; the terrified girl cried for help; there was a momentary scuffle in the darkness below them, then with a deafening roar the shotgun exploded in a flash of fire. Miraculously the deadly spray missed the crouching officers, and with the only reaction they could possibly have shown – self-preservation – Richards and Sartain returned fire; six rounds punched into the dark, followed by an eerie silence that rang in their ears. Still the shadow on the stairs inched forward; but obviously panicked, Pagett loosed the other barrel of his weapon, and with a faltering aim shot high into the ceiling of the stairway. Once again the officers retaliated. This time a body crumpled and fell. Gail lay bleeding on the floor, her unborn child killed instantly by a bullet, its mother was to die before the month was out from two others. Pagett was unmarked, and it was only being disarmed before he could reload that prevented him from continuing the bloody battle.

At his trial in Birmingham's Crown Court, David Pagett at least had what satisfaction could be drawn from creating legal history. To sustain a murder charge against him, the prosecution had to establish that Pagett had used the girl as a shield knowing that when he first fired the shotgun at the police officers they were likely to shoot back and possibly kill, or maim, his hostage.

On the two kidnap charges, on the charges

of the attempted murder of Eric Wood and the policemen, the jury found David Pagett guilty; they also convicted him of a lesser charge of possession of a shotgun with intent to endanger life. But on the murder charge they were in disagreement, eventually settling for a verdict of guilty of manslaughter. When sentencing Pagett to seven concurrent twelve-year terms of imprisonment, Mr Justice Park observed: "The use of a hostage by a desperate armed man to achieve safety for himself – and by that use to cause the death of the hostage – is a very grave offence, falling only just short of murder..."

Money in the Bank

The Murder of Mrs ELIZA JANE WORTON by a Person or Persons Unknown in February 1936 by the Birmingham Canal near Tipton and the Trial and Acquittal of FREDERICK WILLIAM OAKLEY

The trial of Frederick William Oakley at Stafford Assizes once again brought to the foreground the recurrent debate on the value of circumstantial evidence versus eyewitness evidence. The problem was not a new one then; almost a century before, in 1850, in Cambridge, Massachusetts, Chief Justice Lemuel Shaw put the question in the case of Professor John White Webster, accused of the murder of Dr George Parkman: "Suppose no person was present on the occasion of death," his lordship posed, "is it wholly unsusceptible of legal proof?" He continued: "Experience has shown that circumstatial evidence may be offered in such a case; that is, a body of facts may be proved of so conclusive a character as to warrant a firm belief of the fact, quite as strong and certain as that on which discreet men are accustomed to act in relation to their most important concerns..."

Murder, of course, may, or should, be taken as a separate category; for though all criminals hope to go unseen, privacy is the very integrity of murder. Given also that a large proportion of murders are committed within the walls of the family home, it is unsurprising that there are few independent eyewitnesses. (It is interestng to reflect that in those days when felons were pardoned for turning "King's evidence", there was a high proportion of accomplices presenting the court with eye-witness accounts.) And so it is in cases of murder that circumstantial evidence plays its most important role. And in none more so than the Oakley case.

Frederick Oakley was a 37-year-old lorry driver who stood accused of the murder of Mrs Eliza Jane Worton, a sailors's wife. The victim's body had been recovered from the Birmingham Canal at Cox's Bridge, at Tipton, and medical evidence was to show that though she had been savagely battered about the head with a heavy blunt instrument – probably a spanner – Mrs Worton had survived some 15 minutes in the water before drowning.

The weight of circumstantial evidence arrayed against Oakley was formidable; but so, too, was the man in whose hands Oakley's defence was entrusted: Mr Norman (later Lord) Birkett, one of the greatest defenders in the history of the Courts.

Oakley, it was stated, drove a lorry for his elder brother, and one of his regular points of delivery was Gadd's Forge, which is where he met Mrs Worton, one of their employees. It had become his habit to give her a lift home on his return journey. Oakley had seen her on the day of the murder, he didn't deny that; but he swore that they parted company at two o'clock in the afternoon, more than eight hours before Eliza Worton's body hit the murky water of the Birmingham Canal.

Two boys testified that they had seen Frederick Oakley sitting in the cab of his lorry – it had 'Oakley Bros.' painted on the side – at ten o'clock. They 'knew' it was Oakley despite only being able to describe the hat he was wearing – "with a shiny peak like a chauffeur's," They knew it was ten o'clock because a local factory had blown its whistle for the late shift. However, according to Mrs Oakley (Frederick's wife), and Mrs Oakley (Frederick's mother), he was at home when they noticed the clock indicating ten minutes past ten.

Routine forensic examination of the prisoner's clothing revealed small, but in the circumstances incriminating, blood spots on his shirt cuffs, and on the seat and knees of his trousers. There was also a small blood smear on the side of his lorry.

This, then, was the evidence which Birkett had to challenge at that Summer Assize of 1936. And never has a defence counsel conducted himself more admirably, or more successfully.

On the matter of Oakley's presence or not on Cox's Bridge at ten o'clock on the night in question, identification rested solely on the description of the hat seen by the two boys; which was a lucky thing for Norman Birkett – he was able to hold up before the jury Frederick Oakley's *actual* hat, a greasy, shapeless old cap in brown with an indistinct pattern. "Look at it," he urged the jury. "This is Oakley's cap. There may be confusion in this world, and there will be confusion till the end of time. But there can be no confusion between this and a shiny peak."

Birkett was equally emphatic that the jury could not safely convict on the evidence of the bloodstains. They were, experts admitted, quite consistent with Oakley's frequent handling of loads of bricks and sharp ashes, and the inevitable small cuts and abrasions to his hands being wiped on his working clothes. It was probable that the blood smear on the side of the lorry had the same origin. But Birkett went further: the medical evidence, he reminded the court, proved that the woman would have bled profusely from her head wounds; this being so, and the body being carried from the lorry to the canal – as suggested by the prosecution re-creation of the crime – why was there no blood in the cab of the lorry? Why was there no obvious staining of the prisoner's clothing?

Oakley made a good impression as a witness, and during the three hours for which he was cross-examined, his demeanour was both candid and convincing. In one of his most memorable speeches to a jury, Norman Birkett addressed them on the subject of his client's character: "... The prisoner has been happily married for fourteen years. He is a loving husband and father, and a man with a good character upon which he can now draw as a man with a credit balance at the bank. That is the man you have to deal with. A man of good character, who, in the twinkling of an eye, according to the prosecution, is turned into a brutal murderer."

The jury were clearly impressed, both by Oakley and his champion, because they returned a verdict of "Not Guilty". And hardly had the words left the foreman's lips when there was such a clamour of approbation in the court, that proceedings were momentarily interrupted; it was clearly a most popular acquittal.

As Seen on the Radio

The Murder of CHARLES WILLIAM FOX by STANLEY ERIC HOBDAY in August 1933 at Moor Street, West Bromwich

It is a never-ending source of amazement how very petty some petty crooks are; astonishing for how little they are prepared to risk reputation and freedom. And when small-minded criminality develops into bloody murder, for how remarkably little reward some killers are prepared to risk their very lives.

On a warm Sunday night in August, 1933,

the still darkness that enveloped Moor Street, West Bromwich, was interrupted by the tinkle of breaking glass. Mrs Fox snapped awake. Convinced she had not been dreaming, she nudged the man who lay asleep beside her: "Charlie! Charlie!" she whispered urgently, "wake up; somebody's broken in; I heard him break the glass. Charlie!" Charlie Fox grunted bad-temperedly under his breath and climbed out from beneath the blankets. Lighting a candle, he crept bare-foot across the room clad only in his nightwear – a vest and underpants – to fulfil his role as 'man the protector'.

Charlie is down in the hallway now, with his wife looking on from the top landing, trying to follow him among the flickering shadows. Going into the sitting-room; suddenly the candle goes out, blown by the draught from an open window. The shadows expand to fill the pre-dawn darkness.

"Charlie; come back up Charlie." A scuffling; a moan. Charles Fox stumbling back up the stairs, tottering through the bedroom doorway... slumping onto the floor without ever uttering another sound.

His wife is on her knees clasping him; she feels the warm, sticky wetness of his blood. In the growing light of dawn she can just see the handle of the knife protruding from his back.

By the time she had stopped screaming, the police had already arrived, alerted by Harold Taylor, a printer just off the night shift, who had responded to Mrs Fox's cry for help.

But Mr and Mrs Fox had not been the only victims of a break-in in that district of West Bromwich on that night in August; to say the unluckiest would be to trivialize their loss, but they were not the only ones.

Bromford Lane is not far from Moor Street, and it is the street in which a man named Newton kept a butcher's shop; and on that Sunday night Mr Newton had had an uninvited house guest. To his – and the police's – astonishment he had found a bowl of soapy water where an intruder had clearly helped himself to a wash; and Newton's own razor – used but uncleaned – floating in the bowl. A work-basket had been taken from the cupboard and a needle threaded apparently to do some running repairs. The butcher had also been relieved of a few scraps of cash, and in a final audacious move, the thief had helped himself to breakfast – a pint of milk!

They say that all criminals, great or small, make one mistake, have one blind-spot. Stanley Eric Hobday was a small criminal in more than his ambition, he was also described by one witness as "an overgrown dwarf". He was also very stupid, because around his breakfast pinta he had left a perfect set of fingerprints. It took Detective Chief Superintendent Fred Cherril of Scotland Yard's Fingerprint Bureau a matter of minutes to identify the thief... and probably the murderer.

Wise in hindsight, Eric Hobday had made himself scarce.

The result was that an unfamiliar announcement was broadcast by the BBC. For the first time in its history, the radio network was carrying the description of a criminal – "wanted by the police in connection with a murder."

Hobday was by this time heading north in a car stolen from near the Bromford Lane robbery; he had got as far as High Leigh in Cheshire when what can only be described as a trick of fate caused the vehicle to leave the road, turn a complete somersault, and land back on four wheels again – much to the astonishment and terror of an Irish labourer who had seen the whole incredible scene unfold before him. Leaving his battered suitcase inside the car, Hobday struck north again, by the more reliable means of his feet. Outside Carlisle he was jostled in a country lane by a herd of dairy cows on their way to the milk-shed.

'Watty' Bowman, the cowman, was the proud owner of a wireless set; an avid listener to the BBC; and as he passed Eric Hobday, he realized he had seen him before. He had seen him on the radio! But cows being cows, and milking time being important as it is to them, it was a couple of hours before Bowman could report back to the farmer about the stranger in the lane.

Within a short time of his receiving the alert from Watty's employer, Police Constable Elder of the Cumberland Constabulary was face to face with the diminutive fugitive from justice. No match for the well-rounded constable Hobday decided, in fiction parlance, to go quietly.

Hobday's luggage had arrived ahead of him; and when he was brought before the detectives back at West Bromwich, his suitcase, recently rescued from the abandoned escape car, was in front of him on the interview-room table.

"Does this case belong to you?"
"Yes. I hid it in some ferns in a place called Haypit's Wood when I had to leave Warstone Fields." (Hobday had been sleeping under canvas in the Fields during the summer, but had been moved on by the owner.)
"Can you describe the contents?"
Yes, he could. A small tent, assorted camping gear, some items of clothing, and a sheath-knife. The contents were unpacked one-by-one in Hobday's presence – tent, camping gear, clothing... but no sheath-knife! That had been left with Charles Fox.

Despite further extensive questioning, Eric Hobday obstinately stuck to his story that he had not seen the suitcase since it was abandoned in Haypit's Wood; he could only suggest that it was stolen from there. In fact, he added, losing it had been a damned nuisance, forcing him to sleep rough, in the open, without a change of clothing.

No mention of the car yet; the Jowett in which the suitcase had been found. That was being given a thorough investigation of its own. For it was not until the expert eyes of Fred Cherrill and his team had found Hobday's fingerprint on the starting handle that he could be proved to have been in it. Once again, a couple of fingerprints had set a man on the narrow path to the scaffold.

The trial was an unremarkable event. It opened in November, 1933, at the Stafford Assizes, under the watchful eyes of Mr Justice Talbot. A motive was established for the murder – if it can be dignified by the term 'motive'. Charles Fox had been supplementing his income as a metal-cutter by working as a doorstep collector for the National Clothing Company; he made his round on Saturdays, and on the day before his death his takings amounted to 14 shillings. It turned out to be the price of his life!

Apart from Chief Superintendent Cherrill's expert testimony on the fingerprint evidence, the remainder of the prosecution case was taken up with scientific proof of Hobday's presence at the two scenes of crime.

For instance: Hobday had been seen by a fellow camper on Warstone Fields brandishing a sheath-knife identical to that used to kill Charles Fox; for instance, the sheath of that knife that had been found in the gutter between Moor Street and the butcher's shop on the night of the murder. Then there was the stubble so carelessly left on Mr Newton's razor – it matched Hobday's. The darning thread in Newton's work-basket matched a mend in Eric Hobday's jacket.

Wisely, Sir Reginald Coventry KC, acting for Hobday, did not call him to the witness stand. "In my submission," he told the jury, "the case for the Crown has not been proved. Think it over, gentlemen," he continued, "is it conceivable that any man, woman, or boy, after foully murdering another human being, and with his hands still bearing the stain of blood, could calmly go off to Mr Newton's house and commit a burglary, sit down and shave himself, his nerves so calm that he could thread a needle and sit down and mend his clothes, and then go off and steal a car..."

The jury obviously felt that it was perfectly conceivable; indeed, that it was just what Eric Hobday *had* done.

The following month, Stanley Eric Hobday featured in Thomas Pierrepoint's diary: "Hobday: 8 am, Winson Green Prison, Birmingham."

Pierrepoint was the public hangman.

APPENDIX ONE
Gaol Fever

This malignant distemper was fatal and frequent in old Newgate and other county jails in different parts of England.

The Assize held at Oxford in the year 1577, called the Black Assize was a dreadful instance of the deadly effects of the gaol fever [Typhus]. The judges, jury, nay, in fact every person, except the prisoners, women and children, in court were killed by a foul air, which at first was thought to have arisen out of the bowels of the earth; but that great philosopher, Lord Bacon, proved it to have come from the prisoners taken out of a noisome jail and brought into court to take their trials; and they alone, inhaling the foul air, were not injured by it. Three hundred, more or less succumbed.

In the year 1730, the Lord Chief Baron Pengelly, with several of his officers and servants; Sir James Sheppard, Serjeant-at-Law; John Pigot, Esq., High Sheriff for Somersetshire, died at Blandford, on the Western Circuit of the Lent Assizes, from the infected stench brought with the prisoners from Ilchester Jail to their trials at Taunton, in which town the infection afterwards spread and carried off some hundred persons.

In 1754 and 1755, this distemper prevailed in Newgate to a degree which carried off more than one-fifth of the prisoners.

Others attributed the cause of this sudden mortality at Oxford to witchcraft, the people in those times being very superstitious. In Webster's *Display of Witchcraft,* we find the following account of the Black Assizes: "The 4th and 5th days of July, 1559, were holden the assizes at Oxford, where was arraigned the condemned, one Rowland Jenkes, for his seditious tongue, at which time there arose such a damp, that almost all were smothered. Very few escaped that were not taken at that instant. The jurors died presently – shortly after died Sir Robert Bell, Lord Chief Baron, Sir Robert De Olie, Sir William Babington, and other Gentlemen. There died at Oxford 300 persons, and sickened there, but died in other places, 200 and odd, from the 6th of July to the 12th of August, after which day died not one of that sickness, for one of them infected not another, nor any one woman or child died thereof... Just at the conjucture of time when Jenkes was condemned, there being none before, and so it could not be a prison infection; for that would have manifested itself by smell or operating sooner. But to take away all scruple, and to assign the true cause, it was thus: it fortuned that a manuscript fell into my hands, collected by an ancient gentleman of York, who was a great observer and gatherer of strange things and facts, who lived about the time of this accident happening at Oxford, wherein it is related thus: 'That Rowland Jenkes, being imprisoned for treasonable words, spoken against the Queen [Elizabeth I], and being a popish recusant, had, notwithstanding, during the time of his restraint, liberty to walk some time abroad with a keeper; and that one day he came to an apothecary, and showed him a receipt [ie. recipe] which he desired him to make up; but the apothecary, upon view of it, told him that it was a strong and dangerous receipt, and required some time to prepare it; but also asked him to what use he would apply it. He answered, to kill the rats, that, since his imprisonment,

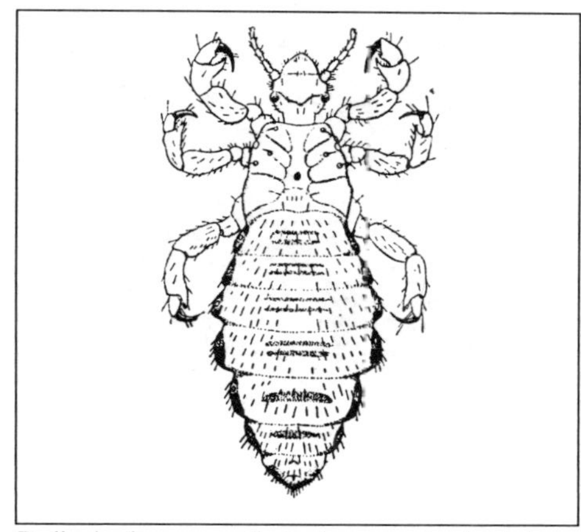

Pediculus humanus, *the typhus-carrying body louse*

spoiled his books. So being satisfied, he promised to make it ready. After a certain time he cometh to know if it were ready; but the apothecary said the ingredients were so hard to procure that he had not done it, and so gave him the receipt again, of which he had taken a copy, which mine author had there precisely written down, but did seem so horribly poisonous, that I cut it forth, lest it fall into the hands of wicked persons. But after, it seems, he had it prepared, and, against the day of his trial, had made a wick of it (for so is the word, that is, so fitted, that like a candle it might be fired) which, as soon as ever he was condemned, he lighted, having provided himself a tinder-box, and steel to strike fire. And whosoever should know the ingredients of that wick, or candle, and the manner of the composition, will easily be persuaded of the virulency and venomous effect of it.' "

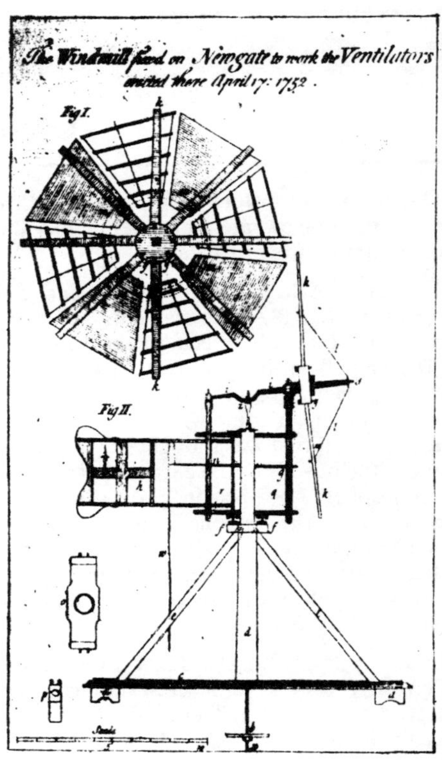

Sir Stephen Theodore Jansen, one of the most philanthropic magistrates of the City of London, took great interest on behalf of the regulation of prisons, and the amelioration of the miseries of the unfortunate prisoners. When Chamberlain of London, in the year 1767, he published a pamphlet addressed to the Lord Mayor, in the cause of gaol fevers. He was Sheriff of London in the year 1750, when the putrid fever, the consequence of filth and foul air, made such dreadful havoc in the Old Bailey Sessions.

A view of 'Old' Newgate showing the windmill installed as part of George Dance's improvements with a view to higher degrees of sanitation. In fact, several of the workmen engaged on connecting up the ventilation shafts died of the Fever.

Sir Theodore strongly recommended a plan similar to that of York Castle, which, he said, covered no less than two acres and a rood of ground, with great plenty of water and other conveniences. He warmly remonstrated against the spot then proposed for the rebuilding of Newgate. He said it did not occupy more than three-quarters of an acre, and that the number of convicts in that prison was more than treble those of York Castle.

In the year 1772 the assizes for the Summer Circuit were adjourned for Hampshire from the 17th of July to the 2nd of September, on account of an infectious distemper in Winchester Gaol. An expositor on this subject, who wrote under the signature of 'A Philanthropist', during that rage of gaol fever, says: "The public may be rather concerned than surprised, at the deplorable consequences of gaol distempers, and at the fatal instances of their contagion. Several judges, sheriffs, magistrates, juries, and whole courts of judicature, have been infected by those contagious diseases, which caused the loss of many valuable lives, particularly at the Old Bailey, and formerly at the assizes at Oxford, all owing to the horrid neglect of gaolers, and even of the sheriffs and magistrates, whose office it is to compel the gaolers, to the most rigorous repeated orders and attention to their duty, without the least indulgence or remission; as the gaolers are (some excepted) frequently low bred, mercenary and oppressive, barbarous fellows, who think of nothing but enriching themselves by the most cruel extortion; and who have less regard for the life of a poor prisoner than for the life of a brute.

The felons of this kingdom lie worse than dogs or swine, and are kept much more uncleanly than those animals are in kennels and sties, according to all accounts from clergymen, who are obliged to go to the gaols. From them I have been assured that the stench and nastiness are so nauseous, that the very atmosphere is pestiferous, and that no persons enter therein, without the risque of their health or lives, which prevents even many clergymen and physicians from going there, and assisting their sick and dying fellow-creatures; so that they live and die like brutes, even worse than many beasts, to the disgrace of human nature.

Every person endowed with the least principle of real humanity, and of true policy, must be affected with such barbarities, neglects, uncleanliness and dangers. A contagion of that kind may spread over a whole country and kingdom; the greatest precaution ought therefore to be taken in time.

The gaolers ought to be forced to have all the rooms sprinkled and fumigated with vinegar every day: for some one hundred prisoners, particularly criminals, are early killed by a sort of pestilence and vermin among them, occasioned by filth and nastiness, and a corrupted air.

All hospitals, prisons and workhouses, should have bathing-places, for the sake of cleanliness and health."

APPENDIX TWO

The Coward's Weapon: 3

OPIUM
(Laudanum, Morphine)

There is no drug so well known as a poison, and, at the same time so rarely used by the murderer, as opium and its derivatives. Whether this is due to the slow action of the poison or to the distinctive smell and symptoms, we cannot say, but the fact remains that the poisoner shuns it.

Opium is the juice of *Papaver somniferum,* the opium poppy. No more beautiful sight can be imagined than to see the whole countryside ablaze with purple and white poppies from which the valuable extract is obtained. The native cultivators guard their fields very carefully when they see that the flowers are about to fall. Then, as soon as the petals have been shed, leaving the familiar capsule containing the seeds, the time for reaping the harvest has come. Armed with a slender knife, wrapped round with cotton or string to within a quarter of an inch of the point, the ryot passes rapidly from plant to plant, making two little slits, one on each side of each capsule. The thick white juice of the poppy oozes out of the slits, and soon dries to a brownish, gummy matter on the side of the capsule. That evening the cultivator goes round again and scrapes the gum off the plants, making more slits for a fresh supply of juice to be ready the following morning. About six incisions in each capsule is as much as the plant can stand, and then it commences to die.

The sticky juice is collected and warmed, and then rolled up into balls which are covered with leaves; this product is crude opium. The refining is effected by means of mixing carefully with water and filtering, then drying the product and treating it with other solvents. It is then ready for conversion into the various forms under which we know it.

The poisoner (and the suicide) at one time principally used Laudanum, which is a tincture of opium, or the purified drug dissolved in spirits, and more recently, Morphine, the alkaloid which gives to opium most of its power.

The characteristics of opium poisoning are as follows: The patient gets drowsy, and is often afflicted by nausea. The face is sometimes swollen and highly coloured, while the pupils of the eyes are contracted, and do not dilate in the dark. Gradually the patient becomes unconscious, as a man who is intoxicated with alcohol. The skin may be cold and clammy, yet bathed in profuse perspiration, although the victim complains of feeling cold. Then unconsciousness sets in, and the muscles get flabby and relaxed in most cases, though occasionally there may be spasmodic contractions. The breathing is slow and noisy, the pulse low. As a rule, there is a strong smell of laudanum if that drug has been taken, but if the victim is suffering from an overdose of morphine there is no smell.

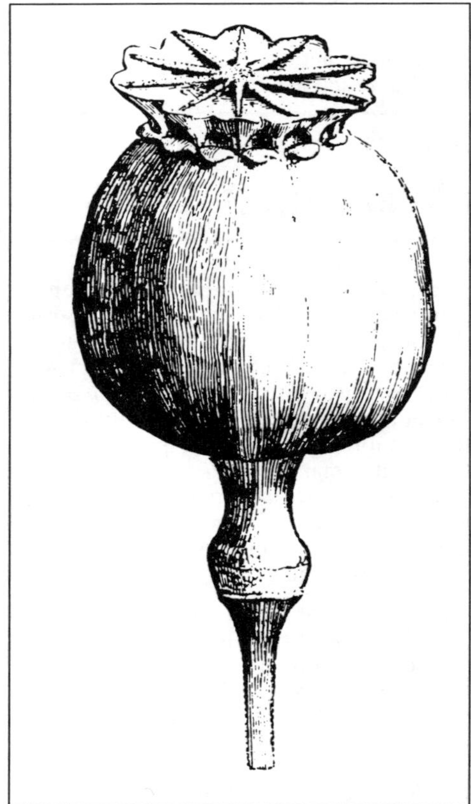

Papaver somniferum: *the Opium Poppy*

The symptoms of morphine poisoning are precisely similar to those of laudanum (with the exception of the lack of smell). Morphine is a fine white crystalline substance, and as little as one grain has been known to be fatal.

ANTIMONY

Like Arsenic [see *Murder Club Guide No. 1*], Antimony is one of the historic poisons. The early Greek and Roman physicians made little cups of the silver-like metal which they sold to their patients as permanent emetic cups. The poisonous properties of antimony were really discovered accidentally. Under the original name of stibium, it was largely used by Egyptian beauties to darken their eyelids and eyebrows; one of the princesses of the house of Usr-maat-Ra was apparently given to experimenting, and selected one of her handmaids to try the effect of a dose of stibium. Needless to say, the maid did not survive the ordeal, and from then, it is said, dates the use of antimony as a poison.

Antimony is found in the metallic state, mixed with arsenic and silver, in nature; but as a rule it is separated from the sulphide which occurs more abundantly than the actual metal. For years, the great difficulty in purifying antimony was getting rid of the arsenic with which it is usually associated.

The poisoner commonly obtains antimony as a tartar emetic, or antimony tartrate, a white powder which leaves a strong taste of metal in the mouth. In doses of more than a grain at a time it is a strong emetic, and for that reason may not have a poisonous effect, being rejected before it has had time to exhibit its lethal properties. Where, however, a deadly dose has been retained, the patient exhibits all the symptoms of poisoning with a strong irritant. There is great heat and burning in the throat, with difficulty in swallowing. This is followed by a violent pain in the region of the stomach, incessant vomiting and purging, faintness and extreme depression. The patient rapidly collapses, though there may be a long period of consciousness, accompanied by cramp. There is usually a premonition of death and a fear of approaching dissolution. Death results either from exhaustion or from gastroenteritis set up by the drug. It is, in short, a most painful death. The chances of survival in cases of antimony poisoning are few, for the irritant nature of the poison is such that the effects of the dose are usually fatal.

So much for the poison when administered in large doses. From the virulence of the symptoms, and the distinctive taste of antimony, it will be seen that the deadly drug is very easily recognised, and for that reason not thought much of by the older poisoners, who preferred a medium which was slower in its operation, and none the less sure. However, science has shown us that antimony, unlike most poisons, is far more deadly when administered in repeated small quantities, than when one large dose is given, and by regulating the doses the victim can be killed without presenting any symptoms incompatible with ordinary disease of the stomach. Thus was it that the infamous Dr Pritchard killed his wife [see *Murder Club Guide No. 8*].

LAUREL WATER

To discourage the attentions of grazing animals certain plants have developed a source of natural cyanide – this is commonly found in the stones of fruiting trees like cherry, plum, and peach, but can also be detected in the pips of apples and pears; more significant quantities are found as a constituent of the leaves of the laurel and cherry laurel. In the human body no worse symptoms than mild heart palpitations accompanied by a headache will be experienced from ingesting a moderate amount of the natural substance; however, it was early discovered in the Middle East that distilation by evaporation from laurel-water resulted in a lethal concentration of the poison.

When crushed, the laurel leaves give off hydrocyanic acid as they ferment, and it was once common for butterfly collectors to use them in their 'killing bottles'. Though the "sweet, sickly smell of almonds" so beloved of detective fiction writers is a great exaggeration, one of the common features of poisoning by the cyanides is the faint odour of bitter almond on the breath or in the stomach. Other cyanide compounds bear different names, like prussic acid, oil of bitter almonds, and Scheele's acid.

As poisons the cyanides are as brutal as they are lethal – 50 milligrams being sufficient to cause death within five minutes by an inhibition of the blood's capacity to absorb oxygen.

One of the earliest recorded misuses of concentrated laurel-water was the killing by Livia of her elderly husband Augustus in August of the year AD 14. The murder was effected by soaking the old man's figs in the poison.

In his *Lives of the Caesars*, Suetonius attributes Augustus's death to a natural bodily disorder, but gives the following account of a characteristically Roman death omen:

> His death, and his deification after death, were pre-known by unmistakable signs. As he was bringing the lustrum [a sacrifice of purification made every five years] to a close in the Campus Martius before a great concourse of people, an eagle was seen to fly several times around him, and then flying across to the temple to perch above the first letter of Agrippa's name. Observing this, Augustus bade Tiberius to recite the vows for the next five years... At the same time the first letter of his name [Caesar] was burned from the inscription on one of his statues by a flash of lightning; the interpretation of this was that he would live only a further one hundred days ['C' is the Roman numeral for 100], and that he would be elevated to the rank of a god because the remaining letters 'aesar' form the Etruscan word for god...
>
> When he had begun the journey, he went as far as Astura and from there, against his usual habit, took a ship at night, and thus contracted an illness beginning with diarrhoea... Presently he crossed over to the port of Naples, though his bowels were still affected by periodic attacks... But while he was returning his sickness worsened and at Nola he was confined to his bed. On the last day of his life, as he was kissing Livia, he passed away with these last words: 'Live mindful of our marriage, Livia, and goodbye.'

APPENDIX THREE
Some Notes on Street Literature

INTRODUCTION

In order to understand the development of the popular Broadsheets[1] commonly called 'penny dreadfuls', it is necessary to be aware of some of the developments in the social classes to which they made their appeal. For example, the enormous effect that the prodigious rate of education in the first half of the nineteenth century had on street literature in general must be noted. Through the good efforts of such philanthropic groups as the dame schools, the Sunday-schools, the British and Foreign Schools Society, and others, England could boast that by the middle of the century more than two-thirds of its population was literate.

Combine this with the strong position that the Broadsheet had already enjoyed since the seventeenth century as the working class's prime source of day-to-day news, and it is not difficult to credit the burgeoning sales of Broadsheets during this period.[2]

And by far the most popular subject was Crime and Punishment – especially if the crime was Murder, and the punishment Execution.

Again, one is led back – if explanations are sought – to the social conditions prevailing in the penny dreadful's hey-day. Led to remember that crimes against the person were far more rampant, far more vicious than anything that can be imagined today. If the tone of the Broadsheets seems to us to exhibit an unhealthy preoccupation with the violent, then it must be taken as a reflection of a time when executions were many, public, and seen by a population brutalized by open spectacles of unparalleled degradation on the scaffold as in the street; major executions were seen in much the same light as a public carnival, and the gallows literature was as much part of the 'support entertainment', as were the hot-potato sellers and the ginger-pop vendors. Charles Dickens wrote of the execution of the Mannings, in a letter to *The Times* dated November 13th 1847, "... A sight so inconceivably awful as the wickedness and levity of the immense crowd collected at the execution this morning could be imagined by no man, and presented by no heathen kind under the sun. The horrors of the gibbet, and of the crime which brought the wretched murderers to it, faded in my mind before the atrocious bearing, looks, and language of the assembled spectators. When I came upon the scene at midnight, the shrillness of the cries and howls that were raised from time to time, denoting they came from a concourse of boys and girls already assembled in the best places, made my blood run cold."

We have, as a matter of record[3], the following statistics for the sales of gallows sheets for some of the most notorious murderers:

James Blomfield Rush [see *Murder Club Guide No. 5*] 2,500,000
Frederick and Maria Manning [see *MCG No. 1*] 2,500,000
François Benjamin Courvoisier [see *MCG No. 1*] 1,666,000
James Greenacre, [see *MCG No. 1*] 1,650,000
William Corder [see *MCG No. 5*] 1,666,000
Flowery Land Pirates 290,000
Franz Müller [see *MCG No. 1*] 280,000
Constance Kent [see *MCG No. 6*] ... 150,000

However, as the increasingly popular penny newspapers[4] gave more detailed, and cer-

[1] Strictly, there are two distinct terms used to describe this type of publication: 'Broadside', being a newsheet printed on one side only; and 'Broadsheet', which was printed on both sides. In accordance with modern practice the latter term is used here to denote both types.

[2] It should be emphasized that, although our special interest here is with the genre of 'gallows literature', broadsheets also transmitted information on religious, political and social matters, and provided humorous and romantic entertainment.

[3] Figures quoted by Charles Hindley, in *Curiosities of Street Literature*, London, 1871.

[4] Prior to 1855 the tax on newspapers via the Newspaper Stamp Duty and the Paper Duty had kept them – at a selling price of about sevenpence a copy – in the preserve of the wealthy.

tainly more accurate, accounts of the murders of the day, so the penny Broadsheets began their decline. The cessation of public executions represented a further major loss of revenue for both the ballad printers and sellers. With crowds at major public hangings rarely numbering less than five figures, it is not surprising that one seller recalls with affection the execution of the Five Pirates of the *Flowery Land,* "Well I never in my time printed so many as I did of the Five Pirates of the *Flowery Land,* and I sold them at the

EXECUTION

OF

FIVE PIRATES

At Newgate, on Monday, Feb. 22nd, for Murder on board the FloweryLand.

H. DISLEY; Printer, 57, High Street,
St. Giles, London. -W.C.

Oh! what numbers did flock to see
Five murderers die on the gallows tree,
For those cruel deeds which they have done,
Their fatal glass is now quite run;
When they were sent to the shades below,
No tears of pity for them did flow,
No mercy did they expect to have,
Only to fill a murderer's grave.

Those five men on the drop did stand.
For their deeds on board the Flowery Land.

Children and mothers they have caus'd to weep,
For those who were slain and sunk in the deep;
We hope they are number'd with the blest,
And with God above their souls at rest;
Their sufferings were great, no tongue can tell,
Welt'ring in blood, on the deck they fell.
On their knees, for mercy they did crave,
But were murder'd and sunk beneath the waves

They've took from wives their husbands dear,
And griev'd their hearts the sad news to hear,
But in the hour of their distress,
God protect them and the fatherless!
For what those murderers did on board the
Flowery Land,
At the throne of God they will have to stand,
On the scaffold their lives did forfeit pay,
Oh, what will they feel on the Judgment day

In the mighty deep, where the billows roar,
Their victims sleep for evermore,
Tho' they parted them from those they love,
We hope their friends will meet them in Hea-
ven above,
Where their sufferings will be all o'er
On another bless'd and peaceful shore,
Where they will feel no grief or pain,
But for ever dwell ne'er to part again.

In the murderers' last hour, the solemn bell,
Warn'd them to bid this world farewell,
To resign their breath they did on the gallows
stand,
Life for life's required by God and man;
The murderers on the fatal morn,
On the gallows did die, expos'd to scorn,
For them there was no sympathy,
When they were launched in eternity.

We hope that this will a warning be,
To all, either by land or sea,
From the paths of virtue never to stray,
And never take precious life away;
Or like those mutineers, your fate may be,
Have to end your days on the fatal tree,
No one for them could pity have,
When they were sent to the murderer's grave.

rate of 3,000 copies per hour, and did altogether 90,000 – that was my share".[5]

Another not inconsiderable factor in the decline of gallows literature was the gradual acceptance by a previously blood-hungry mass, of the new Abolitionist feelings being expressed in Parliament and in academic and public life and, in turn, in the popular newspapers. An enlightened moral sense that found its first success in the Capital Punishment Within Prisons Bill receiving the Royal Assent on May 29th 1868 (three days after Michael Barrett became the last man to be publicly executed in England).

With rare exceptions, the Crime and Retribution sheets did not survive the turn of the nineteenth century. Exceptions took the form of revivalists of the genre, whose notable figurehead is John Foreman, self-styled 'Broadsheet King', whose formidable output since the '60s has spread from Catnach reprints to modern Gallows Ballads. His publication of Ewan McColl's verses on the execution of Timothy Evans in 1950 is a masterpiece of its kind – albeit taking a committed abolitionist stand.

THE TEXTS

In order to maximise the profit from any major act of murder or 'inhuman treatment', it was common for a sequence of sheets to cover a crime – the standard sequence being Discovery/Arrest-and-Trial/Execution. We must remember also that more than one printer would be covering the case, and each employing their own writers to fill in the texts, thus ensuring that the story remained, on the whole, uncomplicated by facts.

[5] Henry Mayhew, *London Labour and the London Poor,* London, 1861.

The **Discovery** sheet was in the main a fine excuse for the wildest excesses of the broadsheet hack, an opportunity to wring the last drop of blood out of every sentence:

> The body lay face downwards, and on turning it over a frightful gash in the throat, extending completely from ear to ear, became apparent, the clothes being deeply saturated with gore.

The **Arrest and Trial** sheets emphasized the inevitability of the sinner being caught out in his sins and punished, not only by an earthly Court, but by a Heavenly one also. Texts were characterized by Courtroom rhetoric of a cautionary and improving nature:

> But this [adherance to the Commandments] seems intirely violated in many instances by our dissipated irregular habits; which tends to the committal of such serious things, and thro' disobeying the scriptural voice brings degraded creatures to an untimely end. According to the Scriptures: "He that sheddeth man's blood, so shall his blood be sheddeth".

Often the Sentence which was passed on the prisoner is included in brief, following a standard pattern.

Execution sheets are again of a familiar format and contain a combination of the following features:

The Trial; This is included in brief, particularly if a separate issue has not already covered it.

The Sentence.

Prisoner's confession; Much importance was attached to extracting a confession from the condemned man, as this provided the composite value of proving God's intervention in the affairs of man, the vindication of the Sentence and, in days more orthodoxly religious than our own, the hope of salvation in the after life for the criminal. Where no confession was forthcoming from the condemned it was considered acceptable for the printer to write one for him.

Copy of Verses, (sometimes called the 'Lamentation'); the Verses were an essential part of the execution sheet, being a summary, in verse, of the life, crimes and apologia of the criminal – almost always written in the first person, though never by the prisoner. Said one hack, "I gets a shilling a copy for the verses written by the wretched culprit the night previous to his execution." It seems that the price was a standard one, "no more nor a bob for nothing." Which reflects in the quality of the verse, being for the most part unimaginative in the extreme. Little attention was paid to the facts of the case under treatment, and scant respect paid to any poetic convention. Sometimes special Broadsheets were issued consisting solely of the Copy of Verses, or Lamentation, with perhaps a standard 'cut' to illustrate them; on the whole these were somewhat better compositions and written to be set to a currently popular tune.

Dying Speech; No matter how many people found it difficult to swallow the logic of a sequence of events that allowed a copy of a Dying Speech to be on sale beneath the gallows many hours before the condemned man stood upon it, it made no difference to the popularity of this traditional section of the 'gallows sheet'.

Execution: Another purely fictitious piece of prose hastily prepared to be in time for the first sales on the day of execution. Clearly as it was written without the benefit of witnessing the event, the accuracy of this section was a matter of the purest chance. Indeed, there are execution broadsheets claiming the "launching into eternity" of prisoners who are known to have been given last-minute reprieves.

THE ILLUSTRATIONS

The illustration of popular broadsheets was by means of woodcuts (the pictures are called 'cuts'), either at the top of the sheet or incorporated into the hand-set text. The quality of craftsmanship was very varied, in addition to which, when a 'shocking event' took the printer by surprise, it was considered de rigeur to use any vaguely appropriate 'cut' that was in stock. Thus it is by no means uncommon to find, say, the murder of a young girl by strangulation being illustrated by a cut of an elderly man being shot.

One particularly endearing eccentricity of the Execution cuts – commonly representing the exterior of a prison during a crowded public hanging – are the holes cut into the block beneath the gallows so that the appropriate number and sex of the malefactors to perish could be inserted. The same principle was also used in stock Courtroom scenes.

COCKS, OR CATCHPENNIES

From the sales figures quoted in the Introduction to this Appendix, it should not be inferred that life for the Broadsheet printer and ballad seller was a bed of roses.

There *were* times when no murders of sufficient merit had been committed; when the Courts were presented with nothing but the common, grey, unhappy queues of petty thieves, blasphemers, and bigamists. At these times almost anything was better than nothing, and some squalid, desperate piece of skulduggery, committed out of poverty and degradation managed to keep the pot boiling.

Nevertheless, necessity did have its brighter side from the point of view of the student of Broadsheet literature; for there developed that kind of sheet called a 'Cock'[6] and later, as we shall see, also a 'Catchpenny'.

These sheets are commonly an idealisation of a Crime and Retribution, containing all those elements so carelessly omitted from real-life drama, thoughtfully remedied by the Broadsheet hacks. For if there had ever been any truth at all in these stories, it was expertly disguised with embroidery.

These, then, amounted to fictions, either cobbled together as necessity dictated, or printed up and left on the shelf as insurance against rainy days. The sheets are usually recognizable from their extravagance, convenience, and reluctance to divulge such verifiable facts as names and dates (unless they be false). Often these 'Catchpennies' are identifiable from the familiarity of their content – a common story-line reappearing with different names and locations and issued by different printers. Two classic themes are the familiar 'Sweetheart foully done down by false lover' and the equally well-worn 'Son mistakenly murdered by his avaricious parents' [see *Murder Club Guide No.3*].

[6] Cocks: Fictitious narratives, in verse or prose, of murders, fires, and terrible accidents, sold in the streets as true accounts. The man who hawks them, the patterer, often changes the scene of the awful event to suit the taste of the neighbourhood he is trying to delude. Possibly a corruption of 'cook', a cooked statement, or, as a correspondent suggests, the Cock Lane Ghost may have given rise to the term.

(*Hotten's Slang Dictionary*)

We are grateful to Charles Hindley[7] for this story of the origin of the term 'Catchpenny', with reference to that legendary broadsheet king of Seven Dials, Jeremy Catnach:

> It is stated that Catnach cleared over £500 by Weare's murder and Thurtell's trial and execution [see *Murder Club Guide No.5*], and was so loth to leave it, that when a wag put him up to a joke, and showed him how he might set the thing a-going again, he could not withstand it, so about a fortnight after Thurtell had been hanged 'Jemmy' brought out a startling broad-sheet, headed 'WE ARE ALIVE AGAIN!' He put so little space between the two words 'WE' and 'ARE' that it looked at first sight like 'WEARE'. Many thousands were bought by the ignorant and gullible public, but those who did not like the trick called it a 'catchpenny', and this gave rise to this peculiar term, which ever afterwards stuck to the issues of the 'Seven Dials Press'.

THE PRINTERS

It can fairly be said that the national headquarters of the Broadsheet printing business was that area of London known as the Seven Dials (close by present-day Covent Garden). The name Seven Dials referred to the design on the base of the obelisk that stood at the centre of the seven streets that radiated from it like the spokes of a wheel – Great and Little Earl Street, Great and Little St Andrews Street, Great and Little White Lion Street, and Queen Street.

The district itself was, at the time of the Broadsheet kings, a sprawling slum, whose former claim to celebrtity was being the point at which the Great Plague of 1665 broke out. At the beginning of the nineteenth century, it was a hotbed of poverty and crime, an agglomeration of tumbledown squalid buildings and verminous streets. But for all this, it had about it a kind of colourful, festival atmosphere, with regular 'beggars carnivals', dancing, drinking... and ballad shouters.

It was in the heart of the Seven Dials that John Pitts opened shop in 1802, followed

[7] Charles Hindley, *Curiosities of Street Literature*, London, 1871.

in 1813 by his great rival, Jeremy Catnach. Between them, these two colourful characters monopolised the revival of the broadsheet market, frequently bursting into print with scalding satires one upon the other. This is an example of Pitts lampooning Catnach:

> All the boys and girls around,
> Who go out prigging rags and phials
> Know Jemmy Catsnatch!!! well,
> Who lives in a back slum in the Dials.
> He hangs out in Monmouth Court,
> And wears a pair of blue-black breeches,
> Where all the 'Polly Cox's Crew' do resort
> to chop their swag for badly printed dying speeches.

There follow some brief notes on the lives of these two protagonists, and on some of the lesser pieces in the Seven Dials publishing game.

John Pitts (1765-1844)

Pitts was born at Effingham, Norfolk, in the year 1765. For some years he pursued his father's trade of baker, but at some unknown date he went to London and exchanged this trade for that of printer. He almost certainly worked for John Evans, a ballad printer, from whom Pitts took over his ballad stock. The Year 1802 found Pitts opening his first works at Great St Andrews Street, Seven Dials where, until the arrival of Jeremy Catnach in 1813, he reigned as broadsheet king. A more sober personality than 'Old Jemmy', Pitts nevertheless had a great sense of mischief, and could never resist the opportunity for a joke at the expense of his rival. One such scandal involved a 'cock' issued by Catnach in 1818, suggesting that "a butcher in the neighbourhood of D— L—" was making his sausages from human flesh. Though not named in the ballad, a mob gathered outside the establishment of Mr Pizzey, butcher, of Drury Lane – and smashed his windows. Catnach was rewarded with six months in Clerkenwell House of Correction for criminal libel, and a gleeful John Pitts gloated in print:

> Now Jemmy Catnach's gone to prison,
> And what's he gone to prison for;
> For printing a libel against Mr Pizzey,
> Which was sung from door to door.

In 1819, John Pitts moved to 31 Monmouth Street where he established his 'Toy and Marble Warehouse', printing also juvenile primers, chapbooks and songbooks. Later, in the 1830s, Pitts was to enter into the spirit of the Murder and Execution sheets, though his first affection was always for traditional ballads. An older, as well as less flamboyant character than Catnach, Pitts's failing eyesight caused him to lose more and more ground in this now quite unequal battle. To his credit, the blind John Pitts continued for many more years to manage his print works, succumbing finally in April 1844 – ironically outliving 'Old Jemmy'.

The Pitts operation was continued after his death by the two beneficiaries of his will, Elizabeth Hodges (see below), and Ann Guichard, in Little White Lion Street.

Jeremy Catnach
Catnach was born the son of a printer living and working at Alnwick in Northumberland. Both father and son later found their way to London where, on the death of the former, Jeremy Catnach established himself at Numbers. 2 & 3 Monmouth Court, Seven Dials, in 1813.

The list of legends surrounding Catnach is endless and, in a great measure, apocryphal. What is not disputed was his great love of money. It was quite fairly said of 'Old Jemmy' that he cared not a jot for the craft of printing; for him it was good enough if there were black marks on the sheet, and they would fetch him a penny in the streets. So terrified was he of the old wives tale that one could catch fever from touching the coins handled by street hawkers, that Catnach would boil his great sacks of pennies in a cocktail of potash and vinegar before carrying them to the Bank of England to exchange for silver. And at the height of his business activities, Jeremy was certainly filling a lot of sacks – he estimated a profit of some £500 on the Thurtell murder sheets alone.

After a full and colourful life the man once described as "a plodding, ignorant, dirty, successful individual" retired and was succeeded in the business by his sister Anne Ryle and James Paul (see below). 'Old Jemmy' died at his home in 1841.

William S. Fortey
Ironically, it was Fortey who, after the death of them both, finally reconciled the rivalries of Catnach and Pitts. Acquiring the stock of both firms (through their successors), William Fortey reissued many of the better items in stock whilst collecting and retaining many others. After Fortey's death in 1901, the collection was auctioned at Sotheby's, and to a large degree was kept together, a great proportion finding its way eventually to Mr George F. Wilson. Through the generosity of Mr Wilson, his collection is now preserved and made available for research in the Printing Library of the St Bride Foundation, London.

Elizabeth Mary Ann Hodges
Housekeeper to John Pitts and, on his death in 1844, the inheritor of Nineteen Guineas and part of the "Rest Residue and Remainder of my goods, chattels..." Mrs Hodges clearly obtained a substantial proportion of the business for she set up in the old Monmouth Street 'Toy and Marble Warehouse' to continue the printing operation. When Monmouth Street was renamed in 1845, the Hodges imprint became 31 Dudley Street; later 'E. Hodges' was to be located at Grafton Street, Soho, where she was still in business as late as 1861.

Henry Disley
Apprenticed to the Birt family of printers in Seven Dials, Disley later worked for Catnach, and then set up on his own. During the 1860s and 70s, Henry Disley was the acknowledged specialist in Murder and Execution sheets.

James Paul
Formerly the manager of Catnach's business, Paul went into partnership with 'Old Jemmy's' sister, Anne Ryle, who took over after his retirement. The imprint became first Ryle and Paul, then J. Paul and Co. until 1845 when Anne Ryle dissolved the partnership.

The Bloody Gardener's CRUELTY,

SHEWING HOW THE **MOTHER** OF A Young Nobleman BRIBED THE **GARDENER** TO COMMIT ***MURDER*** ON A Young Shepherdess.

BECAUSE **HER SON HAD FELL IN LOVE WITH HER** And she wished them not to be **MARRIED.**

THE GARDENER Found out, and afterwards ***Hung in Chains.***

Come all you constant lovers, & to me lend an ear
And mind this sad relation which I do give here,
'Tis of a maiden fair,
A shepherd's daughter dear,
But love did prove her utter overthrow.

She was of beauteous mould, fair and clear to behold,
And by a noble Lord she courted were,
But was too young we find,
As yet fond love to mind,
Yet little Cupid did her heart ensnare.

His parents they were all of high degree,
They said she is no match at all for thee,
If you'll a blessing have,
Grant us but what we crave,
And wed with none but whom we shall agree.

Dear son we have for you a chosen bride,
With store of gold and beautiful beside,
Of a temper kind and free,
She is the girl for thee,
But not a shepherd's daughter of mean degree.

And if by us you'll not be ruled or led,
You from our presence shall be banished,
No more we will you own,
To be our only son,
Then let our will be done to end the strife.

Madam, said he, if a begging I should go,
I should be contented so to do,
If that I could but have,
The girl that I do crave,
No curs'd gold shall part my love and me.

Was she as poor as Job, and I of royal robe,
And lord of all the globe, she should be mine,
His mother said in scorn,
Thou art most nobly born,
And with a beggar's brat shall never join.

He hearing his mother to say so,
His eyes then with tears like fountains flow,
Saying a promise I have made,
And her beauty betray'd,
Therefore no other for my bride I chuse.

A cruel scheme then for her life she laid,
And then for to act this thing, O then she did,
With her gard'ner she agreed,
To do the bloody deed,
And butcher her forthwith and dig her grave.

To the gardener she gave four score pounds
To murder her and lay her under ground,
All in a grave so deep,
In everlasting sleep,
Hoping her fair body would not be found.

She wrote a letter and sent it with speed,
Saying, my dearest, with haste now proceed,
Meet me this night I pray,
I've something to say,
Poor girl she little thought upon the deed.

The youthful shepherdess of this nothing knew,
But went to seek her true love as she us'd to do,
She search'd the garden round,
But no true love she found,
At length the bloody gardener did appear.

What business have you here, madam, I pray?
Are you come here to rob the garden gay?
Cries she, no thief I am,
To meet my love I'm come,
Which did this night appoint to meet me here.

He spoke no more but straight a knife he took,
And pierc'd her heart before one word he spoke,
Then on the ground she fell,
Crying sweet love farewell,
O welcome, Death, thy fatal stroke.

Was this done now my dear by your design,
Or by your cruel parents most unkind,
My life is thus betray'd,
Farewell vain world she said,
I hope in heaven I a place shall find.

But when he saw her life was really gone,
Immediately he laid her in the ground,
With flowers fine and gay,
Her corpse did overlay,
Intending that her body should not be found.

Now all the time this Lord he little knew,
But went to meet his love as he used to,
He search'd the vallies round,
But no true love he found,
The little lambs were wandering to and fro.

Lamenting greatly for his shepherdess,
Then he did lay him down upon the grass
The heavens he did implore,
To see his love once more,
O then ye Gods above I'm sure,

O whither shall I seek that angel bright,
Who is alone my pleasure and delight,
Pray if alive she be,
Let me my true love see,
Or else my soul will quickly take its flight.

Whereas the woods and groves began to mourn,
The small birds they did sing a mournful tune,
Crying your love is gone,
And left you quite alone,
Then on a mossy bank he laid him down.

He had no sooner clos'd his eyes to sleep,
But a milk white dove came to his breast,
Her fluttering wing did bent,
Which wak'd him out of sleep.
And then the dove took wing and he was blest.

To his mother's garden he did repair,
For to bemoan the loss of his dear,
Here once more the dove he see,
Sitting on a myrtle tree.
With drooping wings she did disconsolate appear.

O dove, disconsolate, why do you come?
Have you lost your love as I have done,
That you dodge me here,
No comfort can I bear,
Then thus the dove replied, and then flew down.

Saying it was your mother ordered it so,
That from her milk-white breast her blood did flow
To the grave he did repair,
But found no true love there.
Homeward then to his mother he did go.

I fear you have kill'd my joy and only dear,
He said, mother most cruel and severe,
For a dove a dove I do declare,
Did all in blood appear,
And said if she is dead her fate I'll share.

His mother hearing what the son did say,
She turn'd as pale as death and swoon'd away,
Then into destraction ran,
And told him what she had done,
And where the virgin's body it then lay.

He said no more but straight took a knife,
And said, now farewell to the comforts of life,
Then into the garden he flew,
And pierc'd his body through,
And said it was curs'd gold that caus'd all this strife.

These two lovers in one tomb were laid,
And many a briny tear for them was shed,
And the gard'ner as we hear,
Was apprehended there,
And hung in chains for being so severe.

Printed by T. Bloomer, 53, Edgbaston Street, B

H. Pyle

Two views of the Ballad Seller: above 'The Long Song Seller' from Mayhew's London Labour and the London Poor; *left, a much idealised view of the itinerant pedlar who included broadsheets and chapbooks among his wares.*

APPENDIX FOUR

Epilepsy, Murder and the Homicide Bill

It is a well-known medical phenomenon that subsequent on an epileptic fit, the patient may enter a state known as "epileptic automatism" where, as the name suggests, he behaves automatically, without rational premeditation, and with either no, or very imperfect, recollection of his actions. If it can be established that a crime was committed by the patient in this state, then a defence can be made that the accused was not responsible for the consequences of his actions.

In fact it is only rarely that this defence is advanced in a case of murder; for it is not sufficient to prove (and the burden of proof here lies with the *defence*) that the prisoner *is* an epileptic, but also that the act of killing was performed in a state of automatism. However, there is a basic connection between epilepsy beyond an expected numerical percentage. Drs Denis Hill and Desmond Pond during research at the Maudsley Hospital in South-East London, observed that of 105 murders in a sample, 18 of them exhibited symptoms of epilepsy. Given a normal population percentage of 0.5, this figure represents a staggering 32 times the expected incidence.

What may be more important is that, aside from the observable fits and subsequent automatism, the possibility of a complete personality change should be allowed for; we can see from encephalogram tracings that a fit involves a massive discharge of energy from the brain cells, which produces appropriate responses from whichever part of the brain it derives.

It may help to identify the three main clinical categories of what are collectively called epileptic fits:

Major epilepsy (called **Grand mal**); this is the most commonly encountered type of fit, and begins in the patient with an overpowering sensation that envelopes the body, and can take the form of a burst of sound, or of

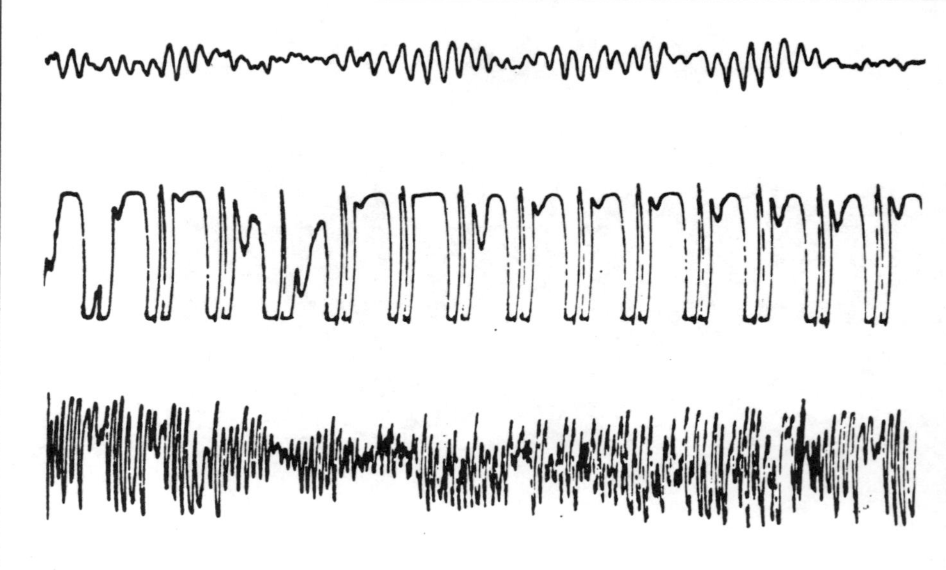

Electroencephalograms, recording: top, normal brain wave patterm; centre, 'spike and flat top' waves of petit mal; bottom, the sharp spikey waves of grand mal

light, or of heat. This is followed by loss of consciousness, and then the characteristic rhythmic 'convulsions'. This may be accompanied by a foaming at the mouth and holding the breath. When consciousness returns the patient feels tiredness usually accompanied by headache and confusion.

Minor epilepsy (called **Petit mal**); These are the minor losses of consciousness of which the patient himself may not even be fully aware. He may suddenly stop in the middle of speaking, or drop something that he is carrying; the eyelids and facial muscles may twitch slightly.

Psychomotor (or **Temporal Lobe**) **epilepsy**; This has been very adequately described in connection with a celebrated American murder case* by Dr D.T. Davidson Jnr and Dr William Lennox:

> The behaviour of a person during an automatism, or automatic seizure displays the greatest variety. He may appear to be fully aware of his surroundings and act as a normal person would, or he may be clumsy, speechless, or appear confused, act inappropriately or become surly or belligerent, or display excessive muscular activity such as violent running. In deciding as to whether a paroxysmal brain disorder is responsible for sudden and temporary abnormal actions. What the person did is not as important as whether he remembers what he did.
>
> The person's inability to remember what he did during this period may have three explanations: first his reputed amnesia may be simply feigned. The individual tries to dodge responsibility for his actions by saying he has no recollection of them. A plea for clemency is often based upon the false claim of amnesia. Such a lie may be exposed by indirect methods; a lie detector may be useful. The brainwave tracing should be normal.
>
> Secondly, the amnesia may be real but hysterical, based on some emotional disturbance such as the necessity of forgetting some horrible experience or escaping from an unpleasant dilemma. The person is not confused, but acts rationally and retains knowledge acquired in the past. He does not commit any major crimes in this state. Memory of events may often be recaptured under partial sedation with drugs or by hypnosis. The brainwave tracing taken during as well as before and after such episodes should be normal.
>
> The third type of amnesia is based on pathological rather than on psychological disturbance of brain function. Amnesia for events may attend such conditions as brain concussion, delirious states, complicating high fever, alcoholic intoxication or (in diabetics) an overdose of insulin. Such conditions are readily recognized.
>
> In addition recurrent temporary periods of amnesia may occur in persons who are otherwise mentally and physically healthy, except for possible brainwave disturbance. These episodes may come without warning and without apparent cause. As already stated, actions may be extremely diverse.
>
> These periods of amnesia and attendant actions come suddenly without premeditation or warning. They may last for half a minute or many hours or even days. They are therefore termed seizure phenomena. The only laboratory examination that possesses significance is the finding of paroxysmal disturbance in the electrical rhythms of the brain. However, such abnormality may not be demonstrable always, because the electrical disturbance may not be continuously present or may be brought out only by means of sleep, by hard breathing, or by injections of metrazol, a convulsive drug.

The study of epilepsy and its medico-legal significance is in great part linked with the amendments incorporated into the Homicide Bill of 1957, of which the relevant Clause 2 is reproduced below. This brought under the protection of 'insanity' those clinical conditions not previously covered by the McNaghten Rules. The Bill in a large degree addresses the former obscurities surrounding 'insanity' and introduces the concept of "diminished responsibility".

* In May 1950, in Massachusetts, a man named Elwell stabbed and bludgeoned to death his aunt, wrapped her body in a sheet, loaded it into the boot of his car and drove out to a swamp to dispose of it. Arrested by the police, Elwell had but a fragmentary recollection of the events and was proved to have acted in a state of psychomotor epilepsy.

THE HOMICIDE BILL
(5 Eliz. 2)

A
BILL
TO

Make for England and Wales (and for courts-martial wherever sitting), amendments of the law relating to homicide and the trial and punishment of murder, and for Scotland amendments of the law relating to the trial and punishments of murder and attempted murder.

Be it enacted by the Queen's most Excellent Majesty, by and with the advice and consent of the Lords Spiritual and Temporal, and Commons, in this present Parliament assembled, and by the authority of the same, as follows:

PART I
AMENDMENTS OF LAWS OF ENGLAND AND WALES AS TO THE FACT OF MURDER...

...2.–(1) Where a person kills or is a party to the killing of another, he shall not be convicted of murder if he was suffering from such abnormality of mind (whether arising from a condition of arrested or retarded development of mind or any inherent causes or induced by disease or injury) as substantially impaired his mental responsibility for his acts and omissions in doing or being a party to the killing.

(2) On a charge of murder, it shall be for the defence to prove that the person charged is by virtue of this section not liable to be convicted of murder.

(3) A person who but for this section would be liable, whether as principal or as accessory, to be convicted of murder shall be liable to be convicted of manslaughter.

(4) The fact that one party to a killing is by virtue of this section not liable to be convicted of murder shall not affect the question whether the killing amounted to murder in the case of another party to it...

APPENDIX FIVE
Trial by Combat

The "Trial by Battle" which was claimed in the case of Abraham Thornton (see page 134) is thus described:

When the privilege of Trial by Battle was claimed by the appellee, the judges had to consider whether, under the circumstances, he was entitled to the exercise of such a privilege; and his claim thereto having been admitted, they fixed a day and a place for the combat, which was conducted with the following solemnities:

A piece of ground was set out, of sixty feet square, enclosed with lists, and on one side was a court erected for the judges of the Court of Common Pleas, who attended there in their scarlet robes; and also a bar for the learned serjeants-at-law. When the Court was assembled, proclamation was made for the parties, who were accordingly introduced into the area by proper officers, each armed with a baton, or staff, of an ell long, tipped with horn, and bearing a four-cornered leather target for defence. The combatants were bare-headed and bare-footed, the appellee with his head shaved, the appellant as usual, but both dressed alike. The appellee pleaded not guilty, and threw down his glove, and declared that he would defend the same by his body; the appellant took up the glove, and replied that he was ready to make good the appeal body for body. And thereupon the appellee, taking the Bible in his right hand, and in his left the right hand of his antagonist, swore to this effect:

"Hear this, O man, whom I hold by the hand, who callest thyself [James], by the

> name of baptism, that I, who call myself [William], by the name of baptism, did not feloniously murder thy father [Thomas], by name, nor am anyway guilty of the said felony. So help me God."

To which the appellant replied, holding the Bible and his antagonist's hand, in the same manner as the other:

> "Hear this, O man, whom I hold by the hand, who callest thyself [William], by the name of baptism, that thou art perjured, because that thou feloniously did murder my father [Thomas] by name. So help me God and the saints; and this I will prove against thee by my body, as this Court shall award."

Next, an oath against sorcery and enchantment was taken by both the combatants in this or a similar form:

> "Hear this, ye justices, that I have this day neither ate, drank nor have upon me either bone, stone or grass; nor any enchantment, sorcery or witchcraft, whereby the law of God may be abased, or the law of the devil exalted. So help me God and His saints."

The battle was thus begun, and the combatants were bound to fight till the stars appeared in the evening.

If the appellee were so far vanquished that he could not or would not fight any longer, he was adjudged to be hanged immediately; and then, as well as if he were killed in battle, Providence was deemed to have determined in the favour of truth, and his blood was declared attainted. But if he killed the appellant, or could maintain the fight from sunrising till the stars appeared in the evening, he was acquitted. So also, if the appellant became recreant and pronounced the word "Craven," he lost his *liberam legem,* and became infamous; and the appellee recovered his damages and was for ever quit, not only of the appeal, but of all indictments likewise for the same offence. There were cases where the appellant might counterplead, and oust the appellee from his trial by battle: these were vehement presumption or sufficient proof that the appeal was true; or where the appellant was under fourteen or above sixty years of age, or was a woman or a priest, or a peer, or, lastly, a citizen of London, because the peaceful habits of the citizens were supposed to unfit them for battle.

It is needless to say that this remnant of barbarity has ceased to exist, an Act of Parliament, the introduction of which was attributable to the Thornton case, having removed it from the law-books by which our Courts are governed.

Select Bibliography

The following Bibliography makes no claim to completeness, and when one single volume is considered to provide a balanced, reliable account of a crime, this title alone is listed; for example, one in the remarkable Notable British Trials series. Published by William Hodge, the 83 volumes provide an unparalleled panorama of British crime, notably the crime of Murder. It is a matter of regret that the series is now long out of print and only occasional single volumes appear on the second-hand book shelves.

Tribute must also be paid to the publishers of this present series of *Guides* for their consistent, imaginative programme of publishing of true-crime titles; the Harrap list is particularly strong in the field of the forensic sciences. Happily, many of these are either in print or periodically reprinted.

For many of the historical cases (for example, that of George Victor Townley) there are few reliable modern sources. In this event contemporary references (most of them used by the authors in compiling this *Guide*) have been cited, though they are not freely available outside the national archives and book depositories.

As a postscript, this may be an appropriate occasion on which once again to thank the staff of the British Library Reading Room for their unfailing courtesy and expertise. Much of this Series was compiled at desk T9, and it is no exaggeration to say that it would have been far poorer in content were it not for the BL resources.

Select Bibliography

ALLEN, George

The Complete Newgate Calendar, ed. J.L. Rayner and G.T. Crook. Navarre Society, London, 1926.

ARMSTRONG, Herbert Rowse

Notable British Trials, ed. Filson Young, 1922.

Exhumation of a Murderer, Robin Odell. Harrap, London, 1975.

Criminological Studies No. 3: The Case of Major Armstrong. George Newnes, London, 1932.

ASHTON, James, *et al*

Allan and Clara: Murder in the Winnats, Castleton, [18].

BURROWS, Albert Edward

Seven Murderers, Christmas Humphries. William Heinemann, London, 1931.

Companion to Murder, Edward Spencer Shew. Cassell, London, 1960.

CADDELL, George

Curiosities of Street Literature, Charles Hindley. London, 1871.

CLARKE, Mary, and HAYNES, Phillip

[Northampton Public Library and Archive].

COOK, James

Narrative of the Conversion... of James Cook, Elizabeth Lachlan. London, 1832.

Cook the Murderer, C.J. Williams, [London], 1832.

COPELAND, Michael

Derby Evening Telegraph, Derby, 1960-62.

The Times, London, 1960-62.

DONELLAN, John

The Newgate Calendar: or, Malefactors Register. London, [17].

FERRERS, Earl

Tales from the Newgate Calendar, Rayner Heppenstal. Futura MacDonald, London, 1983.

An Account of the Execution of the late Earl Ferrers. London, 1760.

Memoirs of The Life of Laurence, Earl Ferrers. London, 1760.

The Trial of Laurence Earl Ferrers, for the Murder of John Johnson. London, 1760.

GREEN BICYCLE MYSTERY

The Green Bicycle Mystery, A.W.P. Mackintosh. [Private publication, Leicester], 1982. (Published in aid of the Bella Wright Memorial Fund.)

Murder Mistaken: An Analysis of Two Unsolved Murders, John Rowland. John Long, London, 1963.

The Green Bicycle Case, H. Russell Wakefield. Phillip Allan, London, 1930.

GREEN, Leslie

The Sound of Murder, Percy Hoskins. John Long, London, 1973.

Intensive Inquiries, Allen Andrews. Harrap, London, 1973.

HAYNES, Phillip (see CLARKE, Mary)

HAYWARD, George Frederick

London After Dark, Robert Fabian. Naldrett Press, London, 1954.

HOBDAY, Stanley Eric

Cherrill of the Yard, Frederick R. Cherrill. Harrap, London, 1954.

LIGHT, Ronald Vivian (see GREEN BICYCLE MYSTERY)

LOWER QUINTON MYSTERY

The Anatomy of Crime, Robert Fabian. Pelham, London, 1970.

MAJOR, Ethel Lillie

Daughters of Cain, Renee Huggett and Paul Berry. Allen and Unwin, London, 1956.

Murderess, Patrick Wilson. Michael Joseph, London, 1971.

My Forty Years at the Yard, Hugh Young. W.H. Allen, London, 1955.

MILLS, Herbert Leonard

Criminal Calendar II, Richard Harrison. Jarrolds, London, 1952.

Laboratory Detectives, Norman Lucas. Arthur Barker, London, 1971.

NEILSON, Donald

The Capture of the Black Panther, Harry Hawkes. Harrap, London, 1978.

NODDER, Frederick

Notable British Trials, ed. Winifred Duke, 1937.

The Child Killers, Norman Lucas. Arthur Barker, London, 1970.

OAKLEY, Frederick William

Norman Birkett, H. Montgomery Hyde. Hamish Hamilton, London, 1965.

PACE, Beatrice Annie

The Detective Physician: the Life and Work of Sir William Willcox, Philip H.A. Willcox. Heinemann Medical, London, 1970.

PAGETT, David

[Contemporary Newspaper reports provided the factual source of this story.]

PALMER, Dr William

Notable British Trials, ed. Eric R. Watson, 1952.

Palmer: The Rugeley Poisoner, Dudley Barker. Duckworth, London, 1935.

The Life and Career of Dr William Palmer of Rugeley, George Fletcher. T. Fisher Unwin, London, 1925.

They Hanged My Saintly Billy, Robert Graves. Cassell, London, 1957.

PRICE, George

The Annals of Newgate, ed. Rev Mr Villette, the Ordinary of Newgate. London, 1776.

ROUSE, Alfred Arthur

Notable British Trials, ed. Helena Normanton, 1931.

Lord Justice Birkett, Dennis Bardens. Robert Hale, London, 1962.
New Light on the Rouse Case, J.C. Cannell. John Long, London, 1931.
Reasonable Doubt, Geoffrey de C. Parmiter. Arthur Barker, London, 1938.

THORNTON, Abraham
A collection of contemporary booklets, pamphlets and plays relating to the murder of Maria Ashford, various dates and places of publication. [British Library collection.]

TOWNLEY, George Victor
The Trial and Respite of George Victor Townley. London, 1864.

WADDINGHAM, Dorothea
Lord Goddard, Fenton Bresler. Harrap, London, 1984.
Daughters of Cain, Renee Huggett and Paul Berry. Allen and Unwin, London, 1956.
Should Women Hang? Bernard O'Donnell. W.H. Allen, London, 1956.

WALTON, Charles (see LOWER QUINTON MYSTERY)

APPENDICES

GAOL FEVER
The State of the Prisons in England and Wales, John Howard, 1784.

THE COWARD'S WEAPON
Reports of Trials for Murder by Poisoning, George Lathom Browne. Stevens and Sons, London, 1883.
The Coward's Weapon, Terence McLaughlin. Robert Hale, London, 1980.
Poison Mysteries Unsolved, C.J.S. Thompson. Hutchinson, London, 1937.

STREET LITERATURE
Curiosities of Street Literature, Charles Hindley. London, 1871.
The History of the Catnach Press, Charles Hindley. London, 1887.
London Labour and the London Poor, Henry Mayhew. London, 1861.
The History of Street Literature, Leslie Shepard. David and Charles, Newton Abbot, 1973.
John Pitts, Ballad Printer of Seven Dials, Leslie Shepard. London, 1969.
Catchpenny Prints. Dover Books, New York, 1970.

EPILEPSY, MURDER, AND THE HOMICIDE BILL
The Mind of the Murderer, Walter Lindesay Neustatter. Christopher Johnson, London, 1957.

GENERAL REFERENCE BOOKS

The Guilty and the Innocent, William Bixley. Souvenir Press, London, 1957.
True Crime Diary, James Bland. Futura, London, 1987.
Sir Bernard Spilsbury: His Life and Cases, Douglas G. Browne and Tom Tullett. Harrap, London, 1951.
Murderers England, Ivan Butler. Robert Hale, London, 1973.
Memories of Murder, Tony Fletcher. Weidenfeld and Nicholson, London, 1986.
The Murderers' Who's Who, J.H.H. Gaute and Robin Odell. Harrap, London, 1979.
Murder Whatdunit, J.H.H. Gaute and Robin Odell. Harrap, London, 1982.
Murder Whereabouts, J.H.H. Gaute and Robin Odell. Harrap, London, 1986.
The Pleasures of Murder, ed. Jonathan Goodman. Allison and Busby, London, 1983.
Murders of the Black Museum, Gordon Honeycombe. Hutchinson, London, 1982.
Francis Camps, Robert Jackson. Hart-Davis MacGibbon, London, 1975.
Poisoner in the Dock, John Rowland. Arco, London, 1960.
The Concise Encyclopaedia of Crime and Criminals, Sir Harold Scott, Andre Deutsch, London, 1965.
Forty Years of Murder, Professor Keith Simpson. Harrap, London, 1978.
Mostly Murder, Sir Sidney Smith, Harrap, London, 1959.
Cause of Death, Frank Smyth. Orbis, London, 1980.
Companion to Murder, E. Spencer Shew. Cassell, London, 1960.
Clues To Murder, Tom Tullett. Grafton Books, London, 1986.
Strictly Murder, Tom Tullett. Bodley Head, London, 1975. (Republished as *Murder Squad,* Granada, 1981.)
The Black Museum, Bill Waddell and Jonathan Goodman, Harrap, London, 1987.
A Casebook of Murder, Colin Wilson. Leslie Frewin, London, 1969.
Encyclopaedia of Murder, Colin Wilson and Patricia Pitman. Arthur Barker, London, 1961.
Encyclopaedia of Modern Murder, Colin Wilson and Donald Seaman. Arthur Barker, London, 1983.

PICTURE CREDITS

The compilers would like to express their gratitude to the many people who have allowed us access to their collections and given their permission for its use in this series of *Guides.* We apologise in advance to any whose copyright we have failed to trace.

Index

NOTE

Bold type indicates the name of a Murderer.
Italic type indicates a Murder Location.
CAPITALS indicate Murder Method or other key subject.

Abolition of Capital Punishment, 91
ACQUITTALS, Light, Oakley, Pace, Thornton
ALCOHOL (as a complication of Murder), Jones, Pagett
Allen, George, 123
Amos, Catherine, 131
Anonymous Letters, 74
APOCRYPHAL CRIMES, 112-113
Armstrong, Major Herbert Rowse, TD, MA (Cantab), 9, 44 *et seq.*
Armstrong, Katharine, 44 *et seq.*
Ashby-de-la-Zouch, Leicestershire, 66
Ashfield, Maria, 138 *et seq.*
Ashford, Mary, 134 *et seq.*
Ashford, William, 137
Ashton, James, 19 *et seq.*
ASSIZE COURTS:
- Derby: 17, 18, 32
- Hereford: 49
- Leicester: 56, 59
- Lincoln: 75
- Northampton: 78 *et seq.*
- Nottingham: 104
- Stafford: 112, 118, 160
- Warwick: 129, 134 *et seq.*

Bacon, Lord (philosopher), 161
Baguley, Miss Ada, 99 *et seq.*
Baguley, Mrs Louisa, 100 *et seq.*
Bailey, William, 78 *et seq.*
Banks, Dr Cyril (Medical Officer of Health, Nottingham), 102
Barlaston, Staffordshire, 110
Bates Rubber Mills, Leicester, 62
Bedford, Mr (magistrate of Birches Green), 136
Bell Lane (now Orphanage Road), Erdington, 134, 136
Bell, Sir Robert (Lord Chief Baron), 161
Bennett, Arnold (novelist), 110
Bethlehem Hospital, 35
bigamy, 16, 78
Birkett, Mr Norman, KC, 75, 78 *et seq.*, 102, 157-158
Birmingham Canal, near Tipton, 157-158
BIRMINGHAM CROWN COURT, 156
Black Assize, Oxford, 161
Black Boy Chocolate Shop, Alfred Street, Nottingham, 102
Black Museum, 8-9
Black Rod, 69
Blagg, Miss (Hon. Sec. Nottingham County Nursing Association), 100
Blazing Car Murder, 78 *et seq.*
BLUDGEONING, Brodie, Cook, Green, Hayward, Jones, Mills, Oakley, Thornton
Blundell, Sarah, 131
Bolitho, William, 8
Bolus, Mr (surgeon), 138 *et seq.*
Borden, Lizzie, 8
Boughton, Lady, 130 *et seq.*
Boughton, Sir Theodosius Edward Allesley, 129 *et seq.*
Bowman, 'Watty', 159-160
Brandwood Park Road, King's Heath, Birmingham, 154
Brides in the Bath Case (see **Smith, George Joseph),** 8
Brierly Hill police station, Staffordshire, 118
British Broadcasting Corporation, 159
Broadsheet King (see Foreman, John)
Broadsheet Sellers, 166 *et seq.*
BROADSHEETS, 92, 112-113, 166 *et seq.*
Brodie, James, 99
Bromford Lane, West Bromwich, 159
Brown, Alfred, 78 *et seq.*
Brumby, Superintendent (Northampton Divisional Police), 81 *et seq.*
BURNING (as a complication of murder), Rouse
BURNING (as means of disposal of body), Cook
Burroughs, Sir Nehemiah, 106 *et seq.*
Burrows, Albert Edward, 16 *et seq.*
Burton-on-Trent, Staffordshire, 112-113
Butler, Ivan, 8
Byrne, Mr Justice, 104

Caddell, George, 112-113
Calladine, Albert Edward, 16 *et seq.*
Calladine, Elsie, 16 *et seq.*
Calladine, Hannah, 16 *et seq.*
Campbell, Lord, 119
Capital Punishment Within Prisons Bill, 168
Carbon Copy Murders, 14 *et seq.*
Carter, Benjamin, 134
Castle Bromwich, 134, 137
Catchpennies (broadsheets), 112-113, 170
Catnach, Jeremy (printer), 113, 171 *et seq.*
Chambers, Mary (see Price, Mary)
Charles, Mr Justice, 75
Charwelton, Northamptonshire, 92
Cherril, Detective Chief Superintendent Frederick (Scotland Yard) 159-160
Chester Road, near Erdington, 134
Chief Constable of Hereford, 47
CHILDREN (as victims), Burrows
Church Gresley, Nottinghamshire, 100
Churchill, Robert (ballistics expert), 64

circumstantial evidence, 157
Clarke, Daniel (inn-keeper), 134
Clarke, Edmund, 117-118
Clarke, John, 92
Clarke, Mary, 92
Clarke, Mr Nathaniel Gooding, KC, 136
Clewes, Thomas, 52
Clifford, Mrs, 67 *et seq.*
Cock Lane Ghost, 170 (note)
Cocks, or Catchpennies (see Catchpennies)
Coleford, Gloucestershire, 38
Collinson, Mrs Amy, 18
Commissioners in Lunacy, 35-36
Conway, Reuben, 32
Cook, James, 54 *et seq.*
Cook, Nicholas, 19 *et seq.*
Cook, William Parsons, 119 *et seq.*
Copeland, Michael, 14 *et seq.*
Copy-Cat Murders, 14 *et seq.*
Corder, William, 112 (note), 166
Court of Common Pleas, 179
Court of The King's Bench, 137
Courvoisier, François Benjamin, 166
Coventry, Sir Reginald, KC, 160
Cox, Hannah, 134 *et seq.*
Cox's Bridge, Tipton, 157-158
cremation, 102
Crippen, Dr Hawley Harvey, 9, 16
'The Crown' (public house), 78 *et seq.*
Crutchett, Chief Inspector Alfred, 49, 51
Cusop Churchyard, Herefordshire, 49

'Daily Sketch' (newspaper), 78
dandelions, 45 *et seq.*
Darbyshire, John, 131
Davidson, Dr D.T. Jnr, 178
Davies, John (chemist), 45 *et seq.*
De Quincey, Thomas, 7
Deelands Road, No.4, Rubery, Birmingham, 154 *et seq.*
DERBY GAOL, 16, 35
Devon Drive, No.32, Nottingham, 99 *et seq.*
Dinting Airshaft, 17
Dickens, Charles, 75 (note), 166
DISEMBOWELLING, Allen
Disley, Henry (printer), 172
DISMEMBERMENT, Cook
'Display of Witchcraft', 161
Dodson, Inspector, 74-75
'Dog and Gun', Market Street, Leicester, 56
Donellan, John, 129 *et seq.*
DROWNING, Thornton
Dunkley, Susan (writer), 49

Effingham, Norfolk, 171
Elder, Police Constable (Cumberland Constabulary), 159-160
electroencephalograms, 177-178
Ellington, Superintendent (Nottingham police force), 104
Ellistown Colliery, Coalville, 63
Elwes, Mr Richard, KC, 87, 104
EPILEPSY, 123, 177 *et seq.*
Errington, Mr Sheriff, 70
'Estoril', Station Road, Barlaston, 110 *et seq.*
Evans, John (printer), 171
Evans, Timothy John, 168
Evington, Leicestershire, 60 *et seq.*
EXECUTIONS, Allen, Armstrong, Burrows, Clarke, Cook, Donellan, Ferrers, Gordon, Green, Hallam, Harwood, Haynes, Hayward, Hobday, Jones, Major, Mills, Palmer, Rouse, Waddingham
EXHUMATION, 49

Faldingworth Gate, Nr Market Rasen, 75-76
'Famous Crimes Past and Present' (magazine), 7, 30 (note)
Ferrers, Earl, 66 *et seq.*
Fetterhill Farm, Coleford, 38
FIBRES (forensic identification by), 104
Fingerprint Bureau (Scotland Yard), 159
FINGERPRINTS, 159
'Five Towns', 110
'Flowery Land' Pirates, 166-168
'Flying Horse' (public house), 54
Foot, Paul, 9
FOOTPRINTS, 110 *et seq.*
Foreman, John (The Broadsheet King), 168
Fortey, William S. (printer), 172
Fortress Company, Royal Engineers, 63
Fox, Charles William, 158 *et seq.*
Fox, Hannah, 138 *et seq.*
Frost, Samuel, 130
Fuller's chocolates, 46, 51
Furniss, Harold, 7

G.L. (playwright), 138
Gadd's Forge, 157
GAMBLING (as a complication of murder), Jones, Palmer
GAOL FEVER, 42 *et seq.*, 161 *et seq.*
Gardner, Thomas, 76
Gartree Road, Nr Little Stretton, 60 *et seq.*
Gaulby, Leicestershire, 60 *et seq*
Gaulby Church, Leicestershire, 61, *et seq.*
Gaulby Lane, Leicestershire, 60
Gilbert, Fred, 101
Glossop, Derbyshire, 16
Goddard, Mr Justice, 102
Goodwin, Bessie Caroline, 30 *et seq.*
Goodwin, Henry, 30
Gordon, Thomas, 93
Goya, Francisco de, 124
grand mal, 177
Granville Road, Leicester, 63
Great Glen, Leicestershire, 60 *et seq.*
Great North Road, 78
Great Plague of London (1665), 170
Great St Andrews Street, Seven Dials, 170-171
Green Bicycle Mystery, 60 *et seq.*
Green Jackets, 154
Green, Leslie, 110 *et seq.*

Greenacre, James, 166
Grimley, Harry (railway policeman), 112
Guichard, Ann (printer), 172
Guy Fawkes night, 78 *et seq.*

HAIR (forensic identification by), 104, 160
Hall, Constable, 61
Hall, Sir Edward Marshall, KC, 64
Hallam, Isaac, 75-76
Hallam, Thomas, 75-76
Hancock, Robert Selby, 99
Hand, Mr (coroner of Uttoxeter), 123
HANGING IN CHAINS, 56, 108
HANGMEN, Pierrepoint, Thomas
Hardingstone, Northamptonshire, 78 *et seq.*
Hardingstone Lane, Hardingstone, 78 *et seq.*
Harwood, Jocelin, 106 *et seq.*
Hawke, Mr Justice, 18
Hay-on-Wye, Hereford and Worcs, 42 *et seq.*, 44 *et seq.*
Haydn Road, Nottingham, 100
Hayfield, Derbyshire, 18
Haynes, Phillip, 92
Haypit's Wood, 160
Hayward, George Frederick Walter, 18
Heber, Bishop Reginald, 99 (note)
Hemming, Richard, 52
Hendham Vale, Nr Manchester, 30, 31
Henley, Lord (Keeper of the Great Seal), 70
Henley, W.E, 7, 99 (note)
High Holborn, No. 44, London, 54
High Leigh, Cheshire, 159
High Peak, 18
Highfield Street, Leicester, 60, 63
HIGHWAYMEN, Hallam, Harwood
Hill, Dr Denis, 177
Hincks, Dr Thomas, 45 *et seq.*
Hindley, Charles (author), 166, 170 (note)
Hobday, Stanley Eric, 158 *et seq.*
Hodges, Elizabeth Mary Ann (printer), 172
Holroyd, Mr Justice, 136
Homicide Act of 1957, 177 *et seq.*
Honeycombe, Gordon, 8
Honourable Artillery Company, 63
'Horncastle News' (newspaper), 75
Horncastle Police Force, 74
Hotten's Slang Dictionary, 170 (note)
Houghton Lane, Leicestershire, 60
Hounslow Heath, 42 *et seq.*
House of Lords, 69 *et seq.*
Hucknall, Nottinghamshire, 99
HULL PRISON, 75
Humphries, Mr (Chaplain of the Tower of London), 70, 71

Ilchester Gaol, 161
Industrial Revolution, 117
INSANITY, Townley

Jack the Ripper, 9
Jackson, George (road-mender), 136
Jansen, Sir Stephen Theodore (Chamberlain of London), 162
Jardine, David, 7
Jenkes, Rowland, 161
Jenkins, Ivy, 78
Johnson, John, 66 *et seq.*
Jones, Ethel, 117-118
Jones, Joseph, 117-118

Kennedy, Ludovic, 9
Kent, Constance, 166
Kettleborough, Rose, 75
Kinchin, Gail, 154 *et seq.*
Kinchin, Josie, 154 *et seq.*
King's Norton, Leicestershire, 61
Kirkby-on-Bain, Lincolnshire, 74-75
Kirkland, Mr (surgeon), 67-68

Lachlan, Mrs, 56 *et seq.*
'Lantern Pike' (public house) (see *'New Inn'*)
Lawton Hall, Nr Warwick, Warwickshire, 129 *et seq.*
Leech, Thomas Willoughby, 100
Leicester, Leicestershire, 54 *et seq.*
Leicester Castle (court), 64
'Leicester Daily Post' (newspaper), 62
LEICESTER GAOL, 69
'Leicester Mercury' (newspaper), 63
Lennox, Dr William, 178
Lewis, Rev. J. Trevor (Rural Dean), 91
Light, Ronald Vivian, 60
LINCOLN GAOL, 76
Little Hayfield, 18
Little Stretton, Leicestershire, 60 *et seq.*
'London Labour and the London Poor', Henry Mayhew, 168 (note)
London Road, Leicester, 60
Long Compton, Warwickshire, 128-129
Long Compton Church, 129
Longmead Drive, Nottingham, 103
Longton police station (Staffordshire), 111
Lorenzo and Charlie, 112
Lower Quinton, Warwickshire, 126
Lustgarten, Edgar, 8

MaCaulay, Mr, QC, 34
McColl, Ewan, 168
Mackintosh, Mr A.W.P. (writer), 60, 64
McNaghten Rules, 178
Major, Alfred, 74-75
Major, Ethel Lillie, 74-75
Major, Lawrence, 75
'Malefactors Register', 72
Manning, Frederick and Maria, 166
Mansfield Street, Nottingham, 103
MANSLAUGHTER (Murder reduced to), Pagett
Mant, Dr Newton, 32
MARSHALSEA PRISON, 137
Martin, Mr Baron, 32, 35
Martin, Maria, 112 (note)
Martin, Oswald, 44 *et seq.*
Masefield Square, Northfield, Birmingham, 156
Maudsley Hospital, London, 177

Maybrick, Florence, 9
'Mayfield', Hay-on-Wye, 44 *et seq.*
Mayhew, Henry (writer on social matters), 168 (note)
Measures, Mr, 60 *et seq.*
Meredith, Sir William, 66
Metropole Hotel, Leeds, 111, 112
Midland Hotel, Derby, 31
Millen, Detective Sergeant Ernest (Scotland Yard), 110 *et seq.*
Mills, Herbert Leonard, 103-104
Mittimus, Sir George, 138 *et seq.*
Moor Street, West Bromwich, West Midlands, 158 *et seq.*
Morland, Nigel, 8
Morris Minor Cars, 78 *et seq.*
Mother Shipton (witch), 129
Muller, Franz, 166
Munro, Irene, 8
Murder Club, The, 7, 12, 191-192
'The Mysterious Murder' (melodrama), 138 *et seq.*

'The Nags Head' (public house), near Burton, Staffordshire, 113
National Clothing Company, 160
Netherwood Farm, Oddingley, 52
'New Drop', 70, 72
'New Inn' (public house), 18
Newark-on-Trent, Nottinghamshire, 96 *et seq.*
'Newgate Calendar', 93
NEWGATE GAOL, 44, 162
'News of the World' (newspaper), 103-104
Newspaper Stamp Duty, 166
Newton, Mr (butcher), 159, 160
Nodder, Frederick, 96 *et seq.*
'Northampton and County Independent' (newspaper), 80 *et seq.*
Nottingham, Nottinghamshire, 99 *et seq.*
NOTTINGHAM GAOL, 17

Oadby, Leicestershire, 60
Oakley, Frederick William, 157-158
O'Brien, Sergeant (counsel), 34
Oddingley Rectory, Nr Droitwich, 52
'Ode to Death', Percy Bysshe Shelley, 103
OLD BAILEY, 44, 119, 120, 162
Orphanage Road (see Bell Lane)
Orton and Co, Derby, 63
O'Sullivan, Mr Edward, KC

Paas, Mr, 54 *et seq.*
Pace, Beatrice Annie, 38 *et seq.*
Pace, Harry, 38 *et seq.*
Pagett, David, 154 *et seq.*
Pagett, Sheila, 154
'Palmer' Act, 120
Palmer, Annie, 119
Palmer, Dr William, 119 *et seq.*
Paper Duty, 166
Parker, the Reverend Mr, 52
Parsons, Dr (professor of Anatomy at Oxford), 131
Parsons, Mr (counsel), 138 *et seq.*
Paul, James (printer), 172
Payne, Miss, of Sulby Abbey, Northants, 56 *et seq.*
Peace, Charles, 16, 17
Peak District, Derbyshire, 19 *et seq.*
Pearce, Miss Emily, 50-51
Pearson, Edmund, 8
Pengelly, Lord Chief Baron, 161
Penn's Mill Lane, Nr Erdington, West Midlands, 134 *et seq.*
Pensnett Village, Staffordshire, 117
PENTONVILLE PRISON, 35
petit mal, 177-178
Pierrepoint, Thomas (hangman), 18, 118, 160
Pigot, John (High Sheriff for Somerset), 161
Pitman, Patricia, 8
Pitts, John (printer), 170 *et seq.*
plays, 138 *et seq.*
POISON: Antimony: 164-165
POISON: Arsenic: Pace case, Armstrong
POISON:Laudanum: 163-164
POISON: Laurel water: Donellan, 165
POISON: Morphine: Waddingham, 163-164
POISON: Opium: 163-164
POISON: Strychnine: Major
Polstead, Suffolk, 112 (note)
Pond, Dr Desmond, 177
Powell, Mr (apothecary of Rugby), 130
Poynter, Anne, 32
Price, George, 42 *et seq.*
Price, Mary, 42
Price, Miss, 112-113
psychomotor epilepsy, 178

Quarry Bank, Nr Stafford, 117
Quibble, Mr (attorney), 138 *et seq.*

Rae, Norman (journalist), 103-104
Rattenbury, Francis Mawson, 8
Rattray, Dr (pathologist), 131
Reader, William (counsel), 136
Red Barn Murder, 112 (note)
Reynard, Mr (counsel), 138 *et seq.*
Reynold, Henry Revell (counsel), 136
Richards, Detective Constable Gerald, 154 *et seq.*
River Aire, Leeds, 112
Robinson, John (a warrener), 99
ROBBERY (as a motive for Murder), Hayward, Hallam, Green
Roche Lynch, Dr (Home Office Analyst), 74, 102
Roughead, William, 8
Rouse, Alfred Arthur, 78 *et seq.*
Rouse, Mrs Lily May, 83 *et seq.*
Roxy Cinema, Nottingham, 104
Rubery, Birmingham, 154 *et seq.*
Rugeley, Staffordshire, 119 *et seq.*
Rush, James Blomfield, 166
Ryle, Ann (printer), 172

Saffron Lane, Leicester, 59
St Albans, Hertfordshire, 78
St Augustine of Hippo, 43 (note)

St Bartholomew's Hospital, London, 119
St Mary's Hospital, Paddington, London, 74
Sartain, Detective Sergeant Thomas, 156
Scott, John (race-horse breeder), 120
Scott, Rev. John, MA, 122
Sebastopol, Battle of, 30
Seven Dials, London, 170 *et seq.*
Sharp, Detective Sergeant Walter, 51
Shaw, Dr Eric (pathologist), 87
Shaw, Chief Justice Lemuel (USA), 157
Shearman, Mr Justice, 17
Shelley, Percy Bysshe, 103
Sheppard, Sir James (Serjeant-at-law), 161
Sherwood Vale, Nottingham, 103
Shew, Edward Spencer, 8
Shirley, Laurence (see **Ferrers, Earl**)
SHOOTING, Ferrers, Gordon, Green Bicycle Mystery, Hemming, Pagett
Shrewsbury, Shropshire, 106
Shrewsbury Races, 119
Simmondley Moor, Derbyshire, 16 *et seq.*
Sims, Mr (Governor of Derby Gaol), 34
Smith, George Joseph, 8, 16
Smith and Wesson ·38 revolvers, 156
Society for the Diffusion of Useful Knowledge, 7
Solicitors (as Murderers), Armstrong
Spilsbury, Sir Bernard (pathologist), 82 *et seq.*
Spooner, Detective Superintendent Reginald (Scotland Yard), 110 *et seq.*
STABBING, Green, Harwood, Hobday
STAFFORD GAOL, 112, 118, 119, 123
'Stag and Pheasant Inn' (public house), 54
Stanton (see Staunton Harold)
Station Hotel, Stafford, 111, 112
Station Road, Barlaston, 110
Staunton Harold, Leicestershire, 66 *et seq.*
Stoneygate, Leicestershire, 60
Stoughton, Leicestershire, 60 *et seq.*
Stoughton Church, Leicestershire, 62
STRANGULATION, Mills, Price
SUICIDE, 35-36, 43 (note)
Sullivan, Ronald, 100 *et seq.*
'Sunbeams for Dark Hours', 56 *et seq.*
Surgeon's Hall, 72
Sutton Coldfield churchyard, 137

Talbot, Mr Justice, 78 *et seq.*, 160
'Talbot Arms Hotel', Rugeley, 119
Tapster, Daniel (inn-keeper), 138 *et seq.*
Tattershaw, Mabel, 104-105
Tatnall, Mr (Keeper of Warwick Gaol), 137
Taylor, Harold, 159
Taylor, Dr W.W. (Home Office Analyst), 102
Thompson, Edith, 9
Thornton, Abraham, 134 *et seq.*, 179
Thorntree, Abraham, 138 *et seq.*
Thorntree, Mr, 138 *et seq.*
Thorntree, Mrs, 138 *et seq.*
'The Three Tuns' (public house), Tyburn, 134
THROAT CUTTING, Allen, Caddell, Hallam, Hayward, Jones, Townley
'The Times Report of the Trial of William Palmer', 121
Tinsley, Mona Lilian, 96 *et seq.*
Tipton, West Midlands, 157-158
tithes, 52
Tower of London, 69 *et seq.*
Townley, George Victor, 30 *et seq.*
'Toy and Marble Warehouse', Monmouth Street, 171-172
TRIAL BY BATTLE (see TRIAL BY COMBAT)
TRIAL BY COMBAT, 137, 179-180
Tucker, Nellie, 86
Turnout, Jacob (constable), 138 *et seq.*
TYBURN, 70
Typhus (see GAOL FEVER)

UNSOLVED CRIMES, Green Bicycle Mystery, Oakley, Pace, Walton

Vaillant, Mr Sheriff, 70, 71, 72

Waddingham, 'Nurse' Dorothea, 99 *et seq.*
Walton, Charles, 126 *et seq.*
Warstone Fields, 160
WARWICK GAOL, 131, 137
Wateringbury, Kent, 106
Watt, James (engineer), 117
Webster, Professor (Home Office pathologist), 104
Wellington Street, Leicester, 54 *et seq.*
West Bromwich, West Midlands, 158 *et seq.*
Westminster Hall, London, 137
Westmore, Rev. W. N., BA (Vicar of Stoughton), 62
'What's the Clock?' (melodrama), 138 *et seq.*
Whatstandwell, Derbyshire, 30
Whispering Knights, Long Compton, 129
White House, Little Hayfield, 18
Whitewall House, Matton, 120
Wigwell Grange, 30
Wigwell Lane, Nr Wirksworth, Derbyshire, 30 *et seq.*
Williams, Dr, 61
Williams, Glanville (author of legal books), 43 (note)
Wills in contention, Armstrong
Wilmot, Tony, 9
Wilson, Colin, 8
Wiltshaw, Alice, 110 *et seq.*
Wiltshaw, Cuthbert, 110 *et seq.*
WINCHESTER GAOL, 162
Winnats Pass, Derbyshire, 19 *et seq.*
WINSON GREEN PRISON, Birmingham, 102, 104, 118, 160
'WITCHCRAFT MURDERS', 126 *et seq.*
Wood, Eric, 154 *et seq.*
Wood, Thomas, 17
Workhouses, 117
Worton, Eliza Jane, 157-158
Wright, Annie Bella, 60 *et seq.*
Wright, William, 75-76
Wyndham, Horace, 7

YORK CASTLE, 162
Young, Chief Inspector Hugh, 74-75

An Invitation To Join
THE MURDER CLUB

The publication of this series of *Guides* has been timed to coincide with the Club's Public Membership launch.

Criminology will no longer be the exclusive domain of scientists, lawyers and writers, The Murder Club enables every one of its Members to become an arm-chair detective.

You, the readers, are invited to join in the Club's fascinating research programmes, to contribute your ideas to its publications and entertainments, its 'Notorious Locations' tours and presentations.

Or simply sit back and enjoy the regular packages of intriguing true-life crime material prepared by The Murder Club *exclusively* for its Members, stimulating the imagination with a little fireside detective work.

Membership benefits for 1988–1989 include, among other features:

★ The Murder Club's own unique badge, membership card, and personal Certificate of Membership. (Dispatched with Introductory Membership Pack.)

★ *The Murder Club Bulletin,* a two-monthly magazine devoted to all aspects of real-life crime – new cases, old cases, cases to marvel at, cases to solve. A fully illustrated miscellany of information and entertainment; plus full news of Murder Club activities in Great Britain and abroad. (Dispatched to Members bi-monthly.)

continued overleaf

THE MURDER CLUB

APPLICATION FOR MEMBERSHIP

I enclose the sum of £25*, being the annual Membership Fee of The Murder Club. I understand that this entitles me to all the benefits listed above and outlined in the introductory Membership Pack.

Name ____________________

Address ____________________

____

____

Signature ____________________

Please send completed form and remittance to:
The Murder Club
35 North Audley Street, London W1Y 1WG

*Due to high overseas postal rates, a small supplement of £5 will be charged to Members outside the British Isles.

★ *Murder World Wide,* a series of illustrated booklets covering Classics of Murder from around the world. Each issue is complete in itself and a printed slip-case will be presented to contain each series as an annual 'volume'. (Dispatched to Members monthly.)

★ *Cabinet of Crime,* a companion series of monthly publications dealing with immortal cases from the annals of British murder. Specifications as *Murder World Wide.*

★ *The Black Museum,* title of The Murder Club's own mail-order catalogue with a difference. A unique illustrated document covering a wide range of publications, facsimiles, posters, prints, photographs and objects, exclusively produced by the Club to enable its Members to build up their own 'home Black Museum' of thought-provoking conversation pieces. (Published annually with bi-monthly supplements.)

★ The Murder-Book Club. A service offered to Members through our contact with the specialist publishers of popular true-crime books. A two-monthly list of available titles will be issued – many of which are available through the Club at lower than publishers' catalogue prices. (Updated bi-monthly.)

★ Concessionary prices and privileges on a wide range of Murder Club and related products, entertainments, and activities.

For Annual Membership including Introductory Membership Pack and monthly supplements, please complete the form overleaf enclosing the sum of £25.

Or send £2.50 (deductible from Membership) for further information.